fashion plate
PORTRAITS

by Elizabeth St. Hilaire

mixed media portraits,
step-by-step

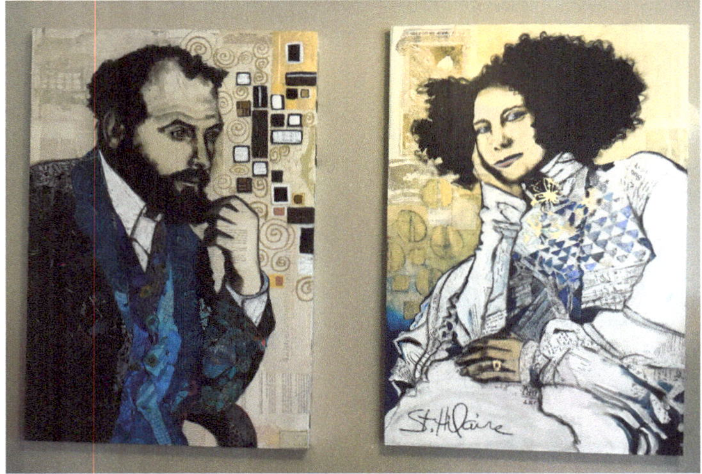

Emilie Flöge and Gustav Klimt, 24x36

For Emilie and Connor

*Thank you for loving me for who I am,
for supporting me in what I do, and for
understanding both.*

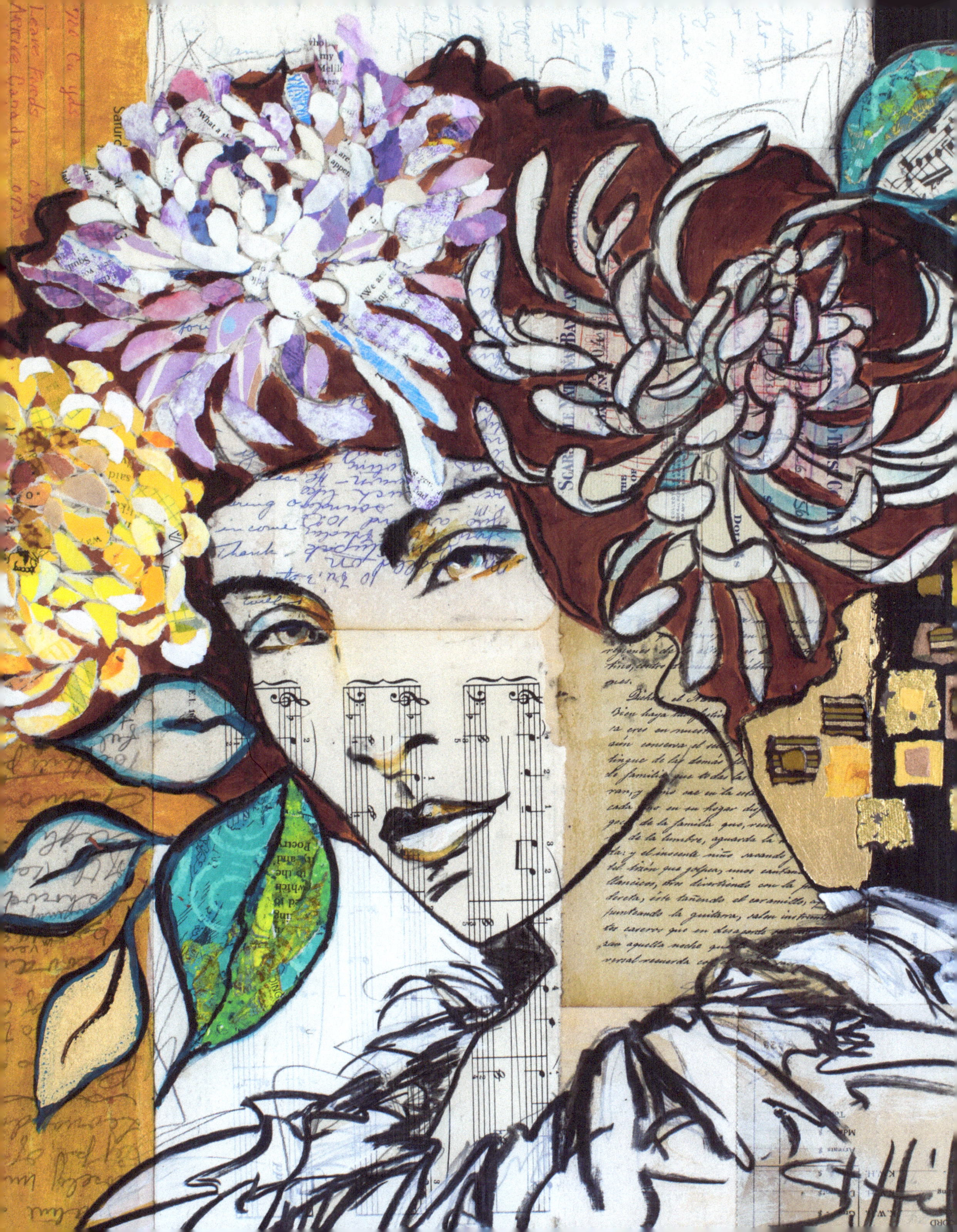

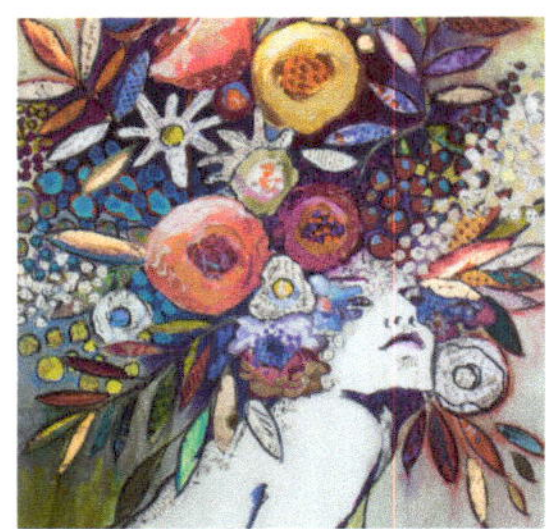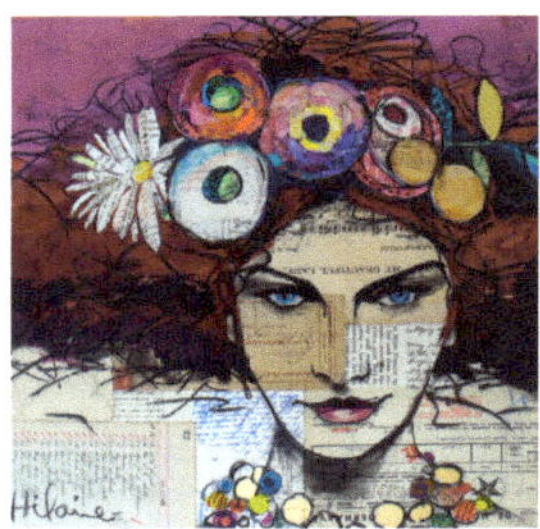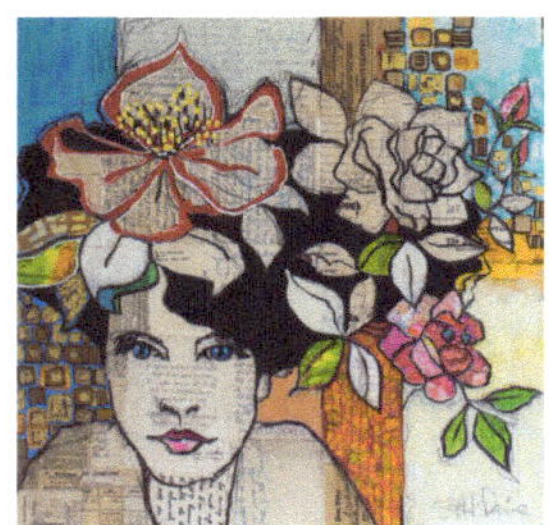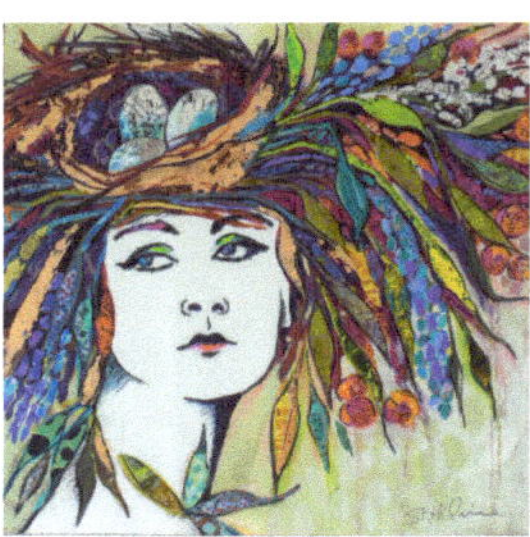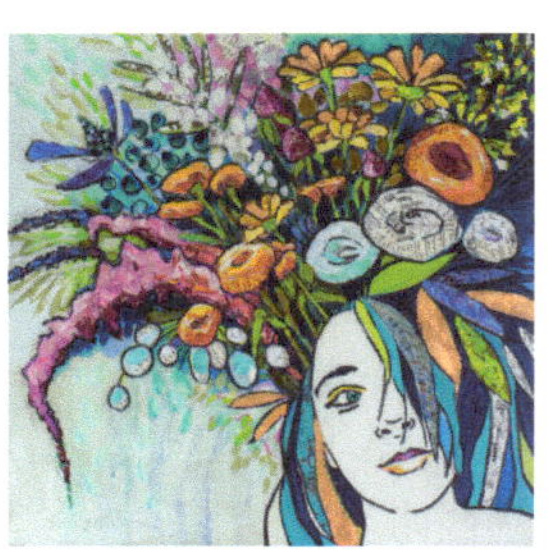

intro

My technique has evolved and changed as a result of experimentation with hand-painted, hand-made, textured, and patterned papers. Layering and weaving, pushing and pulling the colors, patterns, and values makes the collage process like a dance. Undulating, alternating, and overlapping, until the rhythm creates something I love.

In my work I highlight the extraordinary within the ordinary, focusing on intense and vibrant colors combined with a sensibility of design. My collages invite the viewer to look, and having looked, to linger.

fashion plate PORTRAITS

A figurative, painterly mixed media portrait is created by combining collage with an ephemera background, a smudged pastel drawing, and some mark making on top. There's no right or wrong way to do it, there's nothing that I say in this book than cannot be re-imagined by you, the artist.

The painterly appearance of the collage paper application is achieved by treating every bit of torn (not cut) paper like an brush stroke, keeping details loose, and using a variety of texture and shades of paper in every color field.

Creating your own papers for collage offers a custom paper palette with every shade of every color that appeals to you, offering variety and inspiration and possibility.

Utilizing the graphite transfer technique allows artist of any level to successfully transfer a sketch from a photograph, taking the fear out of drawing people.

Join me on this artistic journey where you can explore all that there is to love about mixed media, collage, ephemera, and putting it all together. I hope you will find joy in the process.

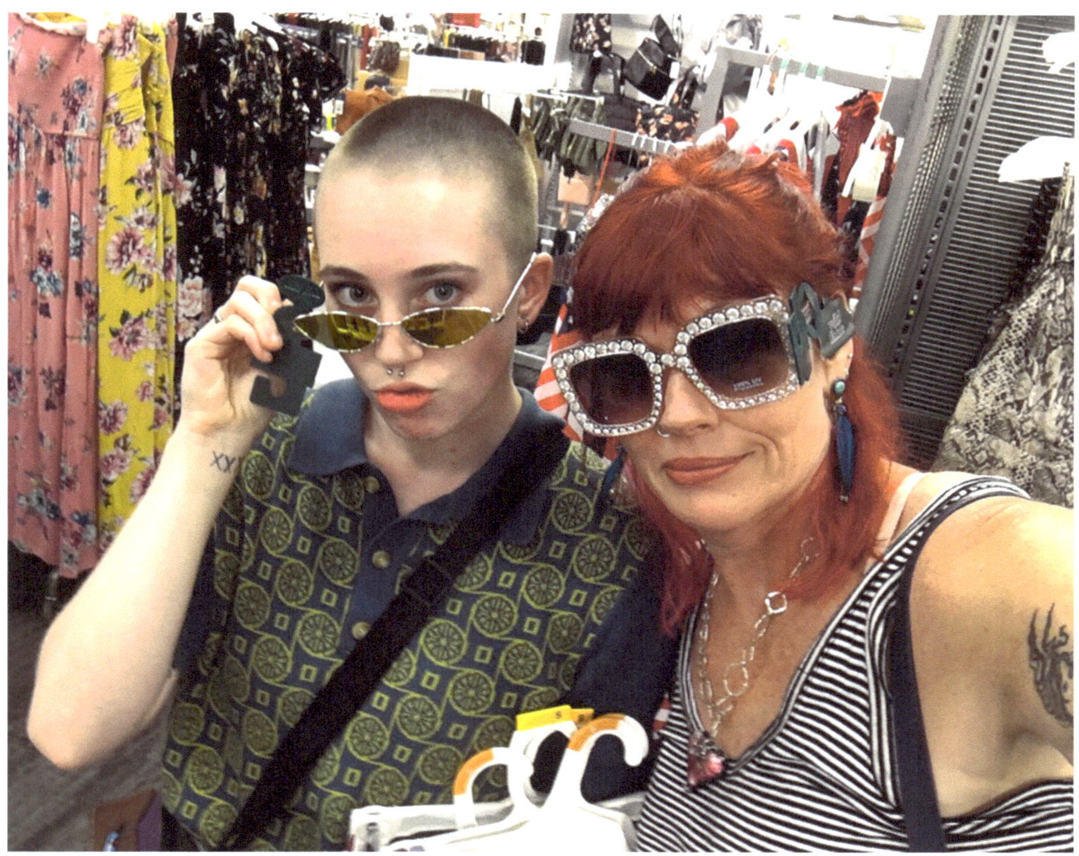

Emilie Elizabeth and I goofing around in Target.

finding your muse

When I was 30 years old, I gave birth to a bouncing baby girl who became a toddling dancer at the young age of three years old. My first portrait of her was from a dance recital when she was about four or five. The dance was titled "North to Alaska" and the costume consisted of lots and lots of fuzzy feathers and shimmery white fabric. I created the portrait of her in soft pastel, my medium of choice in those days.

Over the years I have painted Emilie more times that I can count. She has provided me with endless inspiration and copious amounts iPhone selfies. I could paint her over and over again and never be bored—she's animated and expressive, her sense of fashion and her expressions make for great portraits.

Who inspires you?

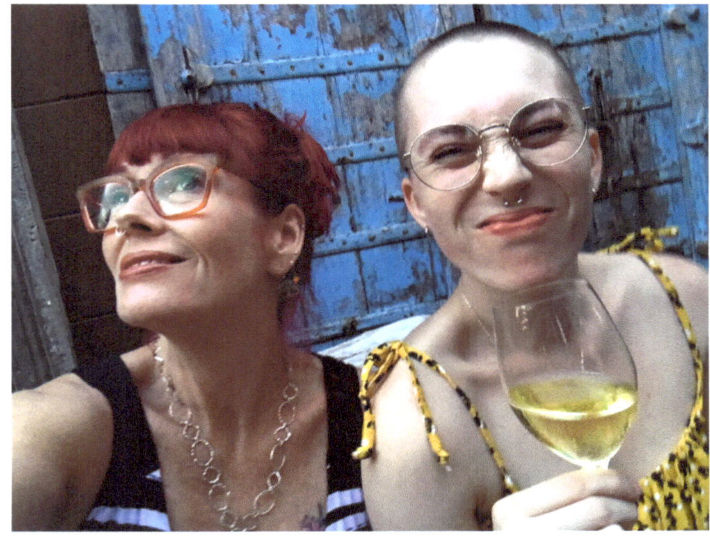

My daughter has been my muse since she was a little kid

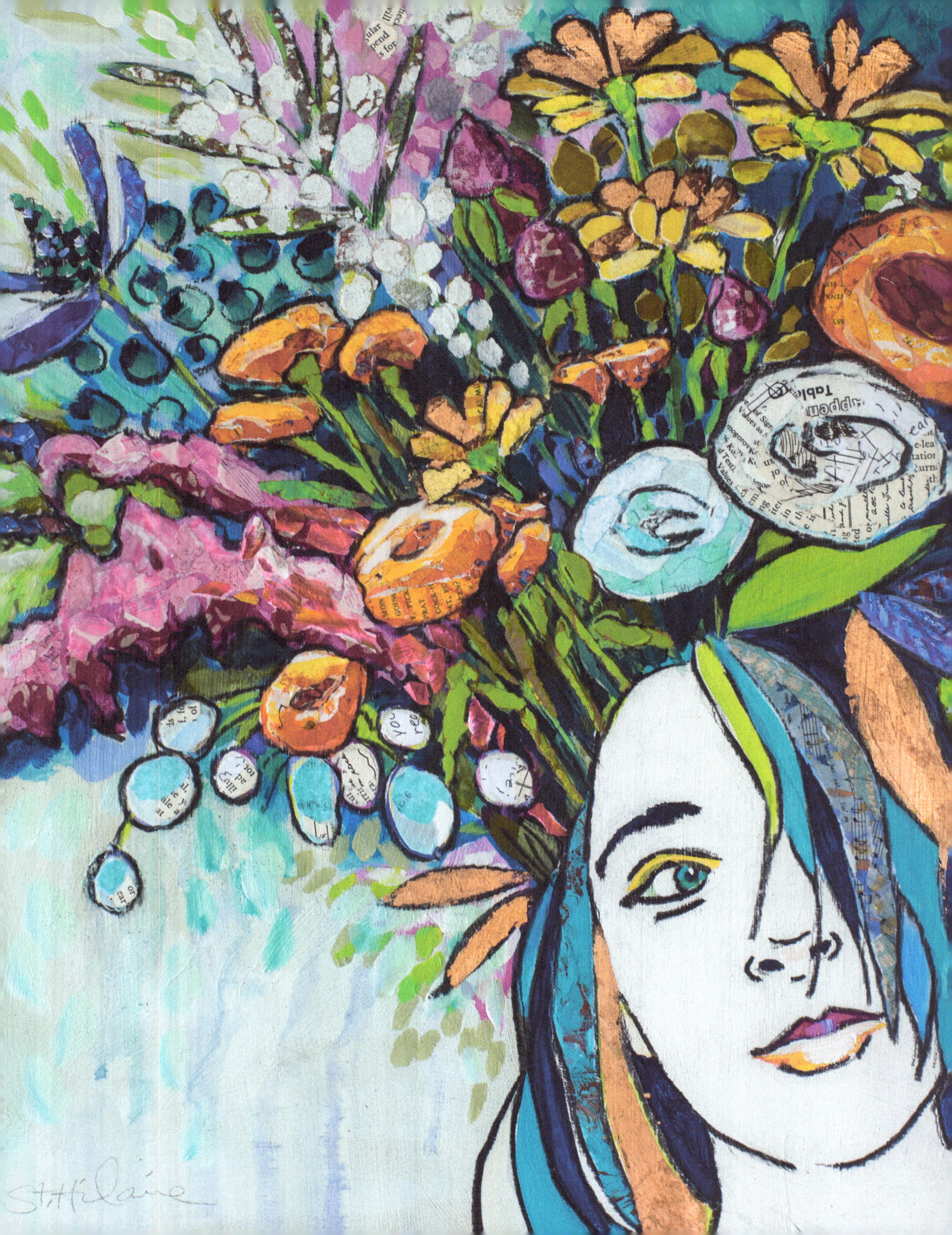
St Hilaire

photo resources

Below are some resources for public domain and copyright free photographs. Use your own photos, use the photos with permission from the photographer, or do you own on-line search for photos in the public domain.

In addition to your muse, you will also need to find inspiration for fashion elements that you can incorporate into your sketch such as floral crowns, jewelry, hats, scarves, etc. You'll want these kinds of elements to incorporate color, collage, and mark making.

If you are interested in painting one of your own photos, you'll want to crop it head and shoulders and size it up to at least 16x20. Working larger than life is easier that working on a smaller scale–small details can present big challenges. A good resource for up-sizing your own image and printing it at home is rapidresizer.com

You may also print out your photo oversized and manually crop it (scissors) to fit your substrate; this is the low-tech approach, but it works!

Websites to check out:

Pinterest: Public Domain People

Unsplash.com

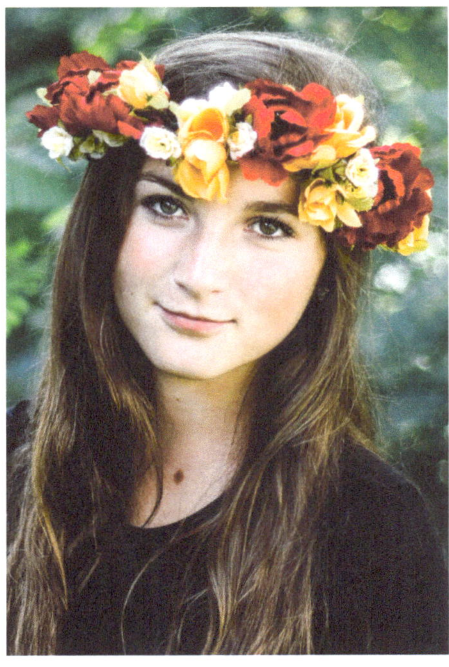
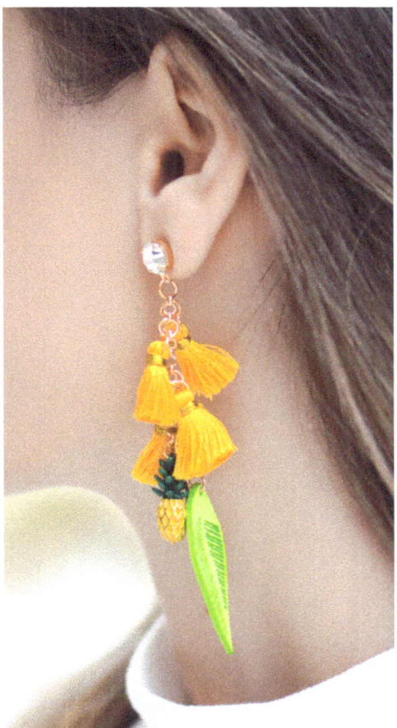
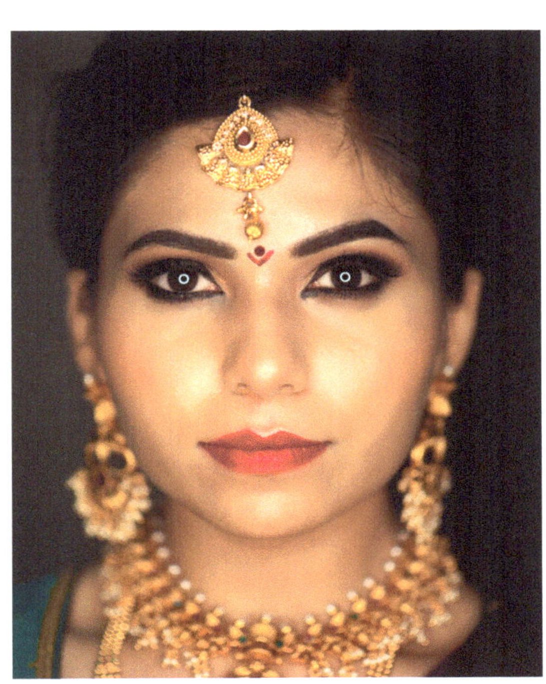

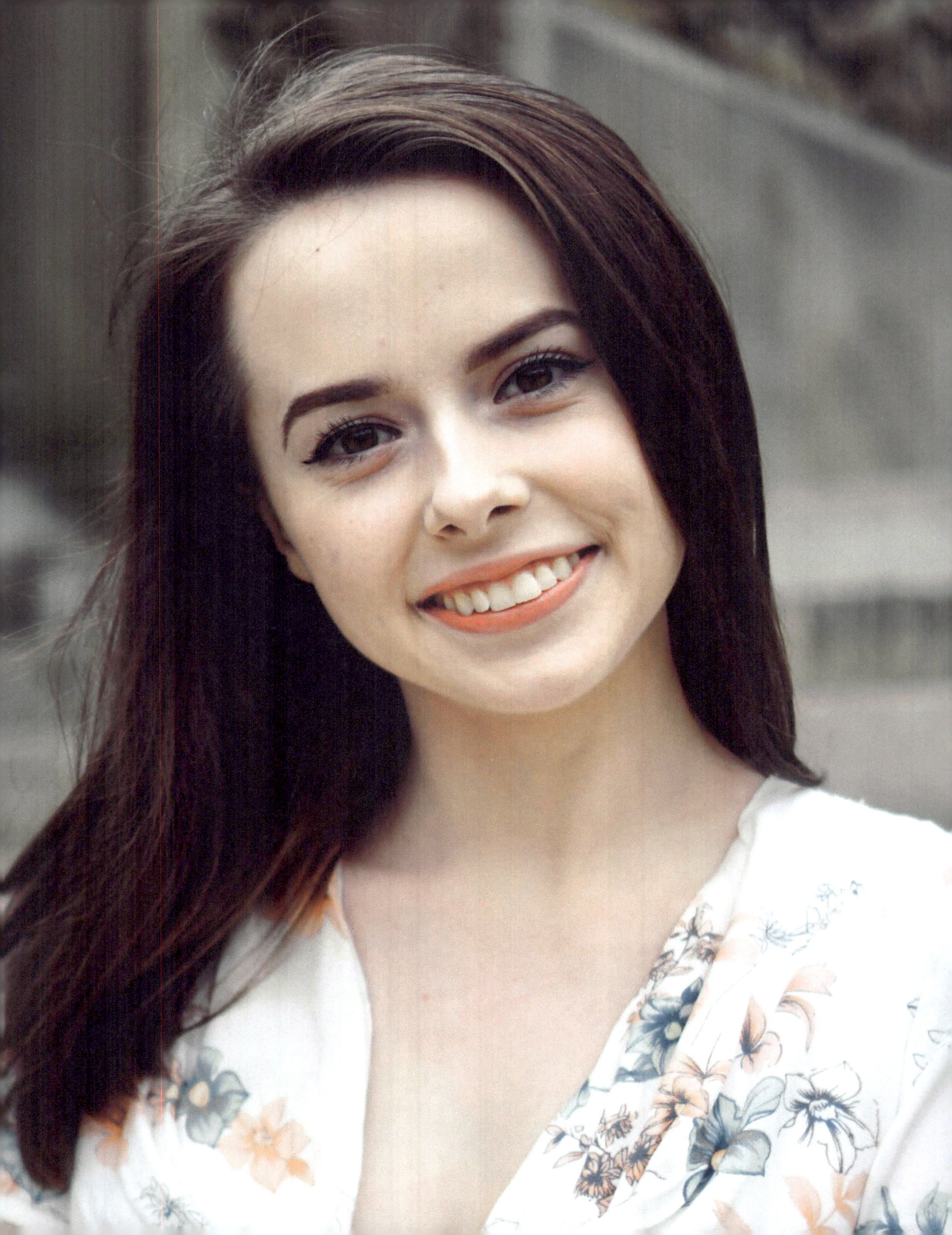

gathering supplies

Gathering and collecting art supplies is a source of great joy for every artist. Mixed media collage offers endless possibilities for combinations of supplies. I encourage you to experiment with what you have on hand in addition to what I list below, as you may have already gathered lots of wonderful art tools and goodies that appeal to your personal sense of adventure. Visit my Amazon Resource page: Amazon.com/Shop/Paper-Paintings-Collage-Artwork for a complete listing of (with links) the recommended products for my workshops.

basic supplies

- Graphite transfer paper to transfer your photo to the board as a sketch

- Soft black pastel sticks for sketching and shading (you can also use charcoal, but pastel is more dense and appears more black)

- Blending Stump for blending pastel in small detail areas

- Pink Pearl eraser

- Drafting brush for removing eraser crumbs without smearing your drawing

- Golden Fluid Acrylic Paint Starter Set for under-painting your subject matter and hand-painting your papers. Keep in mind the colors of your portrait and your ability to mix color, purchase additional colors of paints accordingly, I suggest starting with 1 oz bottles.

- Container of white gesso for priming your wood panels and adding white to certain paint colors in order to make them more opaque.

- Container of black gesso for blocking in dark areas with complete opaque effects

- Mona Lisa Gold Simple Leaf with transfer papers

- Mona Lisa Metal Leaf Adhesive

- Wood Painting Panel Let's go BIG. I'm working on a 16×20 deep wood painting panel so that I can wire and hang it without framing. (these come in natural wood and need to be primed first with two coats of white gesso)

- Masterson Sta-Wet Palette system, this will save your paints for up to a week or more! AND I use the palette sheets in my collage when I'm done mixing on them. (They are not shiny)

gel printing

- Gel Press Plate 8×10 and a hard rubber brayer

- Joggles 9x12 Stencils Designed by Me!

- Punchinella or sequin waste or honeycomb ribbon

- Texture rubbing plates

- Small spray bottles for the soap bubble spritz

- Rice paper–there are many different kinds, the pad on my Amazon Page is what I like the best. You may find others at your local supply store, but please avoid super thin rice papers, as they tear easily.

- Variety of found papers sheet music, maps, hand written notes, old book pages, kids homework, love letters, vintage books, personal ephemera, fun stuff! This we will use to create the base layer of the collage, so gather enough papers to cover the surface of your board.

ephemera base layer

- Liquitex Gloss Gel Medium this is the collage glue, I use gloss because it keeps the colors more vibrant and rich, matte products dull the intensity of your colors

- Paint Brushes, I like Princeton Catalyst short handle #8 filbert specifically for glue application. For painting, please use what you have on-hand in your studio and are comfortable with.

- Princeton Catalyst Polytip Brush long handle, flat, size 20 specifically for gluing down large pieces of background ephemera, this brush is about two inches wide and the bristles are nice and rigid. We will also use this brush to apply the encaustic effect medium

- Golden Extra Heavy Gel Matte for creating the encaustic effect

- Golden Fluid Acrylic Interference Gold Fine for adding that golden glow to the encaustic effect
- Palette Knife for mixing

mark making

- Posca Paint Markers, permanent and opaque, choose your preferred tip, I like the fine
- Stabilo Woodies, these thick pencils will write on top of your collage glue! They require no tooth, they will blend with water (should you choose) or leave them as heavy lines. You'll want to spray vanish Woodies before you apply brush varnish.

signing your work

- Faber Castell Artists PITT Pen, permanent and fade proof in dark sepia brown, medium point
- Uni-ball Signo Gel Pen permanent and fade proof for signing in dark areas. Or use whatever light-fast, permanent, fine point tool you might have in your studio!
- Pencil or charcoal pencil

varnishing your work

- Golden Satin Varnish with UVLS (ultra violet light stabilization) I prefer a satin finish, but you may prefer matte or gloss.
- Krylon Satin Finish Spray for sealing and stabilizing your sketching materials before painting
- Clean, soft bristled, flat, wide brushes for varnishing your work

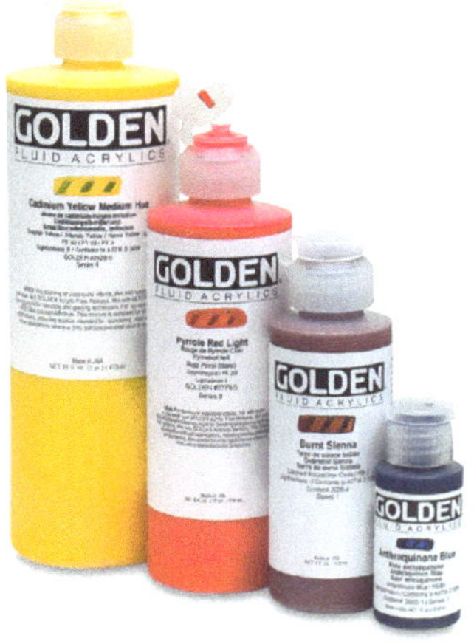

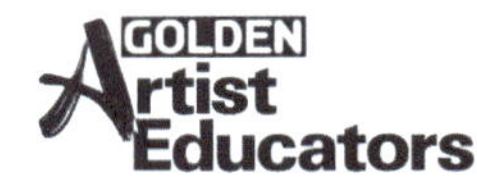

I have been trained by Golden Paints in the use and application of all their products.

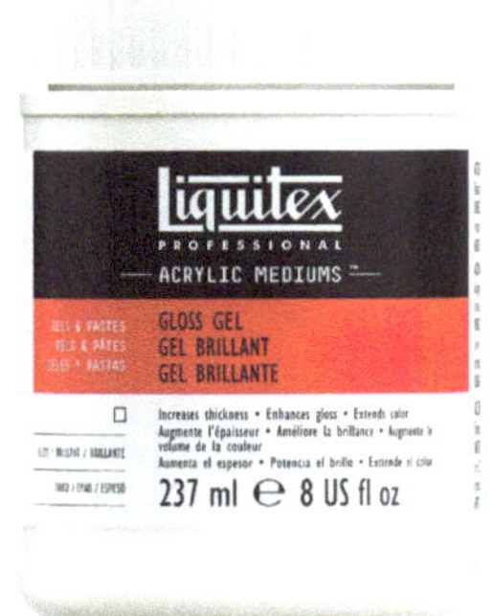

I use Liquitex Gloss Gel Medium as my collage glue, it's thick and stays in place while I work upright at the easel.

a note about rice paper

These acid-free papers are strong and highly absorbent. They are made in the centuries-old Japanese tradition. They are white and natural tones which make an excellent base for creating your own brilliantly colored collage papers. All are available on-line and most can be found at your local art supply store in the Chinese brush painting section.

Rice paper takes the color all the way through and lays flat when glued because of its' absorbent properties. I purchase rice papers on a roll and in a pad. Rice paper comes with and without fibers, both have different applications in collage.

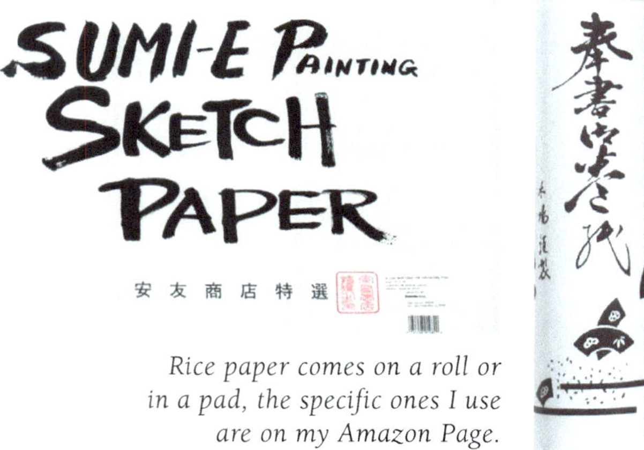

Rice paper comes on a roll or in a pad, the specific ones I use are on my Amazon Page.

painting paper

There are so many papers that are great for collage. I paint anything from old maps to printmaking paper to rice paper to my kids homework.

I am also a fan of found papers, so check out your local used book store or library for some old books that you can take the pages out of. This paper is often great quality, the text adds another layer of creativity in the hand painted paper process, and the books are typically inexpensive.

I have learned through experimentation that glossy coated paper stock is not good for collage. This type of paper tends to cockle and that means the viewer's eye knows it's paper, even from afar. Since I want my artwork to appear as a painting, all papers must lay completely flat.

I also enjoy purchasing decorative papers from my local art supply store with fibers, metallic patterning, and textures. I grab these papers in white or natural tones so that I can paint them any color from yellow to black. In painting paper, experimentation is key, and practice makes perfect.

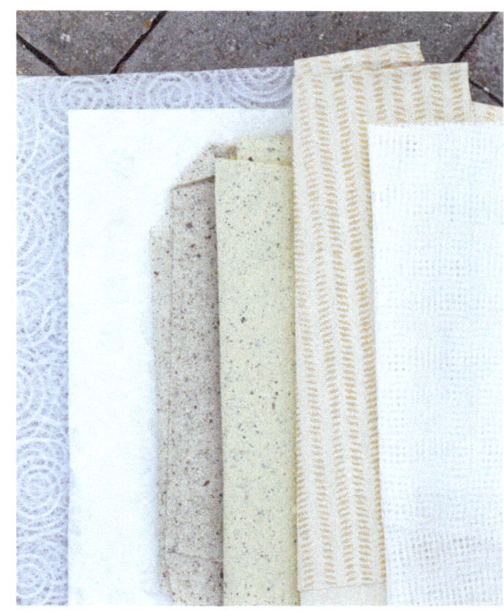

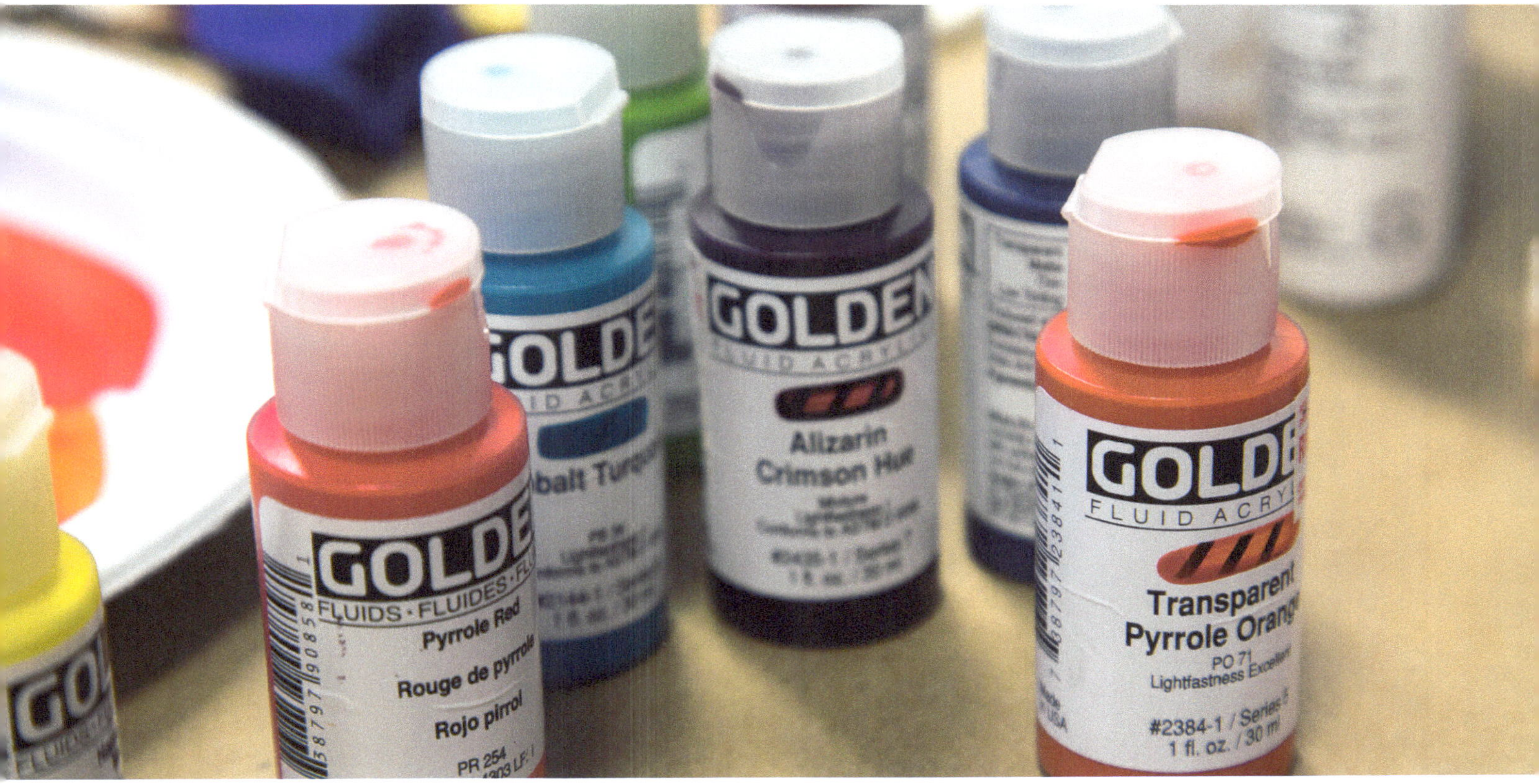

Some samples of my natural toned art store purchased decorative papers. I like the fibers, textures, inclusions, and lace cut patterns.

I prefer Golden Fluid Acrylic colors for painting my collage papers and my under-painting. These paints are light-fast, durable, and flexible. They are wonderfully versatile, professional quality acrylic colors with the consistency of heavy cream. Visit them on-line and request a color swatch chart for accurate color representation at *GoldenPaints.com*

Fluid Acrylics are highly pigmented and translucent, this is important. Every layer of paint allows the previous layer to shine through. This is the effect of translucent paints, they multiply and blend as you lay one technique of painting paper over another.

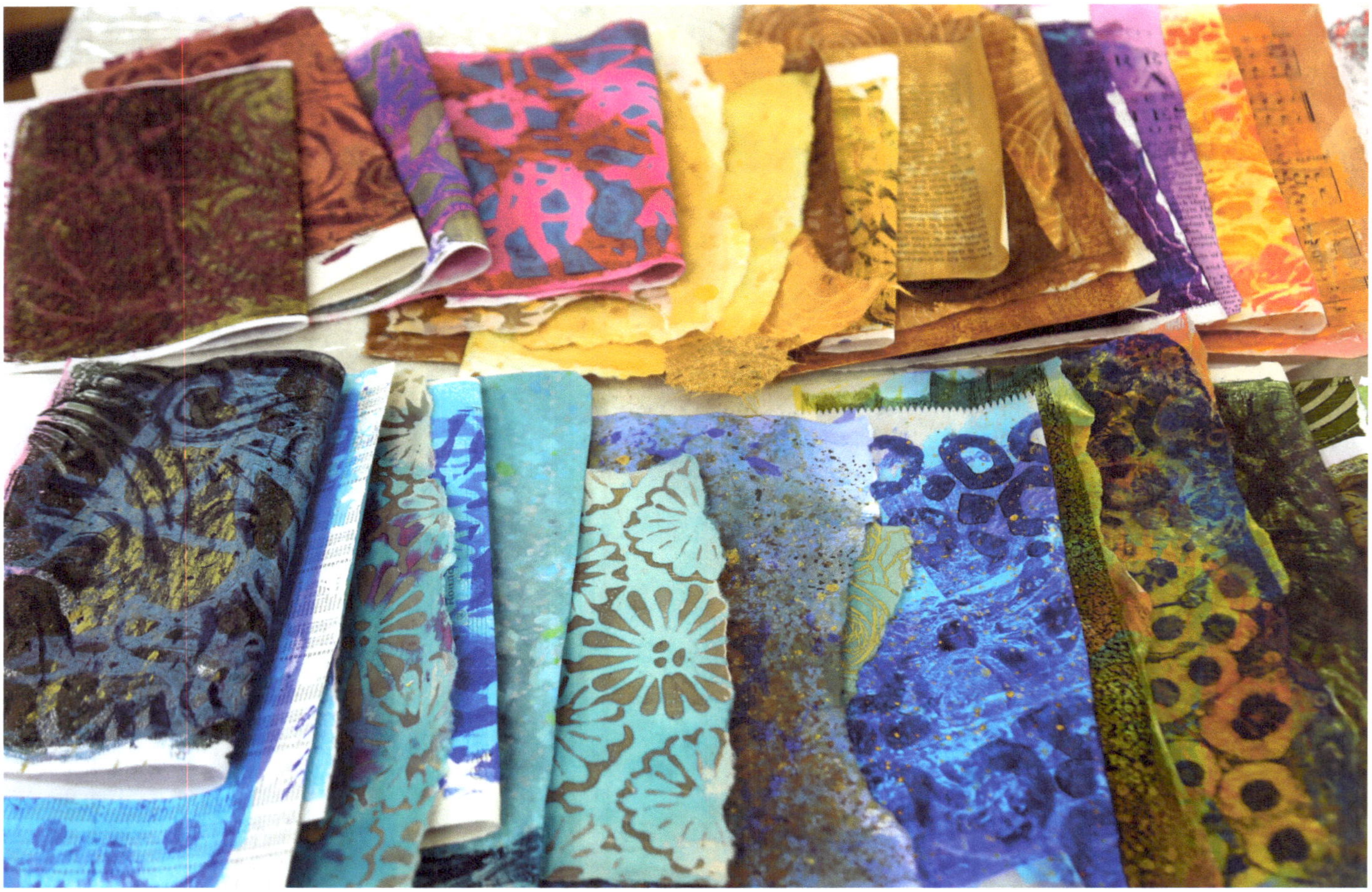

Create a paper palette in all the colors and shades of your portrait.

why paint your own paper?

In the beginning, I used pre-colored papers in my collage work. I found the most richly colored, textured, patterned papers in the art store and I collected and coveted them on every trip I took. On a trip to New York City I must have spent over $100 on sheets of luxuriously colored papers at the store Kate's Paper.

What happened next was sad, but true. Most pre-colored papers fade! These papers are possibly colored with dye and not pure pigment (the color that is the base of all fine art paints and pastels). Dye fades over time, depending on its exposure to sunlight. It will break your heart to see a collage fading right in front of you, little by little, as the years go by. At first you might not even notice it, until you look at a photo of the artwork on your computer, and all of a sudden you realize that your original just does not look as vibrant as it used to.

To combat this dilemma, I started painting my own collage papers. I use Golden Artist Colors Fluid Acrylic paints, these are professional grade paints. Painting my own papers offered me a whole new world of possibilities of color, texture, pattern, shading...A perfect _paper palette!_

Fluid Acrylic paints are an excellent choice for painting your own collage papers. You can water them down extensively and they keep the same level of vibrancy, making them excellent for dripping and splattering.

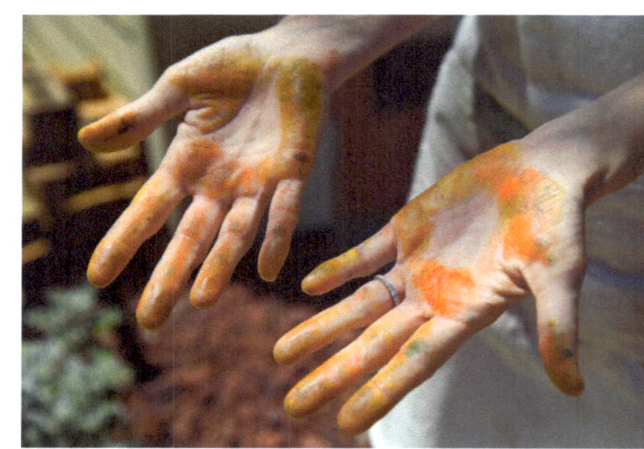

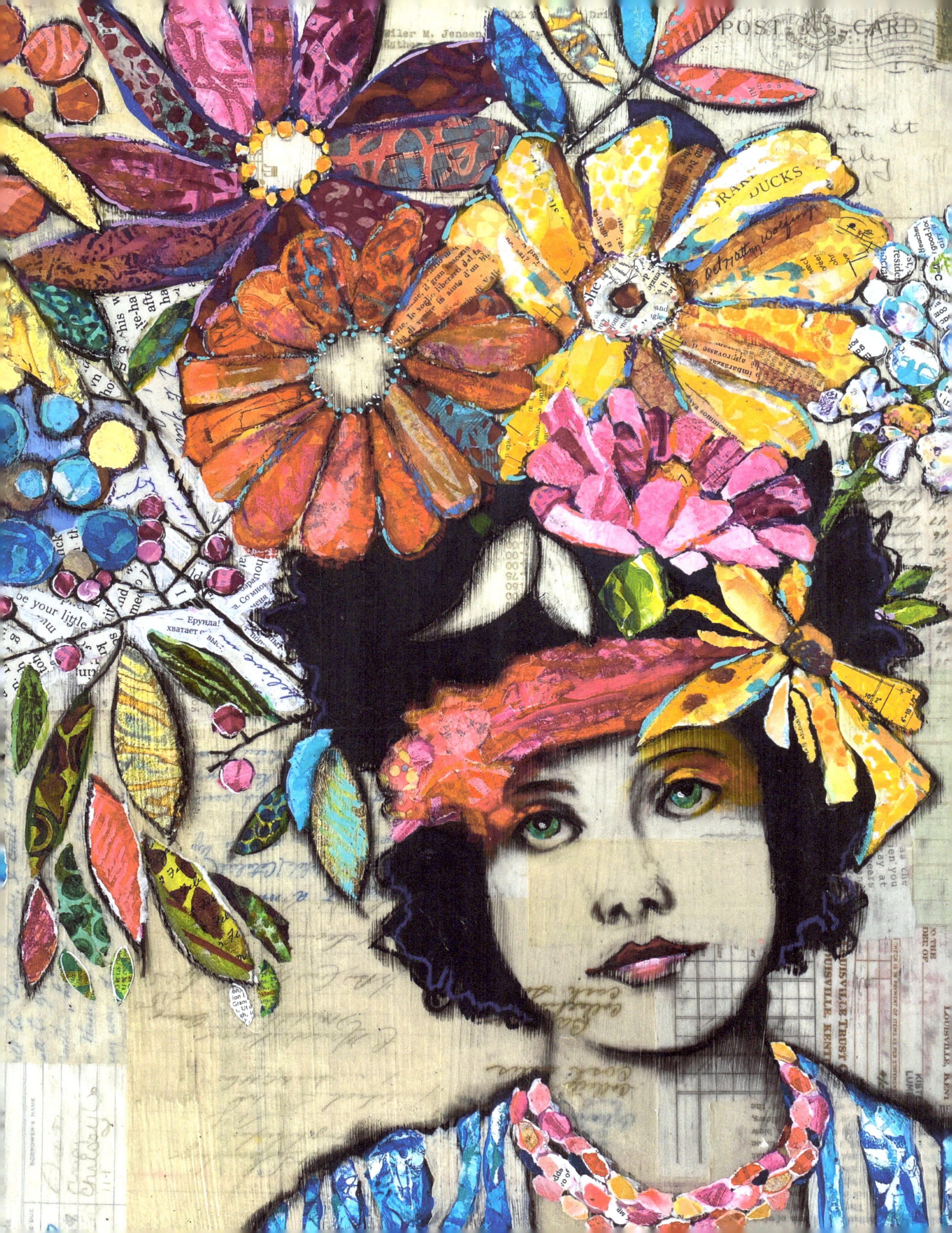
POST CARD

PAPER

variety is key

Keep in mind that you'll be painting papers in a full range of values, from the deepest darkest shadow color to the very lightest highlight color and *every* color in between. The portrait to the left makes use of a wide range of papers in the floral headpiece, the jewelry, and the clothing. Every one of those petals employs a different pattern and layering of techniques.

You can never have enough paper, because each paper brush mark and petal must be different from the one that is glued down next to it. Why is this so? Because if you glue the same paper next to itself, visually the two pieces become one. In order to create a collage that looks like a painting, we must maintain individual paper brush marks–this means within every value of every color there must be many *different* papers.

color organization

In my studio I divide my papers into nine plastic drawers of color. If a paper includes two different colors, I tear it in half and put it in both drawers.

When you are ready to collage, it's much easier to find the perfect value of green when you have organized your colors so that all of your green is in one place. I use three sets of three clear, stacked drawers by Sterilite. They pull out of their framework easily so that I can set them on my taboret one-at-a-time and easily dig through the color I am looking for.

Storage solutions are personal. Although nine plastic drawers work for me, you may need more or less depending on your own organizational process.

Visit my Amazon shopping resource page for my favorite art products.

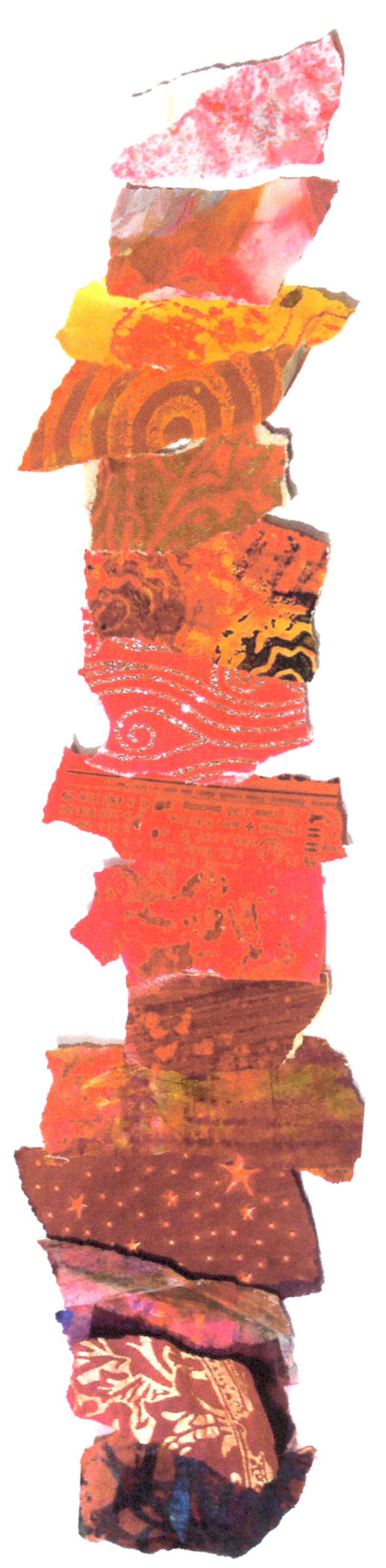

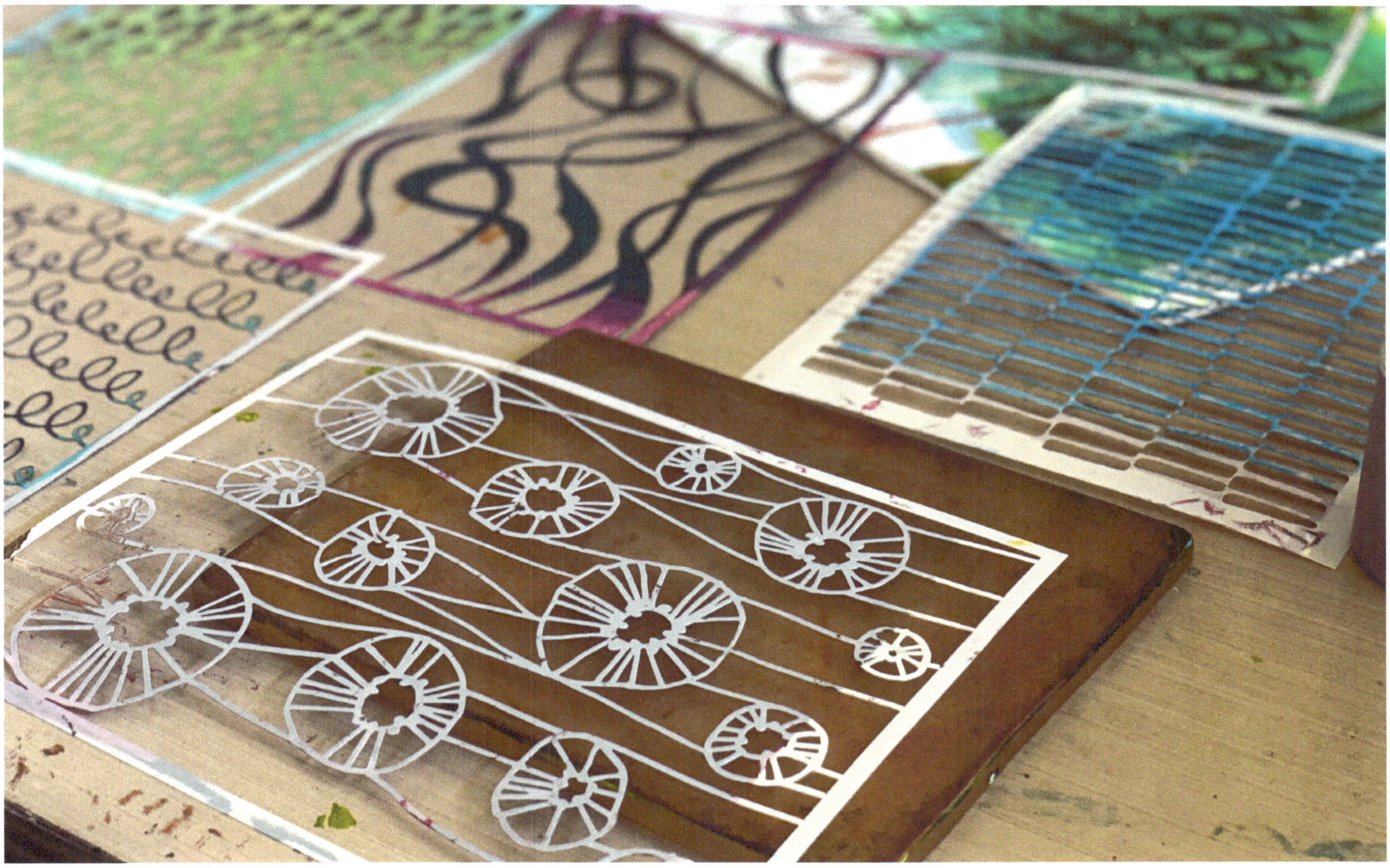

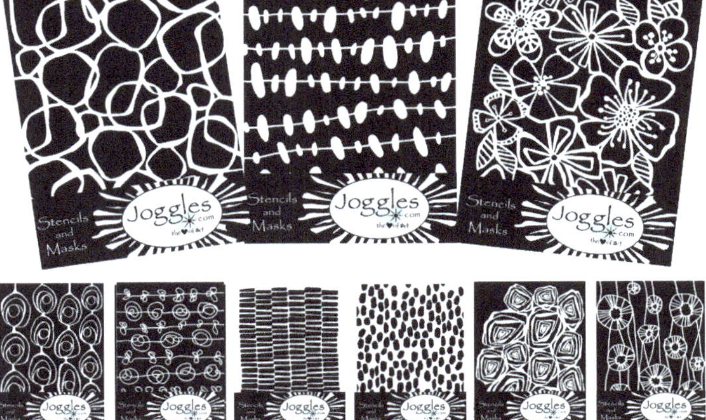
My stencil designs work great with the 8x10 Gel Plate

my stencil designs

I create about 80% of my hand painted paper through the monoprinting process using a reusable gel printing plate by Gel Press and my own stencil designs with Joggles.com. I am super excited about my line of stencil designs which debuted in 2019. I have designed my stencils for the purpose of hand painted collage paper. What does this mean? I am focused on line quality, shape, thickness, and design.

I've created over 45 9x12 stencil designs for Joggles.com

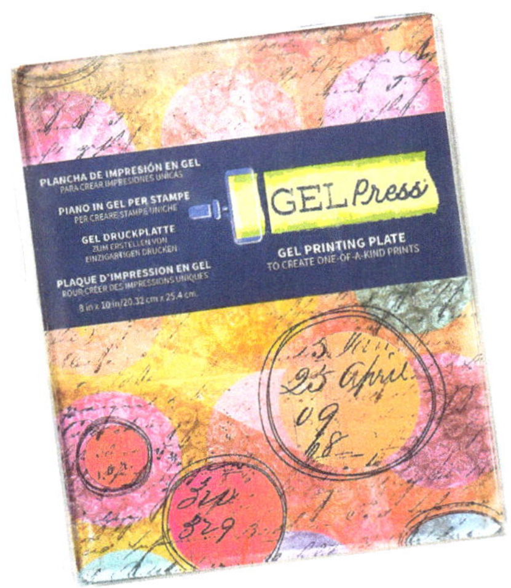

Many of you already have stencils in your stash. If you are looking to add more or you are new to stencils, you might like to try some of my 9x12 designs which are perfectly sized for the 8x10 Gel Press Gel Plate.

Visit **Joggles.com 9x12 Stencils and Masks** to view my collection of designs.

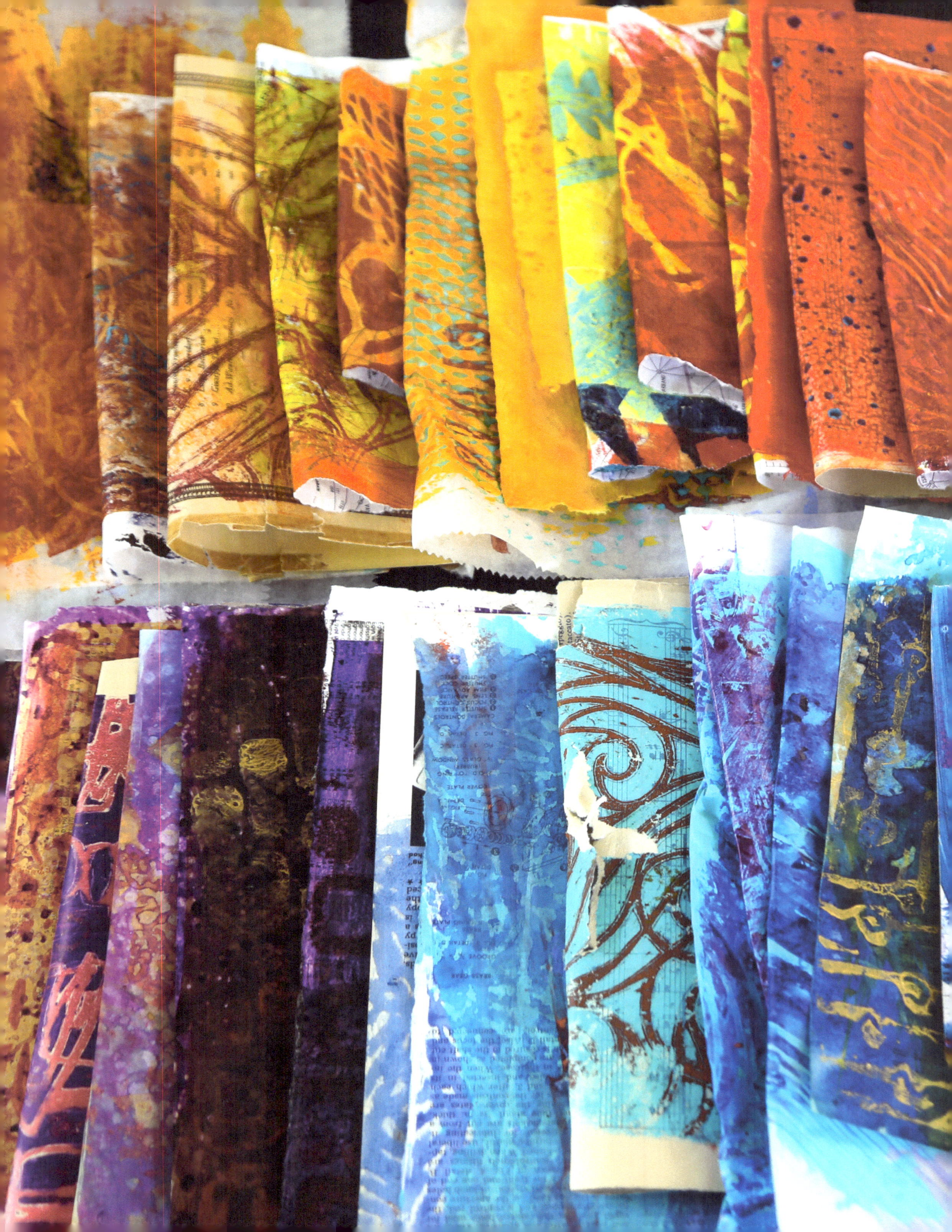

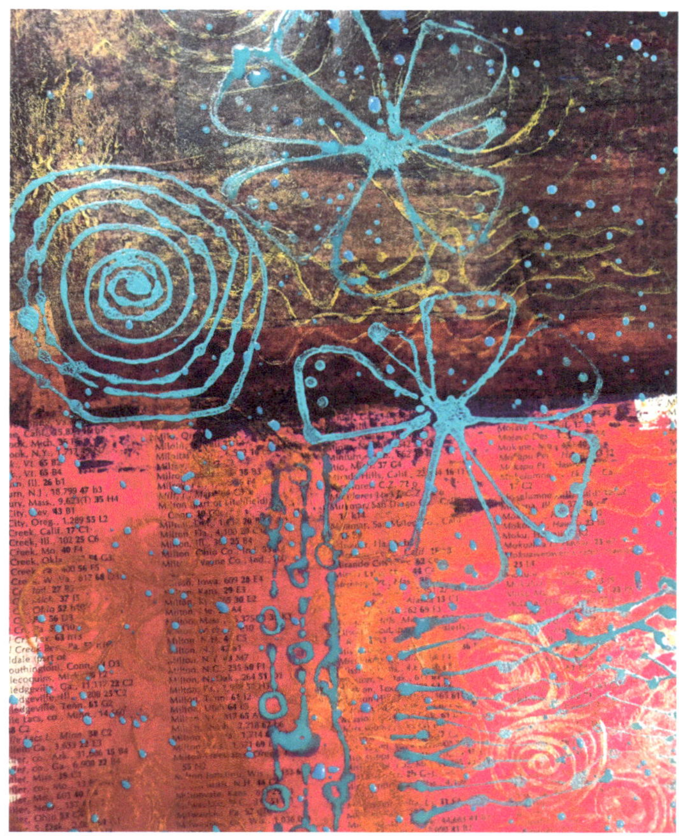

COMBINATIONS: RubberMoon stamps with splatter over an old atlas page

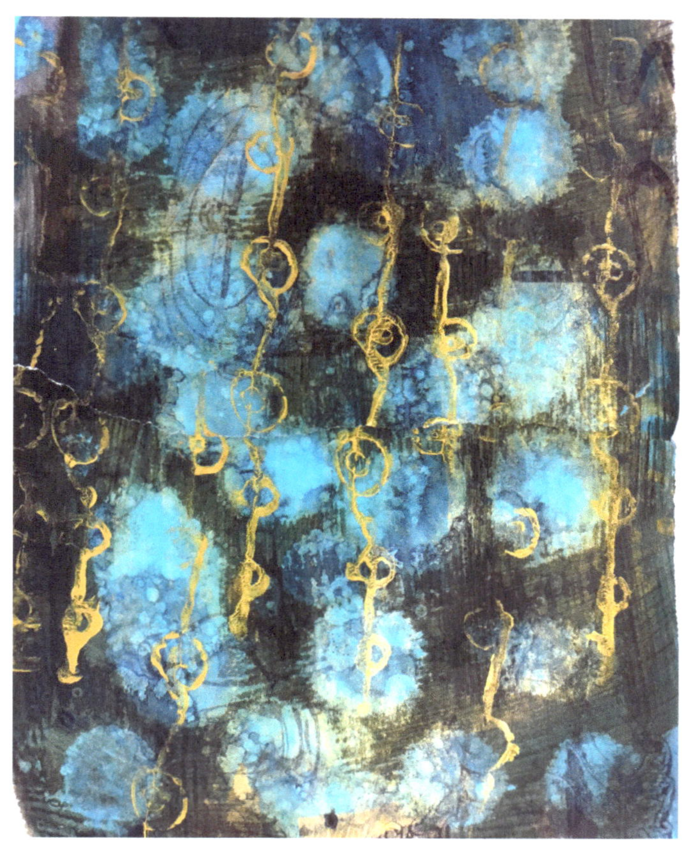

COMBINATIONS: RubberMoon stamps with metallic gold over blotted alcohol resist on an old book page

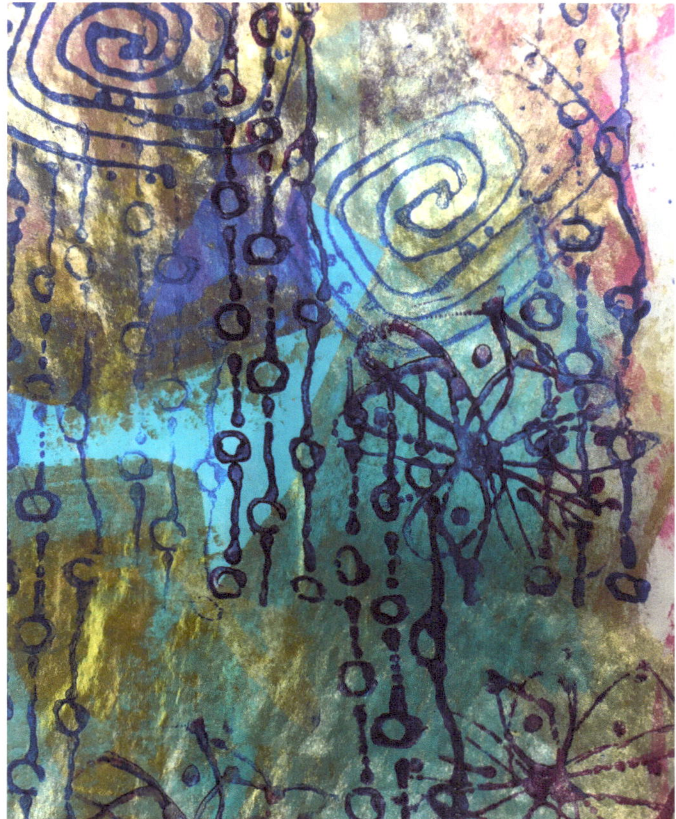

COMBINATIONS: RubberMoon stamps overlapping with metallic paint over credit card scraping on deli paper

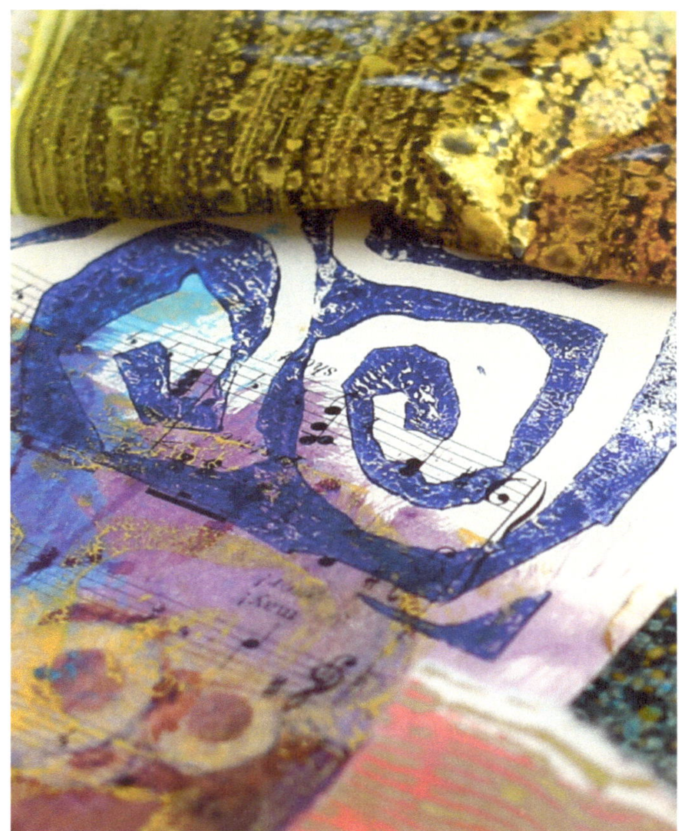

COMBINATIONS: RubberMoon stamps overlapping with alcohol resist and plastic card scraping on sheet music paper

painting paper
techniques

Stamping
Materials:

- Art stamps from RubberMoon.com
- Paint Brush and/or brayer
- Fluid Acrylic Paint or permanent, archival ink pad

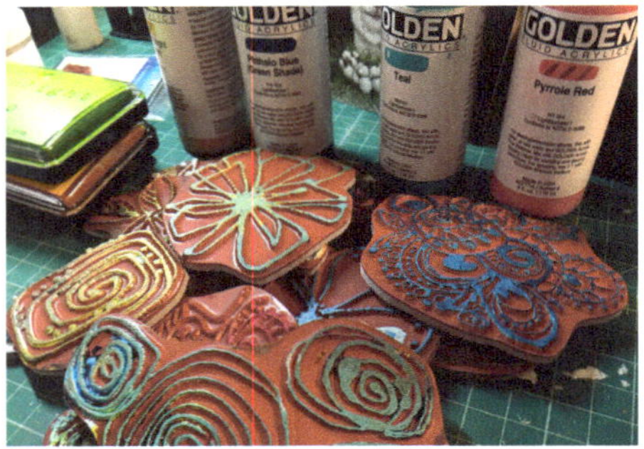

My designed stamps with RubberMoon

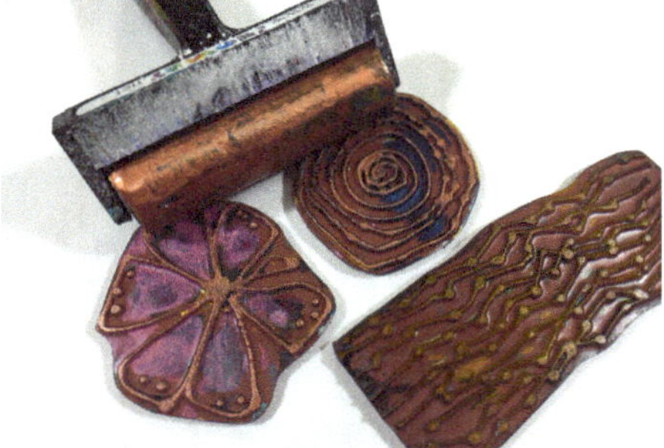

Add paint to stamps

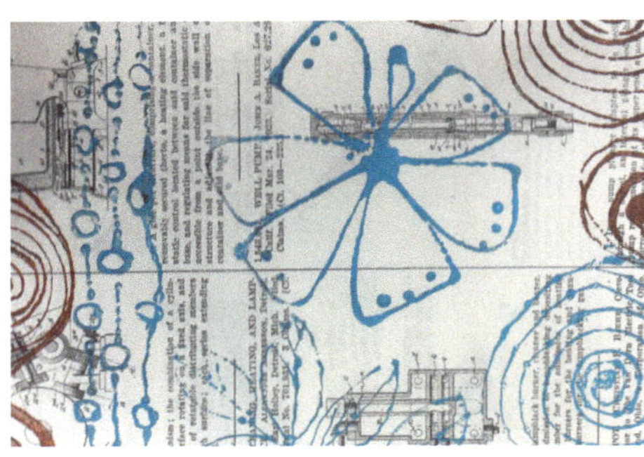

Press stamps onto paper

I typically use my brayer to spread Golden Fluid Acrylic paints directly onto art stamps of my own design with RubberMoon. I use the brayer so that the paint stays on the patterned area of the stamp and does not fill into the negative spaces. You can clean your stamps with baby wipes immediately after spreading paint on them, you can also use a toothbrush with The Masters Brush Cleaner to get dried paint off them. It is not recommended that you soak them in water. I typically print my stamp multiple times in order to remove as much paint as possible before wiping them down.

Companies such as Ranger offer stamp pads that are permanent and fade proof. You can use these for your paper painting or you can use acrylic paint, the effects are different and the choice is yours.

Stamping is just one of the techniques you will use in creating hand-painted papers. The idea is to take one sheet of paper through multiple techniques, adding layer upon layer of texture and pattern. This multi pass process is what makes your papers rich and painterly.

Using your archival ink pad or painting your stamp with acrylic paint, make impressions in multiple colors,

overlapping the images over the surface of a white sheet of rice paper or a paper that you have already layered with other techniques. Once the stamped impressions dry, try adding a wash of color over them to tone down any white areas of the base paper. Colors next to each other (analogous) on the color wheel offer harmonious effects, and colors more close to opposite on the wheel offer more intense and color vibrating effects, both are effective in different applications.

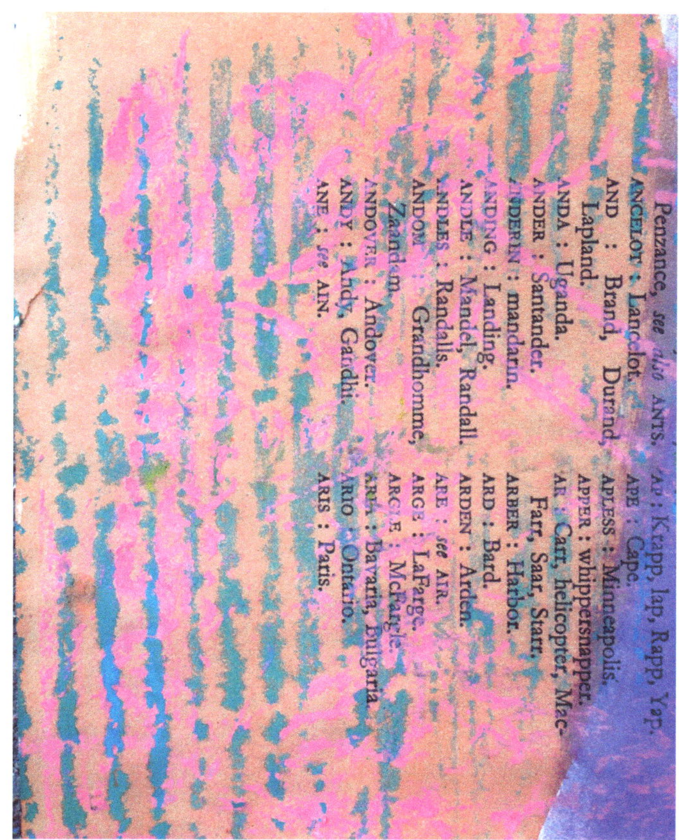

COMBINATIONS: Corrugated cardboard stamping combined with crayon resist & washes of color over an old book page

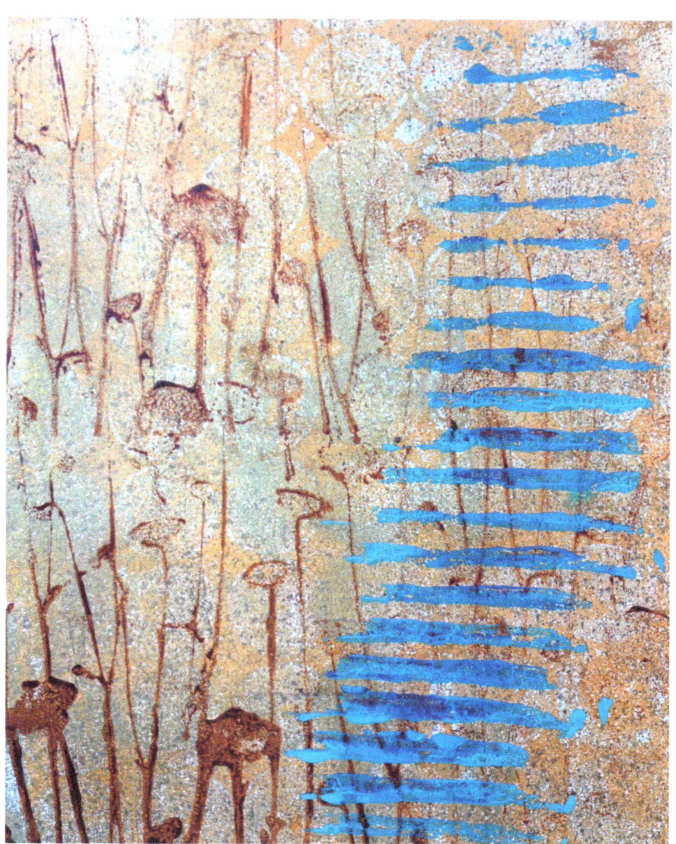

COMBINATIONS: Corrugated cardboard stamping over subtle sink liner stamping with commercial rubber stamping

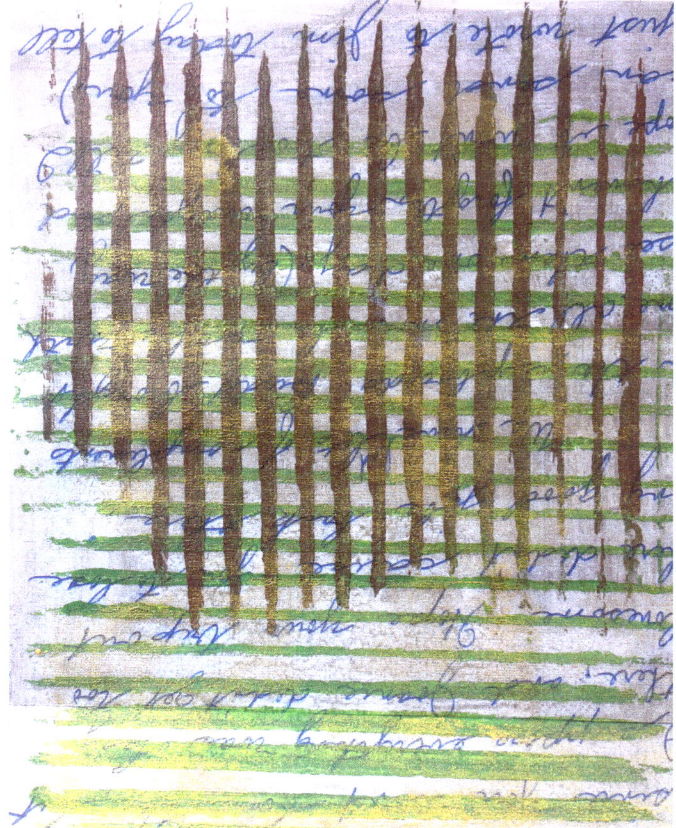

COMBINATIONS: Corrugated cardboard stamping with metallic paints over old hand written letter and pale wash

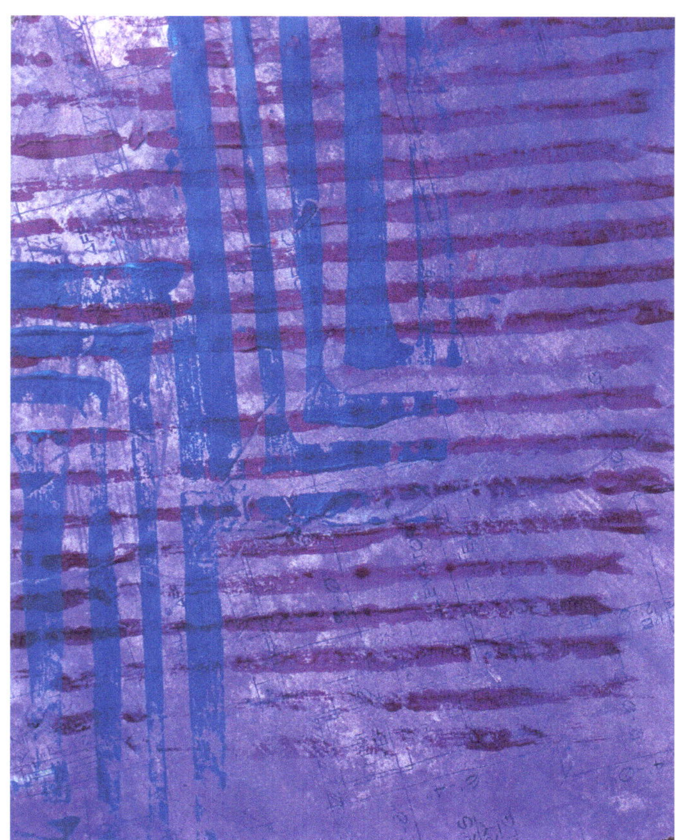

COMBINATIONS: Corrugated cardboard stamping with hand-carved stamp in opposite direction

painting paper
techniques

Corrugated Cardboard
Materials:

- Corrugated cardboard box material
- Gesso
- Acrylic paint
- Paint brush

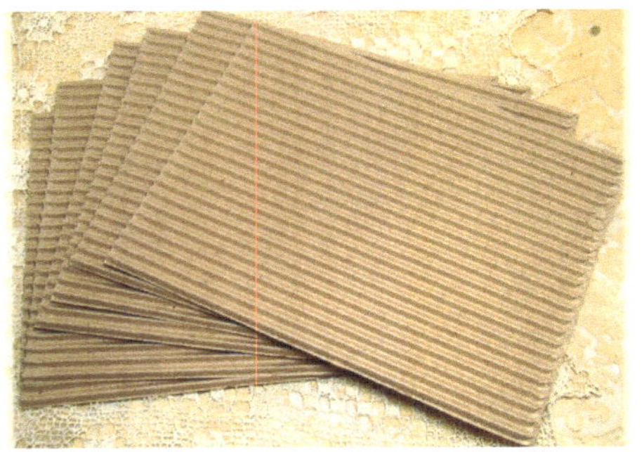

Corrugated cardboard box material

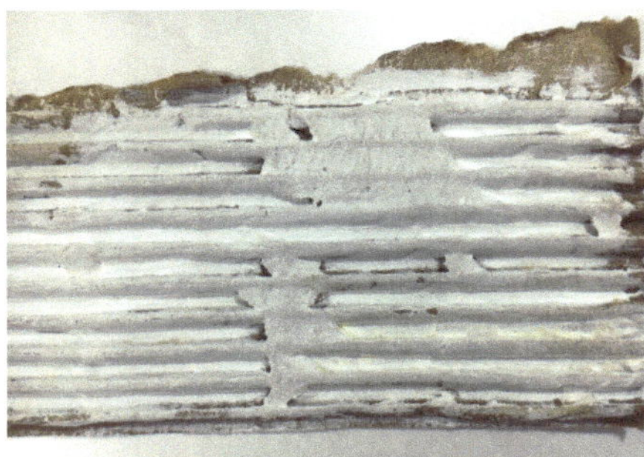

Gesso over corrugated cardboard pieces

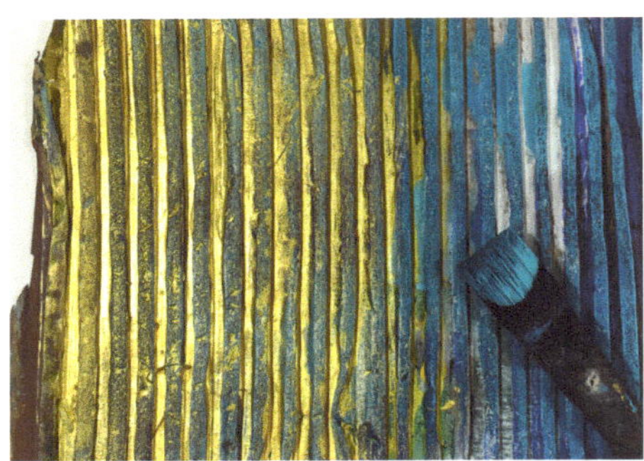

Apply a layer of paint over the cardboard

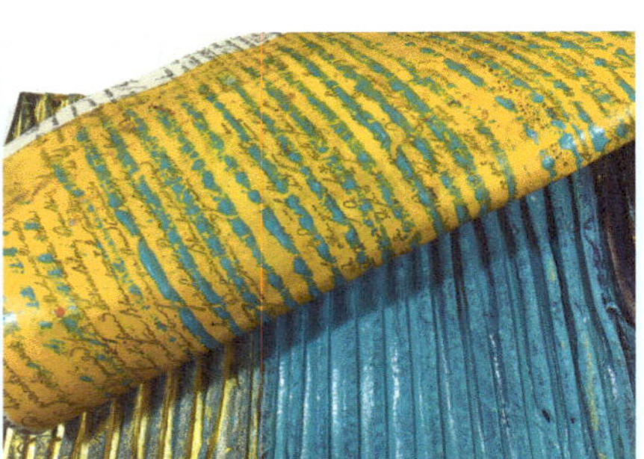

Press the paper onto the cardboard

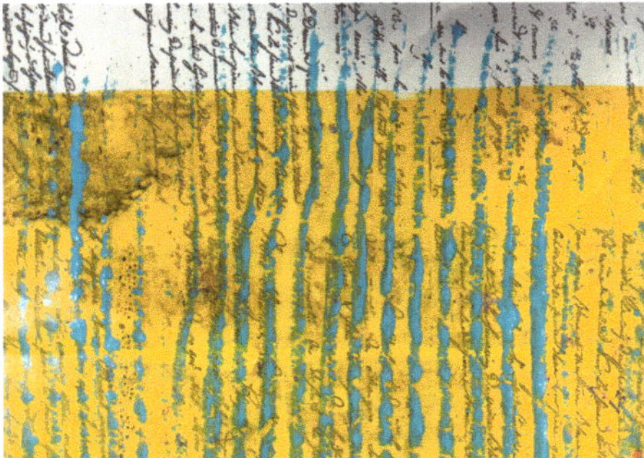

Corrugated lines over a yellow letter

Corrugated cardboard is something that arrives at your door on a regular basis if you are an *Amazon Prime* shopper like I am. If not, you can find free cardboard boxes from your local grocery store or COSTCO. This technique makes a wonderful second or third pass for your already embellished papers. The corrugated lines are much more organic and non-uniform once the cardboard has been pressed several times, it gets better with age!

Separate the cardboard to reveal the corrugation in the middle. Coat the corrugated surface with a layer of gesso on both sides and allow it to dry. This prevents absorption of moisture from the paint, which will deteriorate the cardboard before it gains character.

Apply undiluted paint onto the corrugated surface with a brush. Press the cardboard in either the same or overlapping directions onto any paper surface, experimenting with different types of paper and colors.

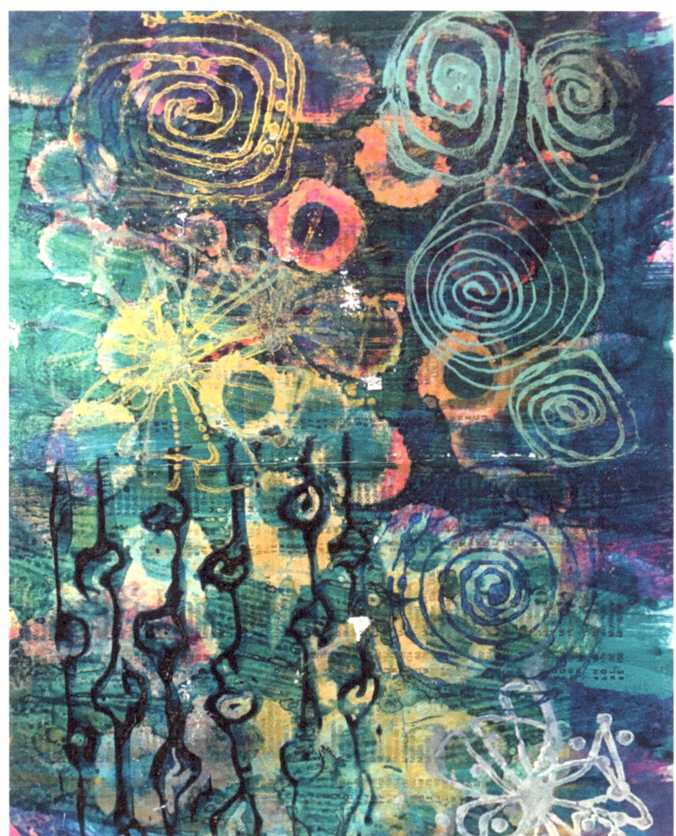

COMBINATIONS: Alcohol resist with rubber stamping

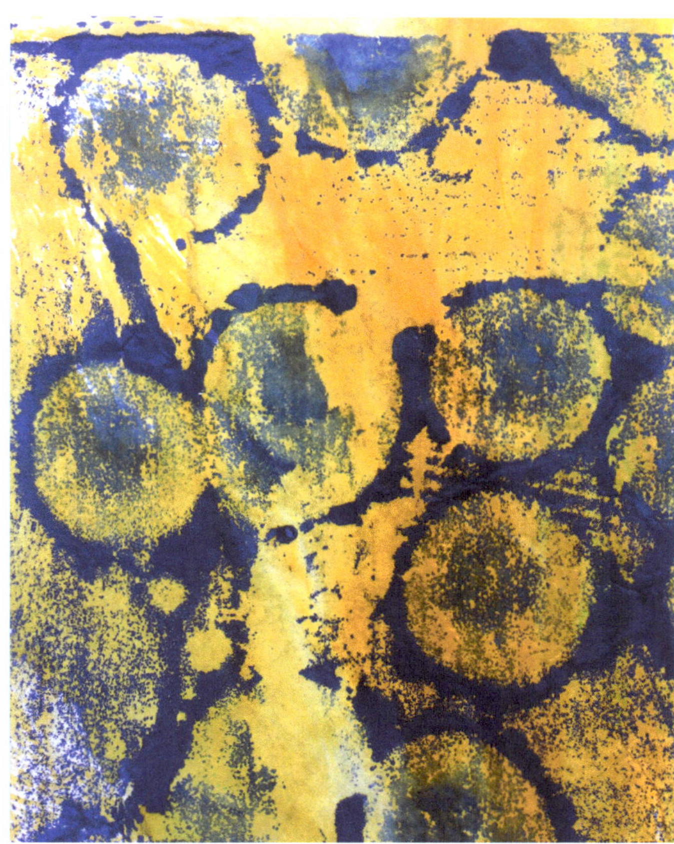

COMBINATIONS: A blotter paper type lift from the alcohol technique onto an absorbent rice paper

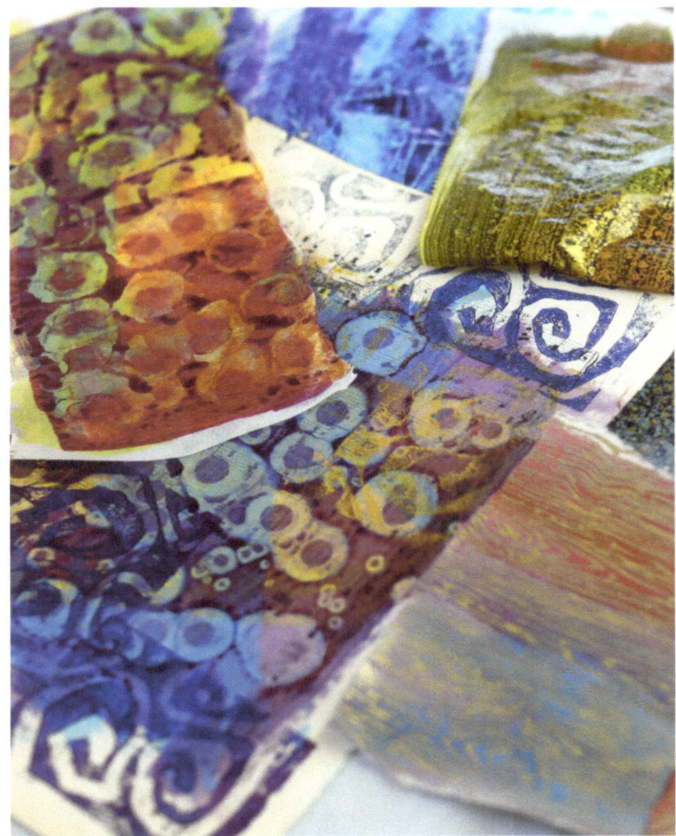

COMBINATIONS: Alcohol resist in various color combos

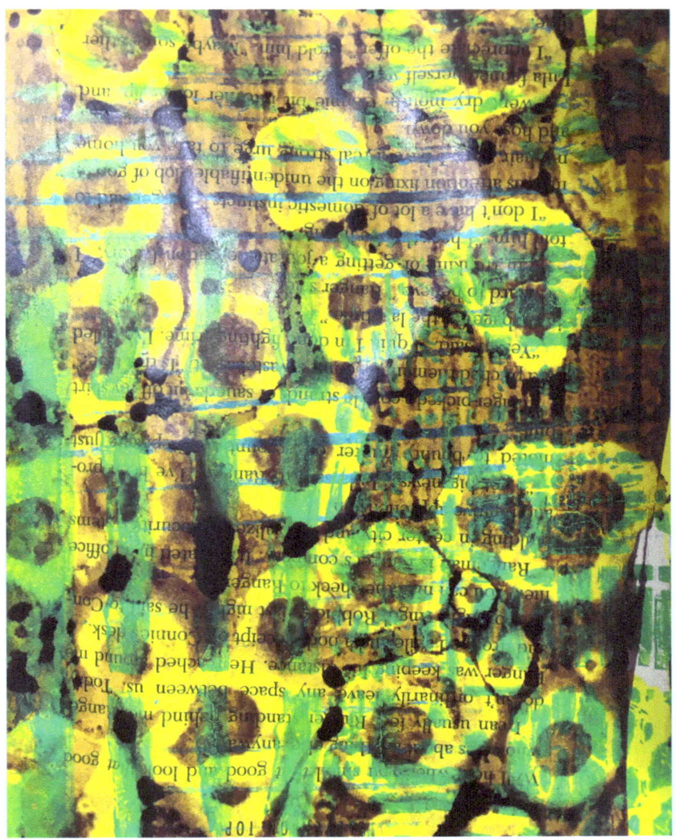

COMBINATIONS: Alcohol resist with cardboard stamping over an old book page

fashion plate **PORTRAITS**

painting paper
techniques

Alcohol Resist

Materials:

- Household rubbing alcohol
- Eye dropper
- Acrylic paint
- Nonabsorbent paper that does not soak up the paint

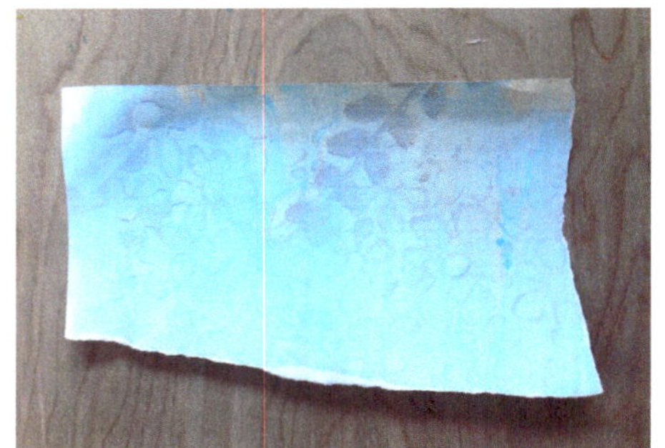

Wallpaper painted a light color and allowed to dry completely

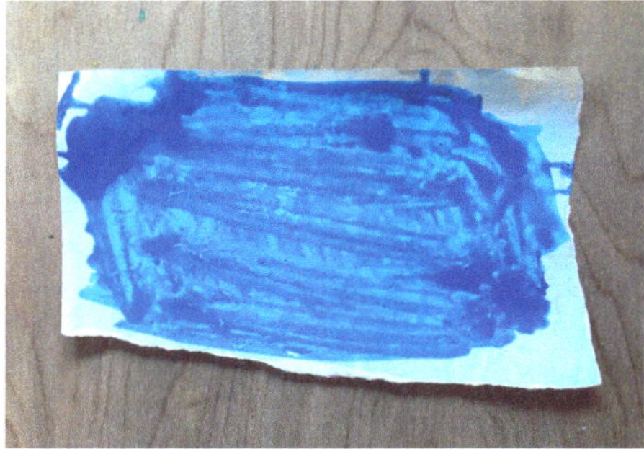

Overlay with a darker color, slightly watered down fluid acrylic paint

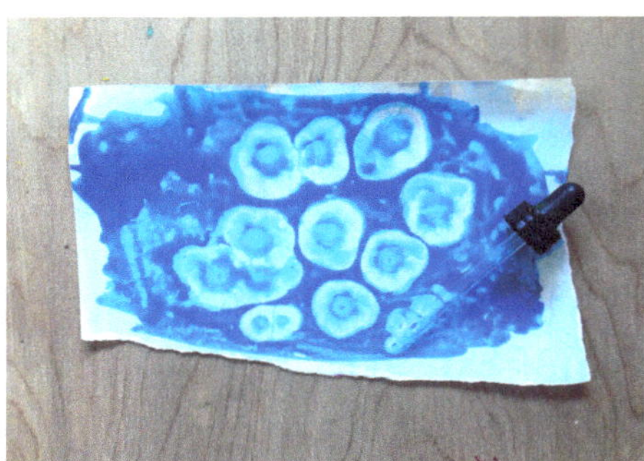

Working quickly, drop alcohol into wet paint with the eye dropper

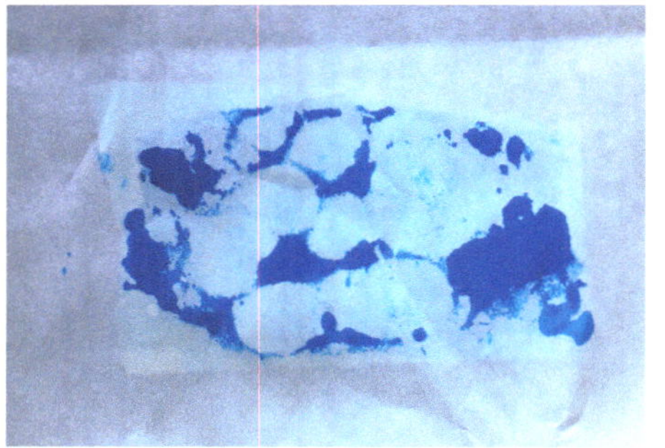

Option: blot off the paint with an absorbent rice paper and a light touch

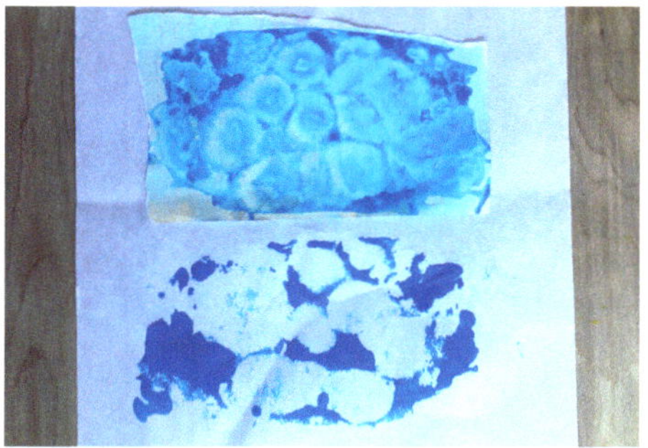

The alcohol pattern is transferred to the rice paper and can obscure the original effect

Rubbing alcohol from the first aid aisle (non-diluted isopropyl) pushes the pigment of acrylic paint away and can offer some wonderful resist techniques.

So many variables come into play with this technique: the type of paper and its' absorbency, the amount of water in the top layer of paint, and how dry the paint is when you drop the alcohol. It's best to experiment with this technique many times to get the best results.

Paint the paper with a light color paint and allow to dry completely. Consider using some of the additive techniques from previous pages.

Overlay a darker watered down fluid acrylic paint on the prepared paper and allow to dry slightly.

Drop alcohol from an eye dropper from varying heights and with varying force to form large and small droplets onto the paper.

Watch the alcohol resist push your top (wet) layer of paint away, revealing the lighter layer underneath. Too wet of paint on top will roll back into the resist space, too dry paint will not move. This technique requires patience and experimentation. If at first you don't succeed, try try again.

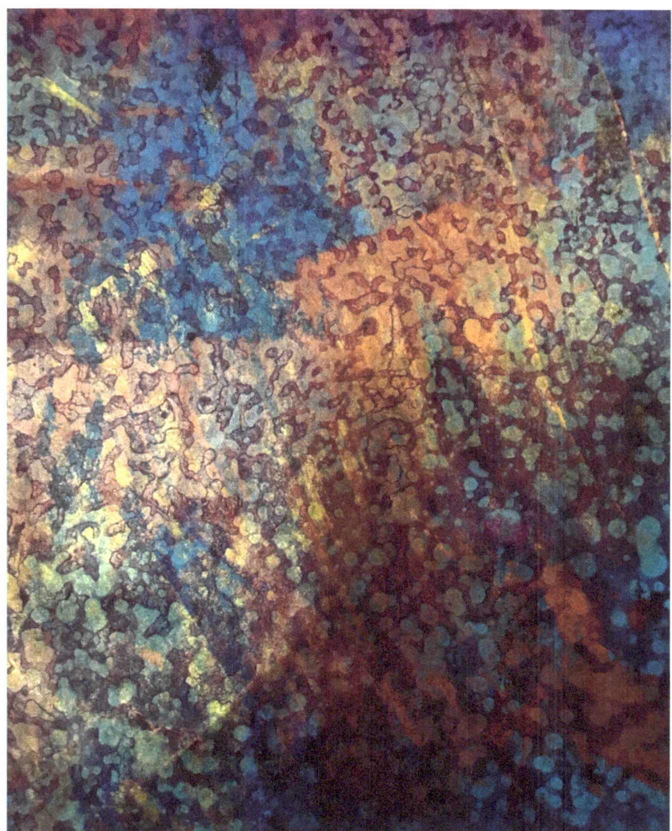

COMBINATIONS: Soap bubble resist over metallic plastic card scraping on deli paper

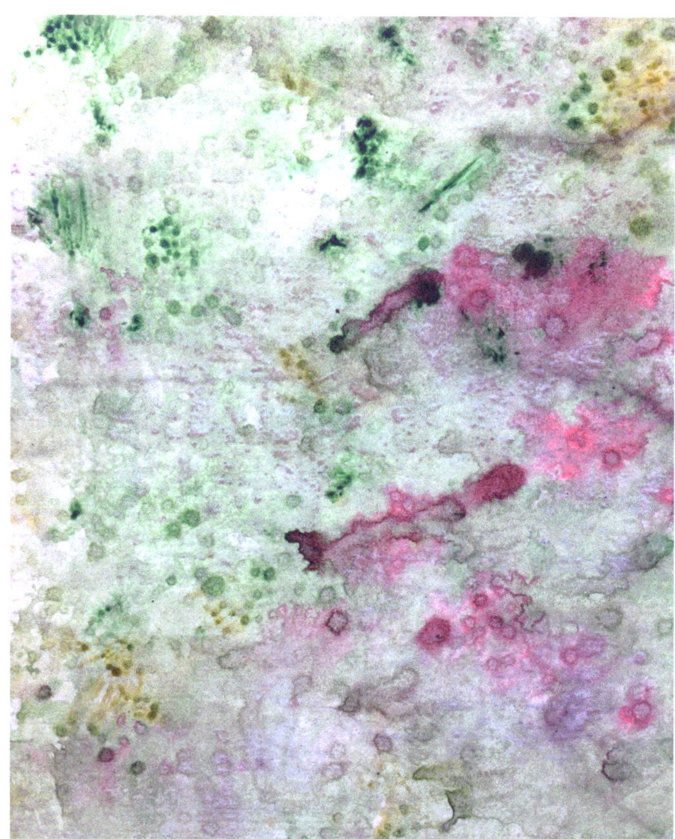

COMBINATIONS: Multiple colors of soap bubble resist on wallpaper, allowed to bleed together

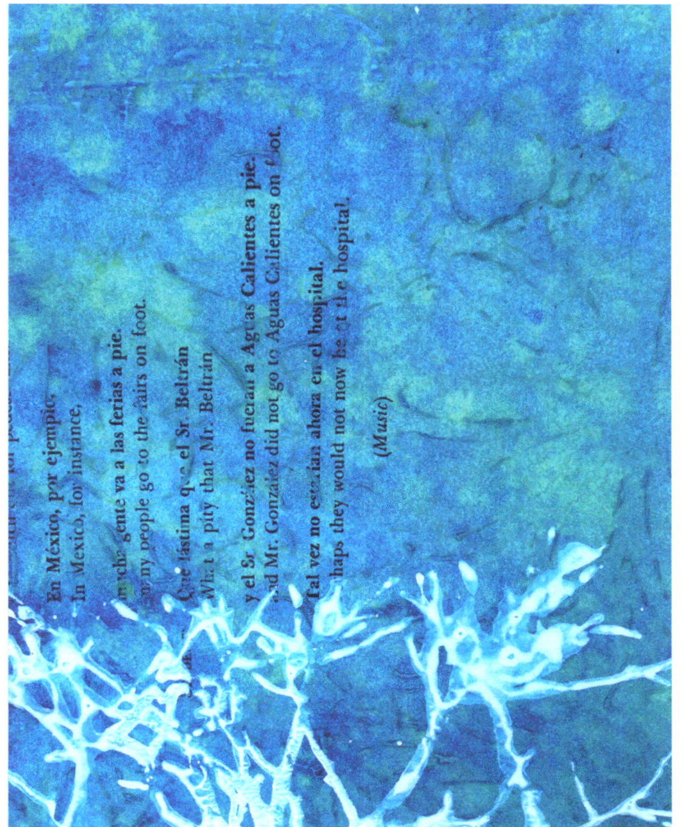

COMBINATIONS: Soap bubble resist over old book page with stenciled pattern in white gesso

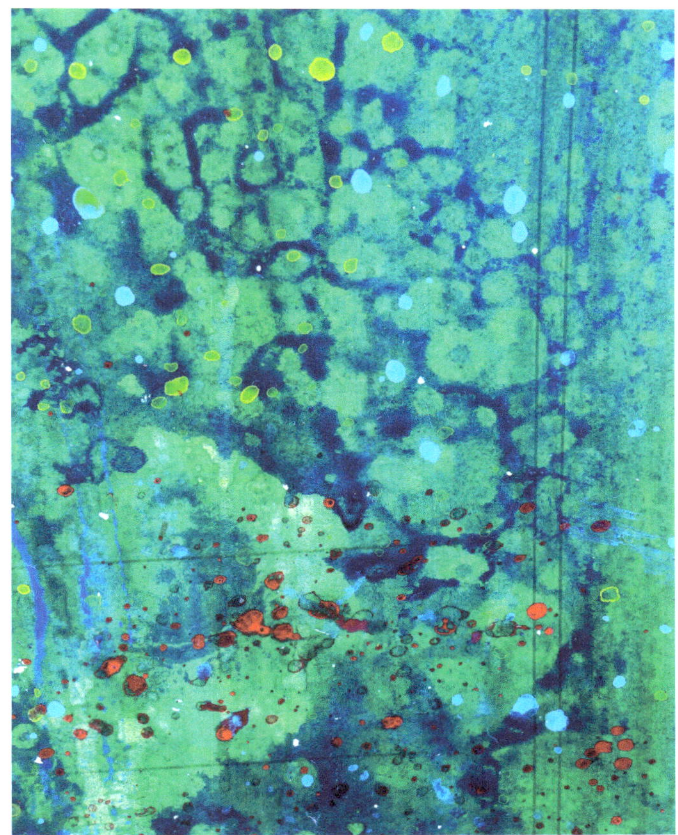

COMBINATIONS: Soap bubble resist over old ledger paper with splattering

painting paper
techniques

Soap Bubble Resist
Materials:

- Travel size spray bottle with a few pumps of dish liquid–Dawn works best
- Non porous found paper
- Acrylic paint
- Paint brush

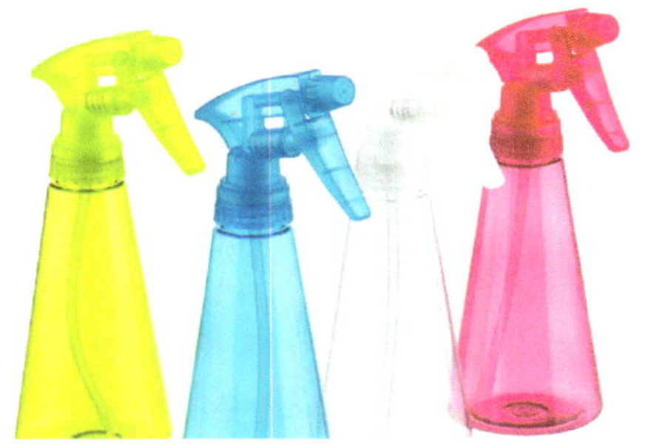

A few tablespoons of dish soap added to a spray bottle and shake

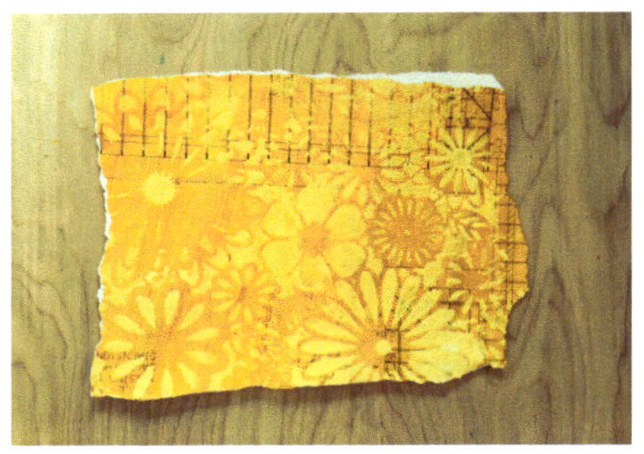

Paper embellished with a stencil pattern in light colors and allowed to dry completely

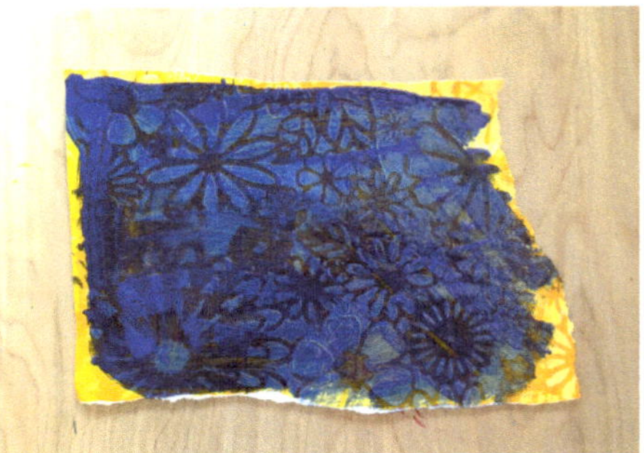

Paint a darker color over the top with diluted fluid acrylics–wet and watery

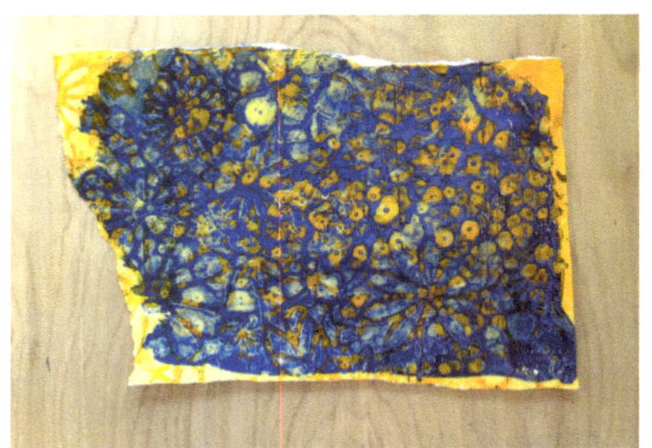

Working quickly, spritz the soap into the wet paint. A pattern will emerge as it resists

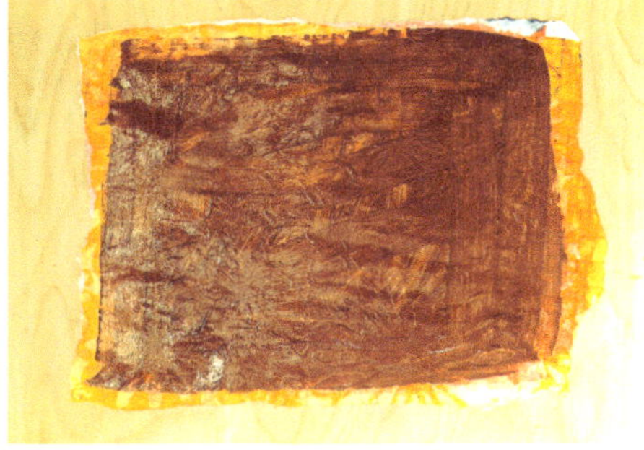

Different paper, paint colors, and water dilution can produce different effects

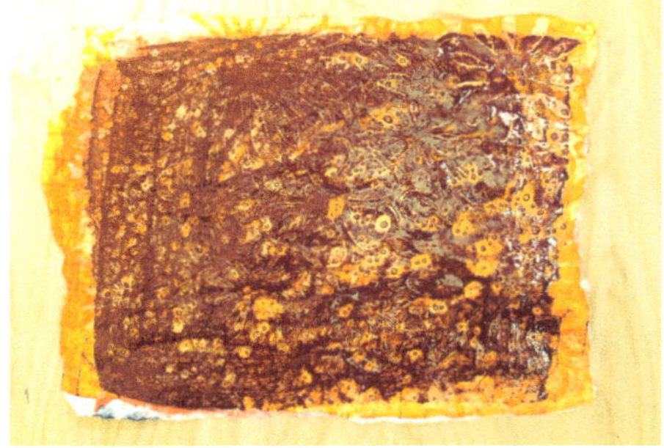

Working quickly, spritz the soap into the wet paint. A pattern will emerge as it resists

Use a piece of paper that will not allow the paint to soak all the way through. Coat paper with a light colored acrylic paint. Allow to dry completely.

Brush over the top of your painted sheet with a darker color of diluted fluid acrylic paint. (Much like the alcohol technique on the previous page).

While the top layer is still wet, gently spray the soap bubble mixture and allow the droplets to fall onto the paper. Try to spray the soap mixture up in air and let it fall straight down onto the paper in small droplets.

Watch the soap bubbles repel the top layer of paint in a small pattern of spots that sometimes continue to grow bigger and bigger.

There are many variables that come into play with this resist technique, so experimentation is paramount. The amount of water in the diluted top coat plays a role, the amount of drying time before spraying the soap bubbles plays a role, the color of the paint can even play a role. Experimentation is key.

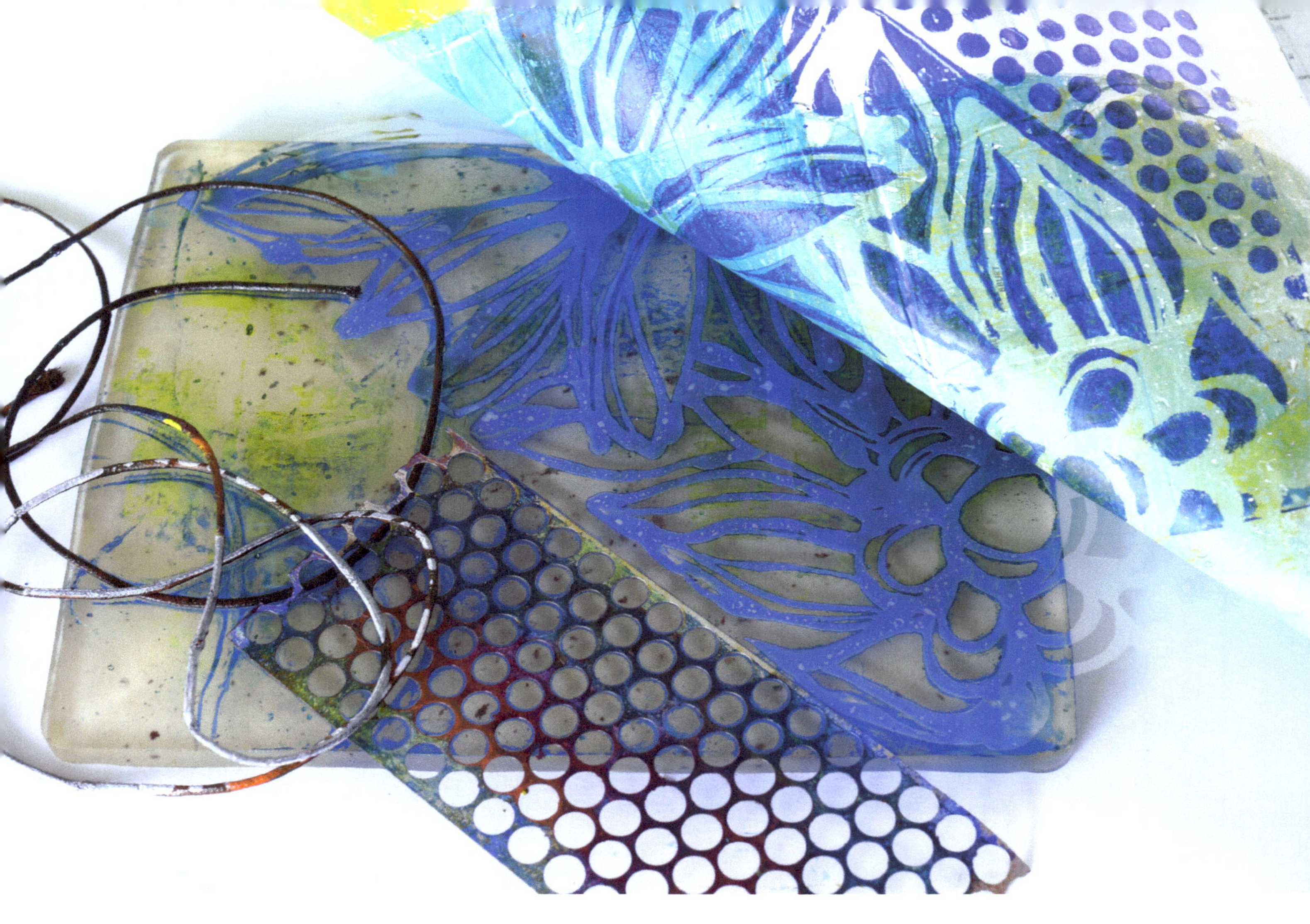

Gel Plate
monoprinting madness!

The Gel Press printing plate has become all the rage with mixed media artists, and yet I find at least two or three people in my Paper Paintings Collage Workshop who have yet to experiment with it. You are in for a treat.

This Gel Press printing plate looks and feels like gelatin, but is durable, reusable, and stores at room temperature. It doesn't take up room in your fridge like a home-made one, it's easy to clean and always ready for printing. Monoprinting on a Gel Press printing plate is simple and fun. The gratification is immediate, and the prints have endless creative uses.

It is my hope that you will experiment with all of the techniques in this book before you pick your favorites. The effects I get with some of my classroom demonstration papers make the students ooh and ahhh, but they don't necessarily always find them to be the techniques they choose for themselves. Why not invite some friends to join you? Clear a table top and have fun Gel printing papers together, then swap and trade and expand your inventory with the styles and color palettes of fellow paper painters . I've gotten some of the best papers in trade that I would have never made on my own.

 fashion plate **PORTRAITS**

color combinations

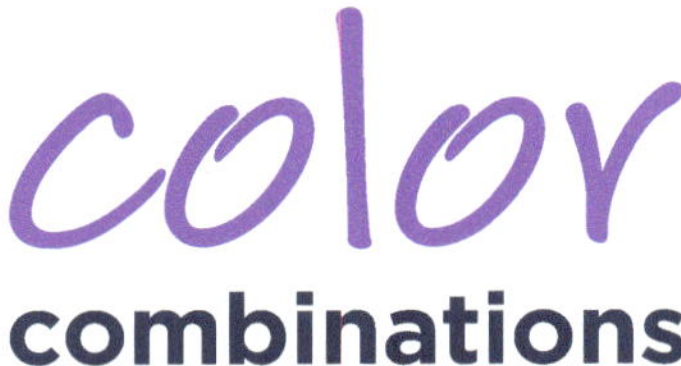

gel plate techniques

Starting with light colors and working your way down to darker colors is the way to go with fluid acrylics, which are the paints I prefer in my process. Because fluid acrylics are translucent, a light color will not show up very well over a darker color. For this reason, I start light and every subsequent layer is a little darker. I also like to use colors that are next to each other on the color wheel for harmony, or colors that are across from each other for discord. I suggest experimenting with both to see what appeals to you.

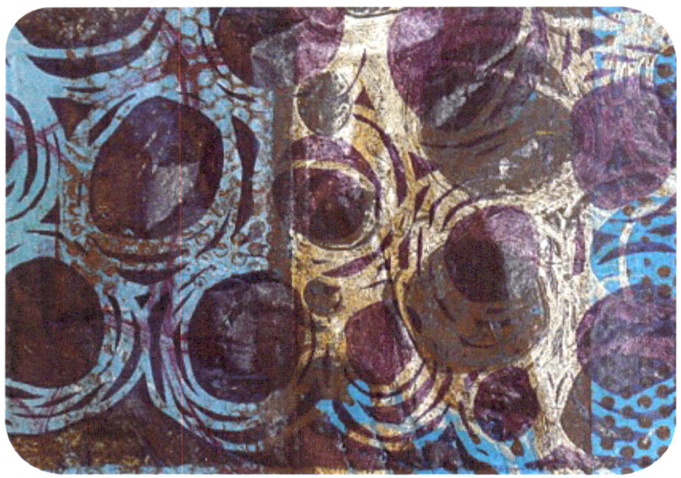

Harmonious colors start with light blue, to dark purple, to opaque gold on top.

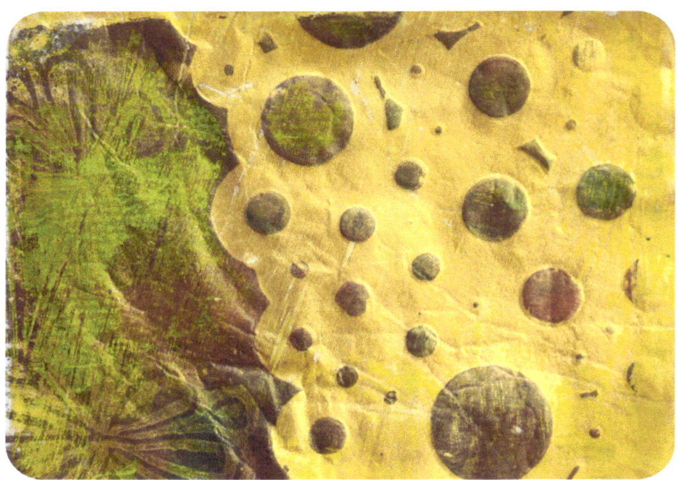

Creating an overall glow by utilizing metallic paint for the base and translucent, darker colors on top.

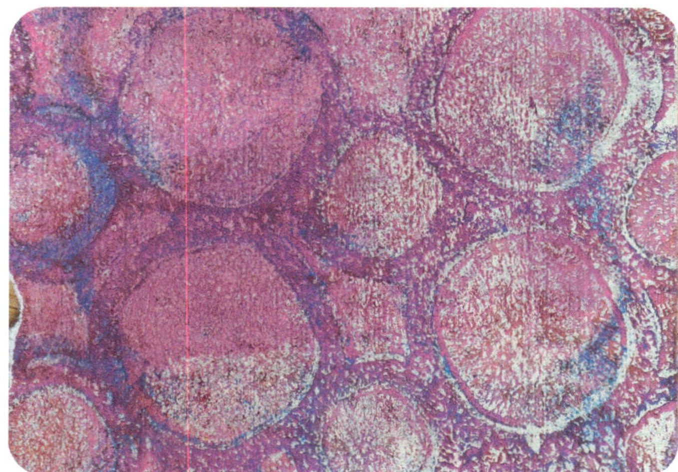

Creating harmony by staying with colors that are next to each other on the color wheel. Staring with magenta, adding darker purple.

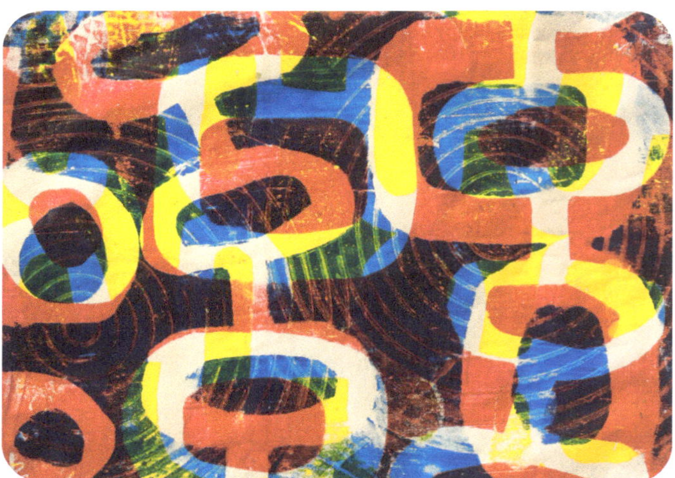

Creating discord with opposite colors. Starting with yellow, adding red, and lastly blue. Working light to dark, starting from white.

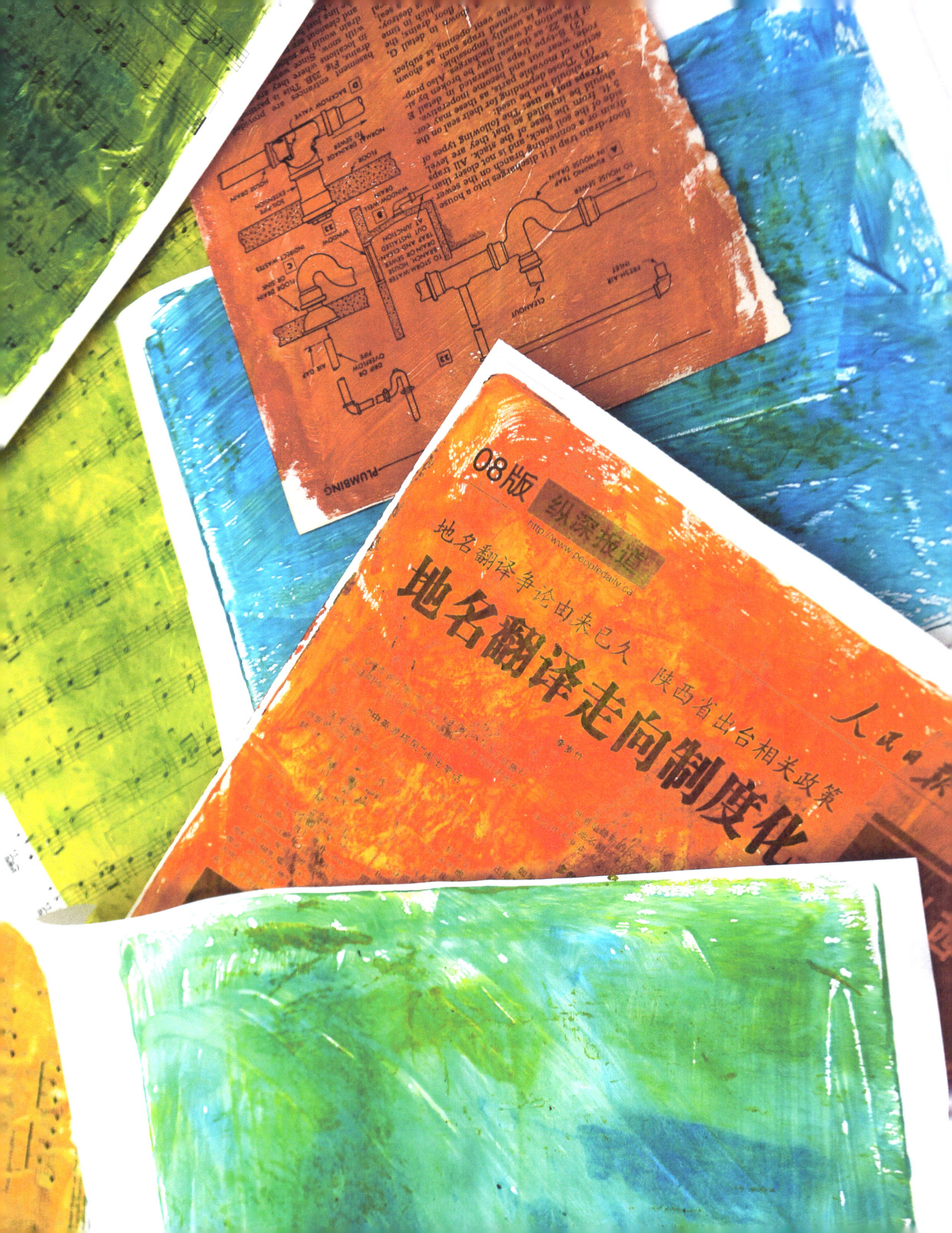
PLUMBING
08版 纵深报道
http://www.peopledaily.ca
地名翻译争论由来已久
陕西省出台相关政策
地名翻译走向制度化
人民

gel plate *techniques*

starting with light colored solids

I find, in fine art Gel printing, that starting with a light colored solid base is the way to go. I prefer not to have any high contrast white areas in my final prints, as I am hoping to achieve a painterly, fine art feeling. In order to eliminate the whites, without having to wash over the print post production, I always start with a solid base layer. I do not clean my plate between base layers, this process makes use of any residual paint on the plate from layer to layer. I call the leftover dried paint the crust. Your subsequent layers pick up the crust along with the newly applied paint—creating unexpected and beautiful results.

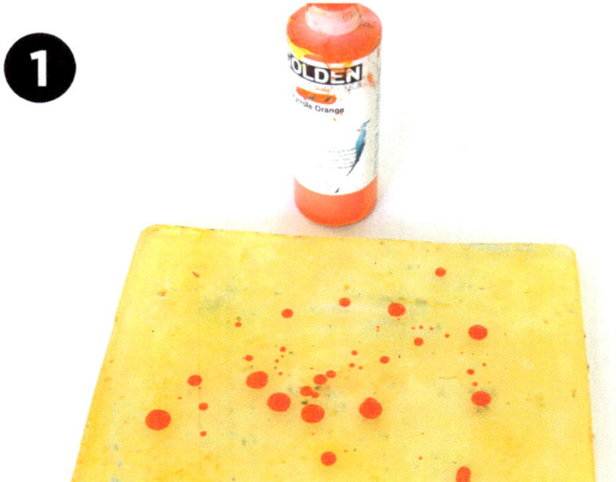

The brayer gives thin, even coverage for a few drops of paint applied directly to the plate.

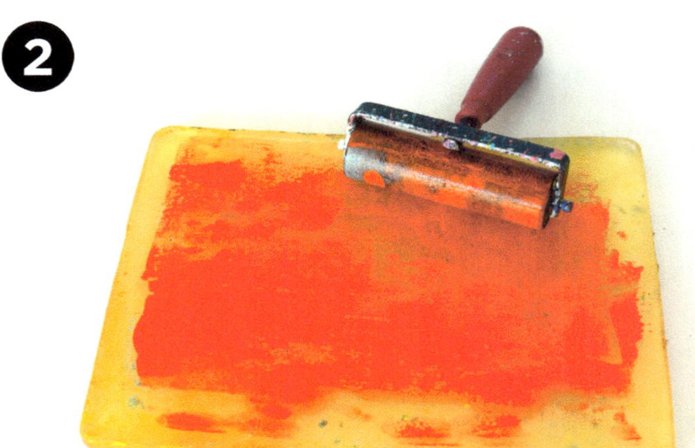

Roll the paint out to evenly cover the surface of the plate with the brayer.

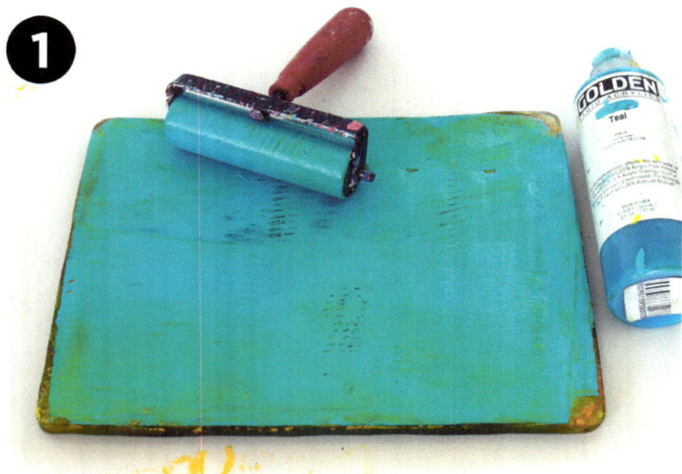

Start your printing process with a light colored solid.

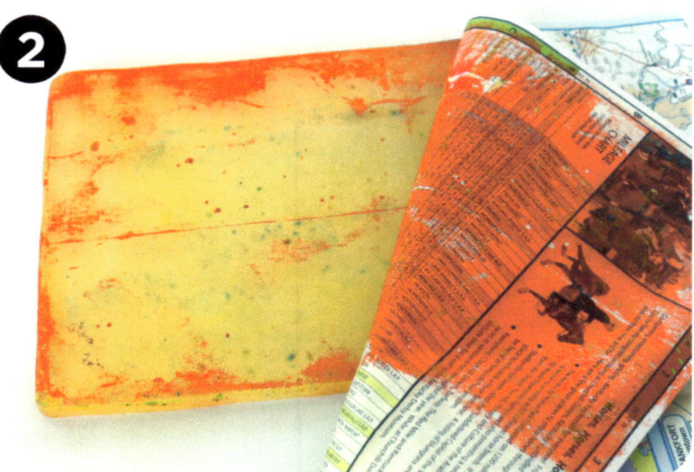

This will act as a base for subsequent, more complex layers

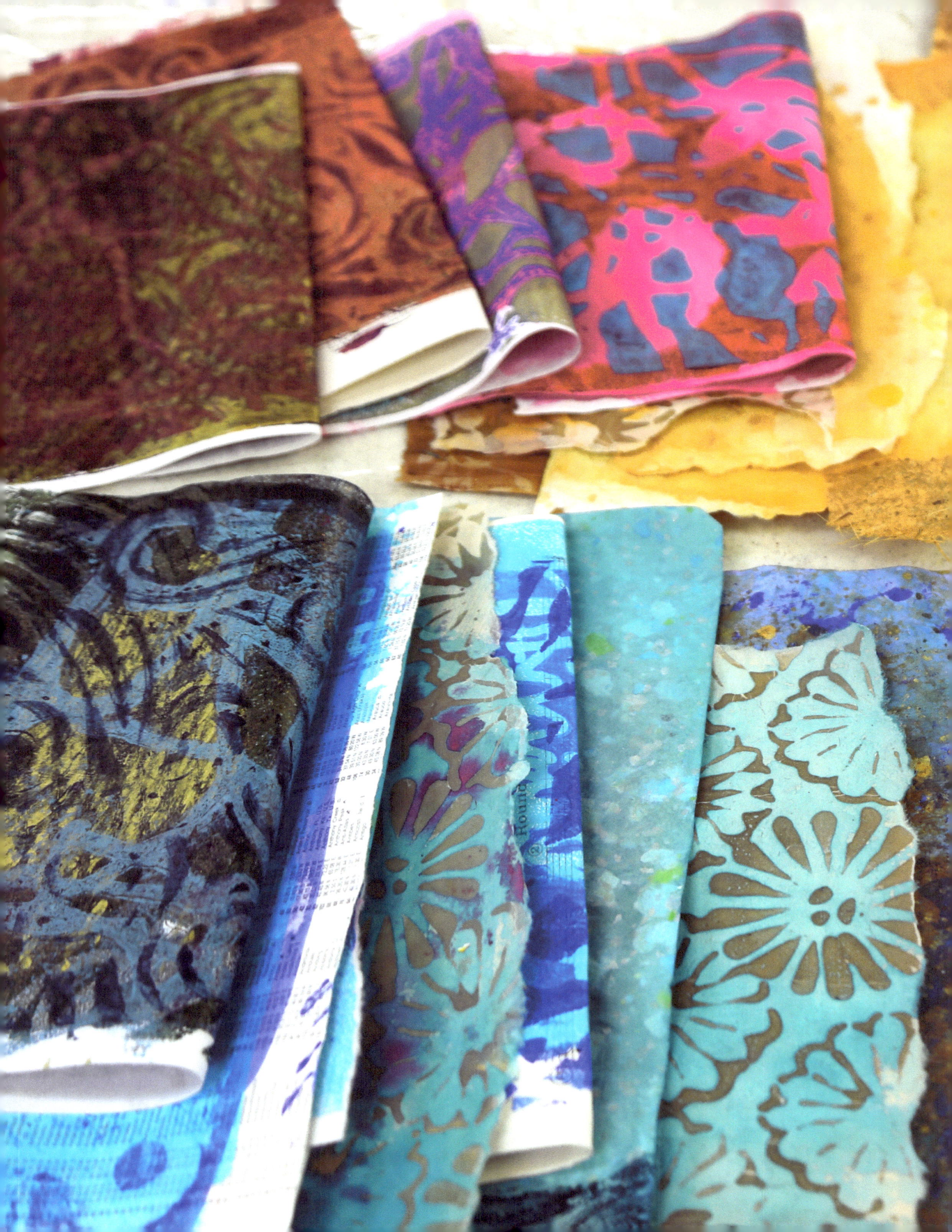

building layers

through translucency

Once you have your light colored base layer(s) printed on several small sheets of paper or an oversized sheet of paper, your goal is to start multiplying prints over and over with the techniques to follow in this book. Because Fluid Acrylics are translucent, every Gel printed layer you apply from here on out is going to show through and multiply with its predecessor. My typical rule of thumb is to combine a minimum of three layers in my Gel Prints, this creates rich papers for collage with lots and lots of depth. Varying the techniques of your layers creates even more visual interest. That being said, stencils tend to be the favorite technique of the Gel Press printing plate for my workshop students. My advice? Be bold, branch out, try different things!

The idea behind starting with a light colored base layer is that your prints don't include the white of the paper, which offers high contrast and can appear busy. High contrast can be distracting in collage papers, apple red should be layers of rich reds, intense oranges, deep yellows; adding white to this palette would be distracting.

I often multiply a print made using scraping tools over a print made with stencils, and then layer that print over one made with hand cut masks. This is the multi layered Gel print process I use for creating collage papers.

Keeping in mind my palette, I'll implement three or more colors (working from light to dark) that are analogous (next to one another) on the color wheel. I love the combination of blues and greens (cool colors) layered over each other through different techniques.

Every rule is meant to be broken! Experiment with combining opposites across the wheel as well.

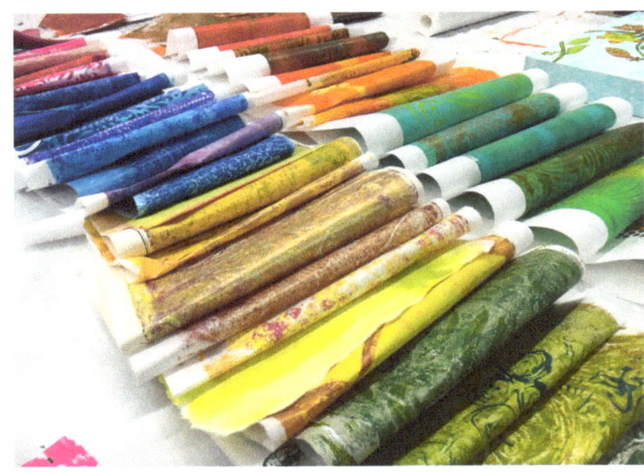

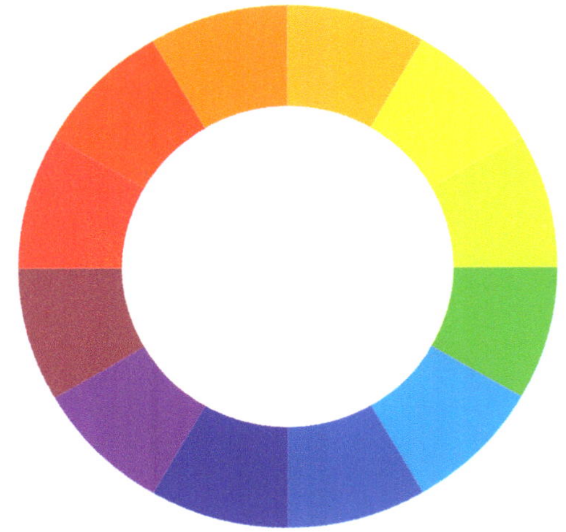

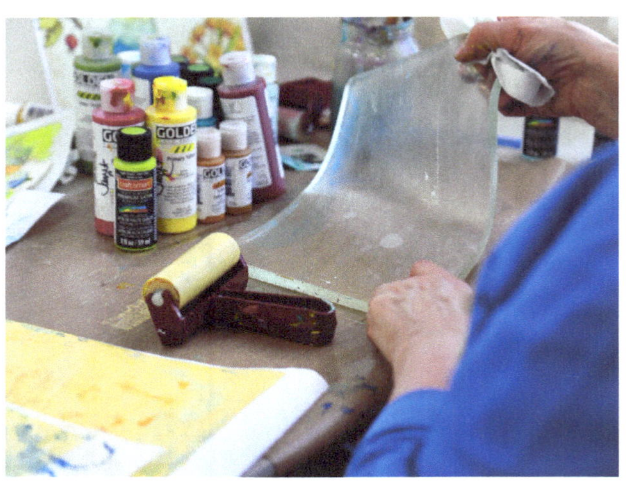

Making use of analogous colors.

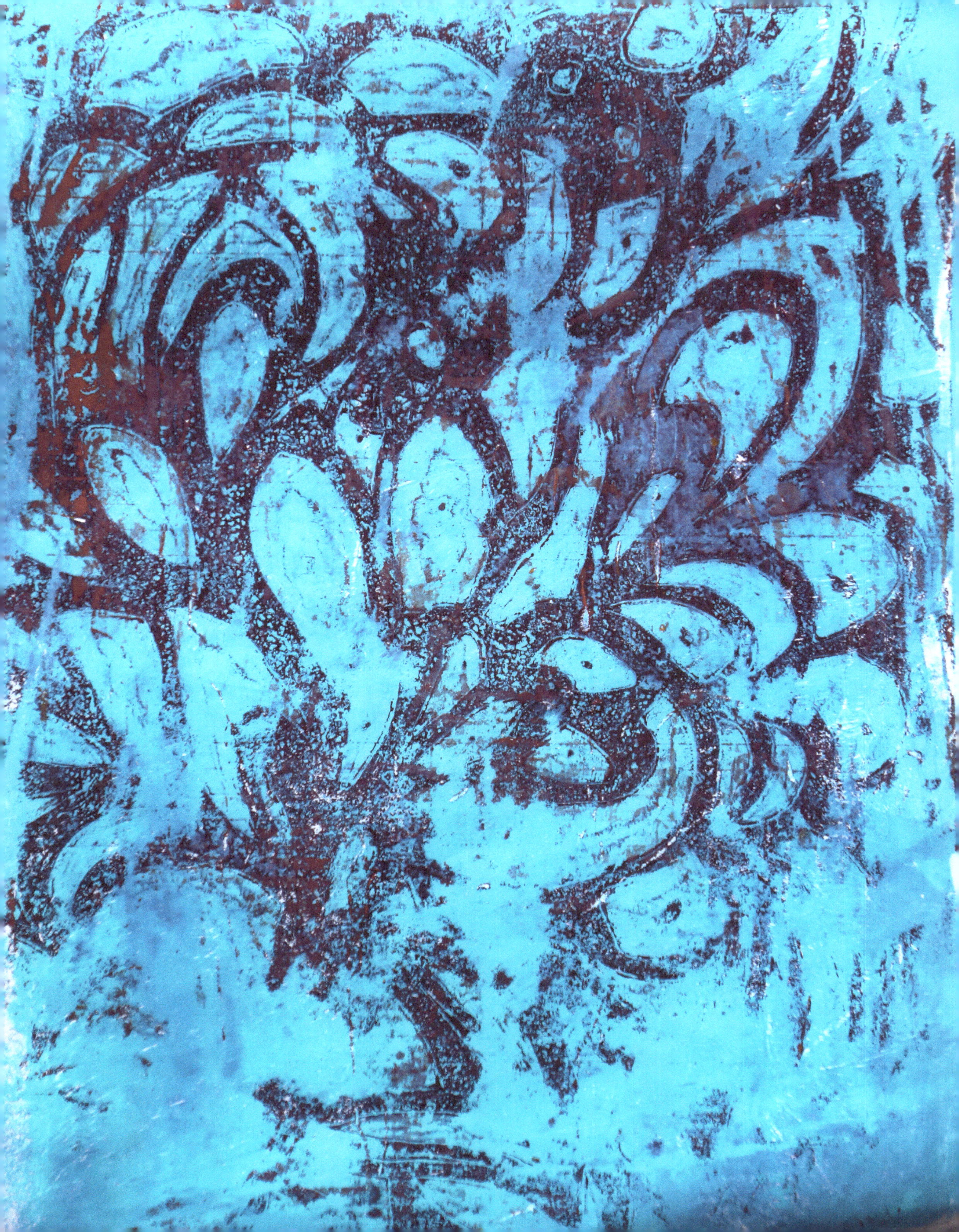

gel plate techniques

stencils

with ghost prints

Layering ghost prints one over the next (working light to dark) offers rich, painterly printed paper. The more layering the better, when you are trying to achieve painterly, fine art prints. Ghost prints can either be pulled immediately onto a -prepared light colored solid, or they can be pulled together with a second layer of paint.

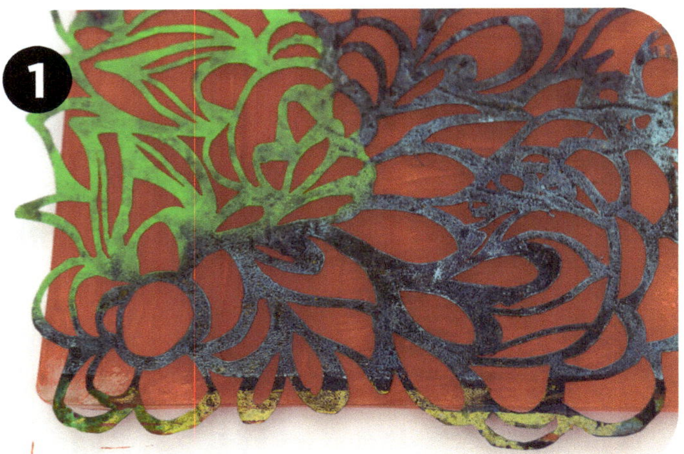

Lay the stencil over a thin layer of paint on the plate.

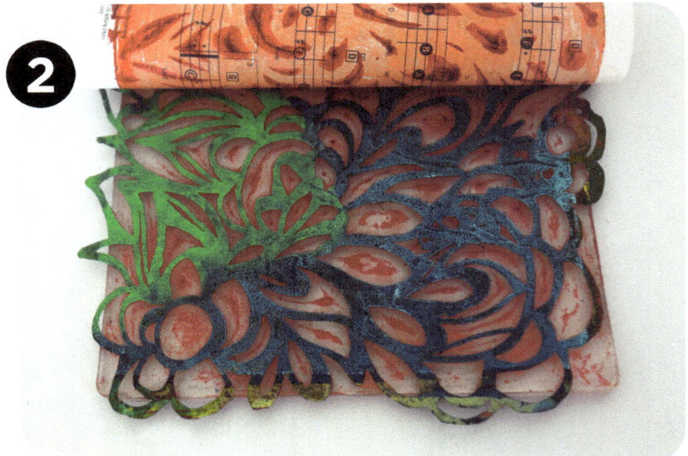

Press and pull a print from the plate

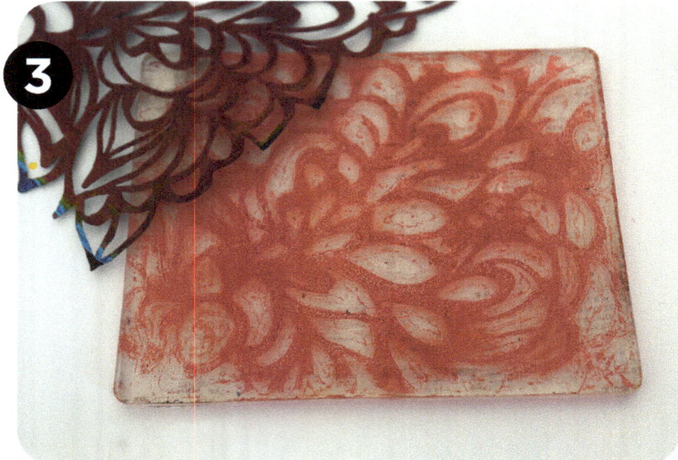

Paint left behind becomes the ghost print, or second print, after removing a stencil.

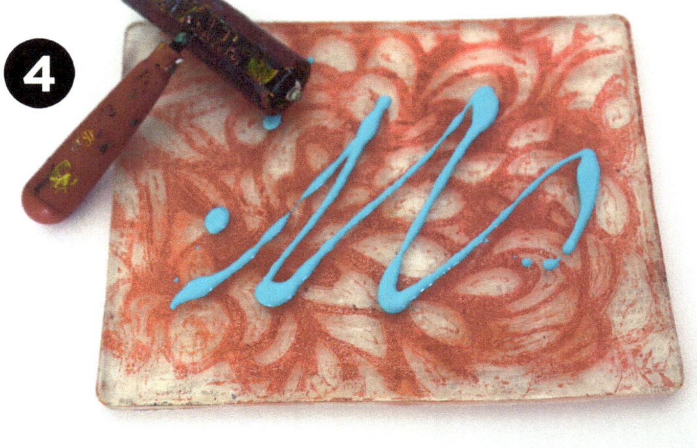

Add a thin layer of a lighter color paint over top of the dried ghost layer, pull the print of both layers together (left).

Passenger Ships

By international law, any ship with space for more than 12 passengers is a passenger ship. They range from freighters with passenger cabins to *ocean liners* or *express liners* built for speed and luxury.

Ocean liners are ordinarily passenger carriers, [though] ordinarily they also carry mail and some light-bulk cargo. A large one may have cabins, or staterooms, for 2,000 passengers. Traditionally, passenger accommodations are offered in three levels of comfort: first class, cabin, or second, class; and tourist, or third, class. Liners have fine restaurants, as well as shops, theaters, libraries, swimming pools, and other recreational facilities.

The largest and fastest liners were built especially to ply the North Atlantic Ocean between the United States and Europe. Smaller liners traverse other routes; many specialize in vacation cruises. By the early 1970's, as airlines won a virtual monopoly of routine transoceanic passenger travel, the world's largest liners—France's *France* (66,348 gross tons, 1,035 feet long, 111 feet in beam) and Britain's *Queen Elizabeth 2* (65,863 gross tons, 963 feet long, 105 feet in beam)—were used in the North Atlantic only during the peak tourist season and were employed as warm-seas cruise ships in the colder months. The record-holding *United States* (see picture on next page) was laid up in 1969.

Cargo, Fishing, and Miscellaneous Vessels

Cargo ships include *freighters* or dry-cargo vessels, and *tankers*. Freighters which carry full loads of a single commodity—such as grain, ore, lumber, or sugar—are known as *bulk carriers*. Most freighters, however, are designed to carry general cargo—parcels of all kinds of materials and manufactured goods. Increasing in popularity are *container ships*, which carry general cargo prepacked ashore in easily handled containers of a standard size—usually about 8 × 8 × 20 feet.

Tankers carry liquids. Their hulls are divided into tanks, which are loaded and unloaded by pumps. Most tankers carry crude oil or petroleum products—gasoline, jet fuel, or lubricating oil. Specialized tankers are built to carry such cargoes as orange juice, other vegetable oils, molasses, liquefied gases, and molten sulfur. Some tankers can also carry grain and similar bulk cargoes.

In recent years tankers have increased spectacularly in size. In 1957 there were only 13 tankers of more than 40,000 deadweight tons. By the early 1970's there were over 1,000 tankers of more than 40,000 tons operating as part of the world fleet and more than 100 of these were over 200,000 tons.

Fishing vessels include small craft, which handle the fishing equipment, and "mother ships," aboard which the catch is processed. Whaling vessels also fall into this group (see Fisheries; Whale).

Among miscellaneous vessels are tugboats (barges are non-powered vessels), dredges, and icebreakers. Tugboats tow barges and assist large ships into and out of harbors. Barges carry liquid and dry cargoes in coastal and inland waters as well as equipment for offshore construction or drilling (see

CARGO LINER. The *James Lykes* (9,887 gross tons, 470 feet long, 69 feet in beam) operates in the Atlantic Ocean.

BULK CARRIER. The *Johnstown* (10,013 gross tons, 626 feet long, 70 feet in beam) is a Great Lakes ore carrier.

TANKER. The *Cities Service Baltimore* (20,188 gross tons, 633 feet long, 90 feet in beam) is a medium-sized tanker. Today's largest tankers are more than 1,000 feet long.

BULK CARRIER. The *Marore* (14,089 gross tons) is a seagoing ore carrier. It resembles a tanker and is more strongly built than are Great Lakes bulk carriers.

gel plate
techniques

stencils

combining and layering

Layering stencil mask prints one over the next (working light to dark) offers rich, painterly printed paper. Combine stencils with elements such as leaves, string, and place mats for more diversity of patterning.

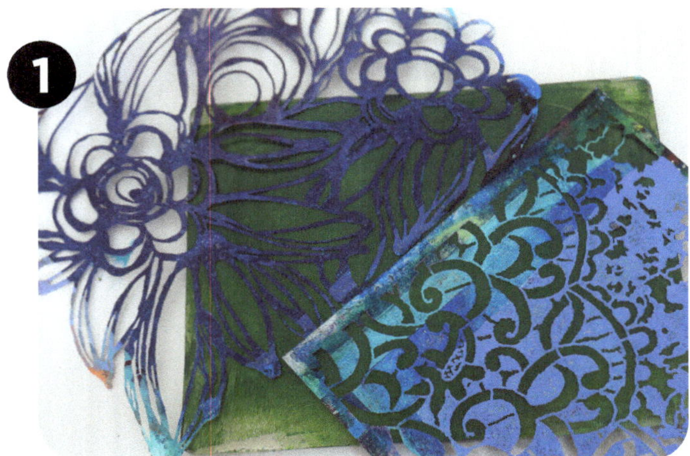

Combining two stencils on dark green paint.

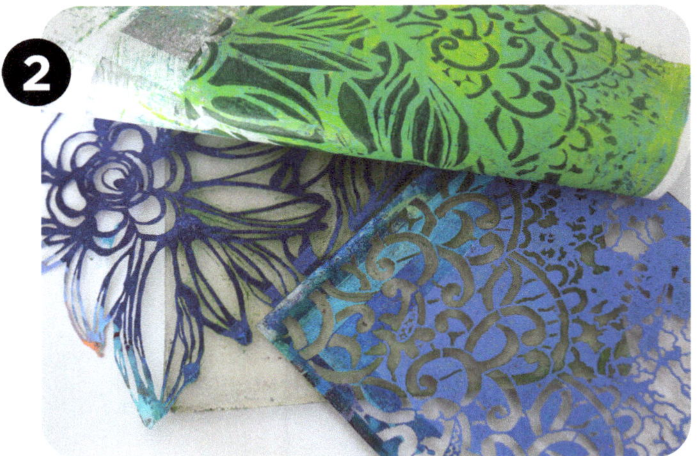

Pulling the multi stencil print on a light green solid.

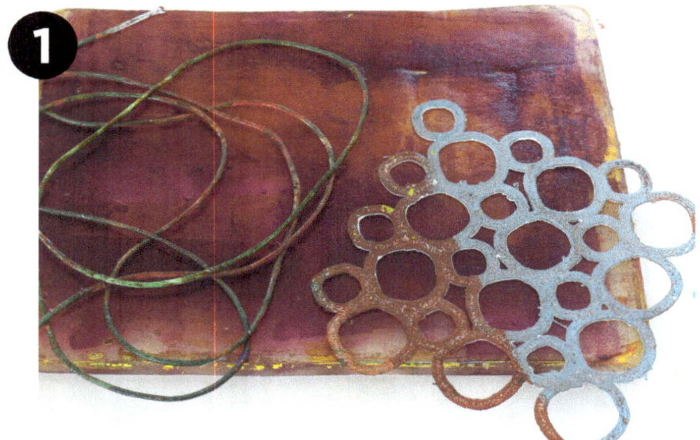

Combining a stencil with string (or other found masking material) on one print.

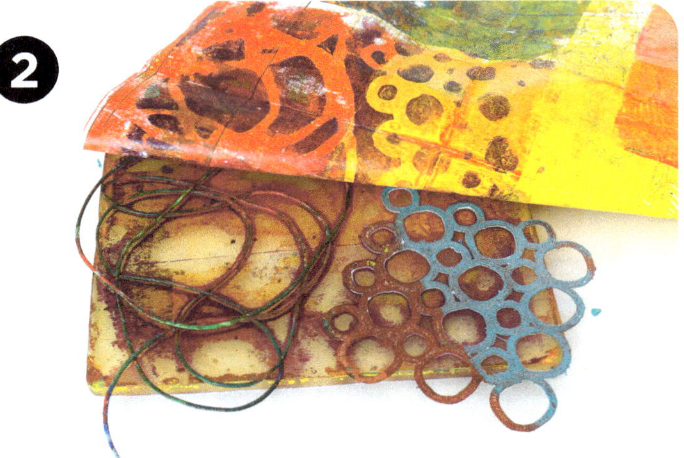

Pulling the print over a mixed solid base layer.

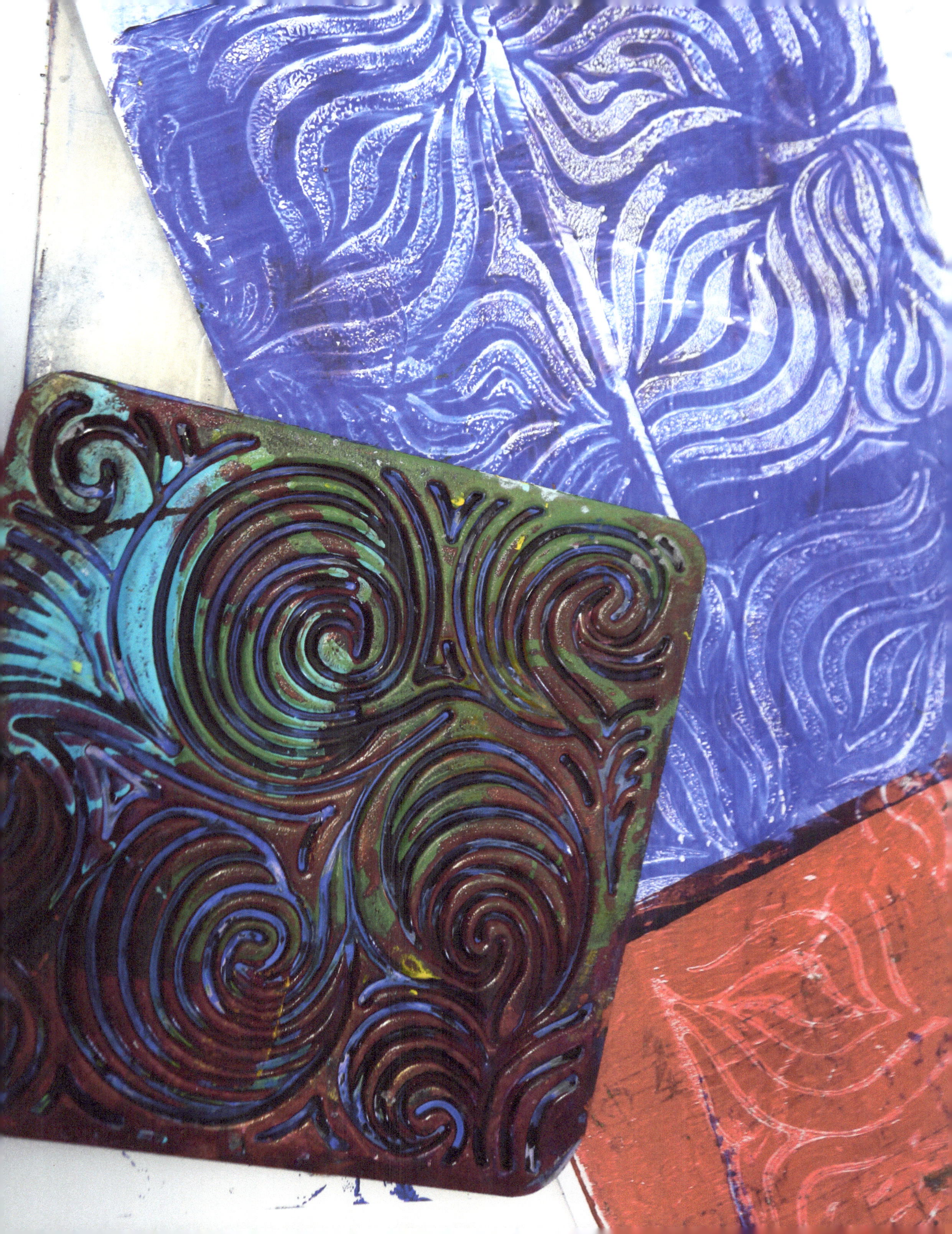

gel plate *techniques*

plastic rubbing plates

There are many ways to apply texture to Gel Prints, commercially produced texture plates being just the beginning. Other elements that can be used include, the bottoms of shoes, the circle end of a paper towel roll, potato mashing tools, yoga mats, needle point mesh... The possibilities are endless. Look around you and start thinking about the everyday items in your life and how they would work when pressed into paint on the Gel Press printing plate. It's a whole new world.

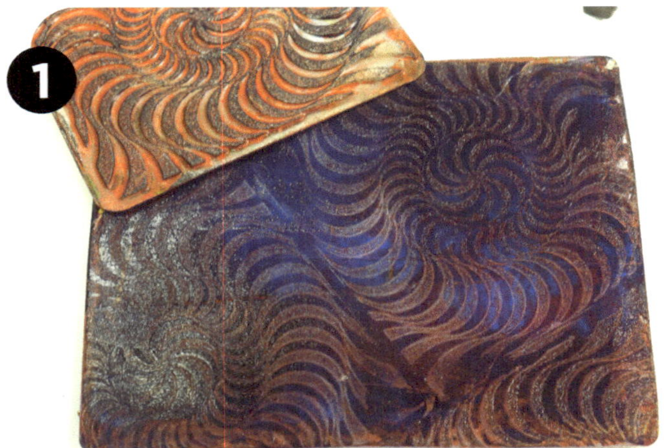

Press a clean, dry rubbing plate into a wet layer of paint to create a pattern by removing paint.

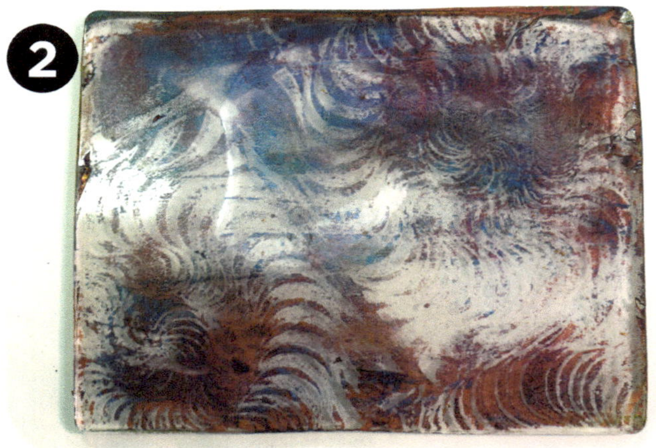

After the first print of the rubbing plate, let the residual paint dry on the plate.

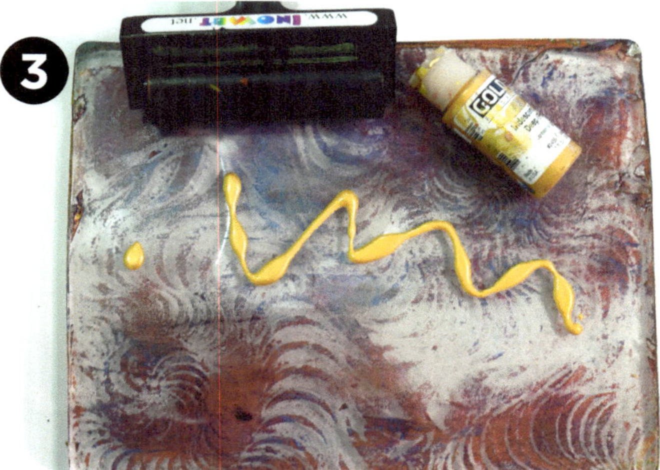

Apply a gold metallic over the residual paint.

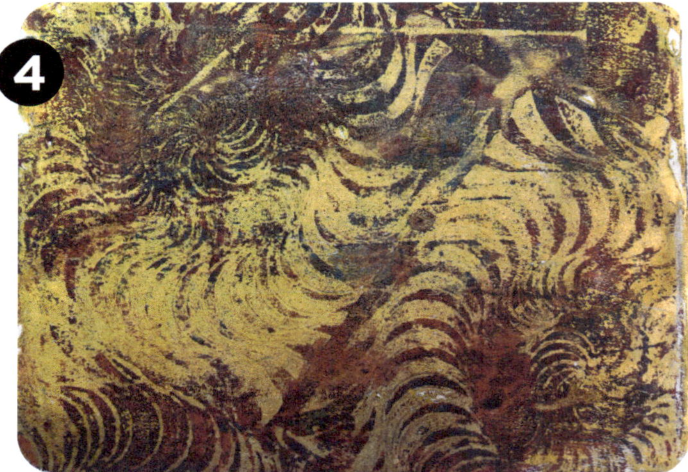

The gold metallic paint and the residual paint are pulled together to create one print, as shown here.

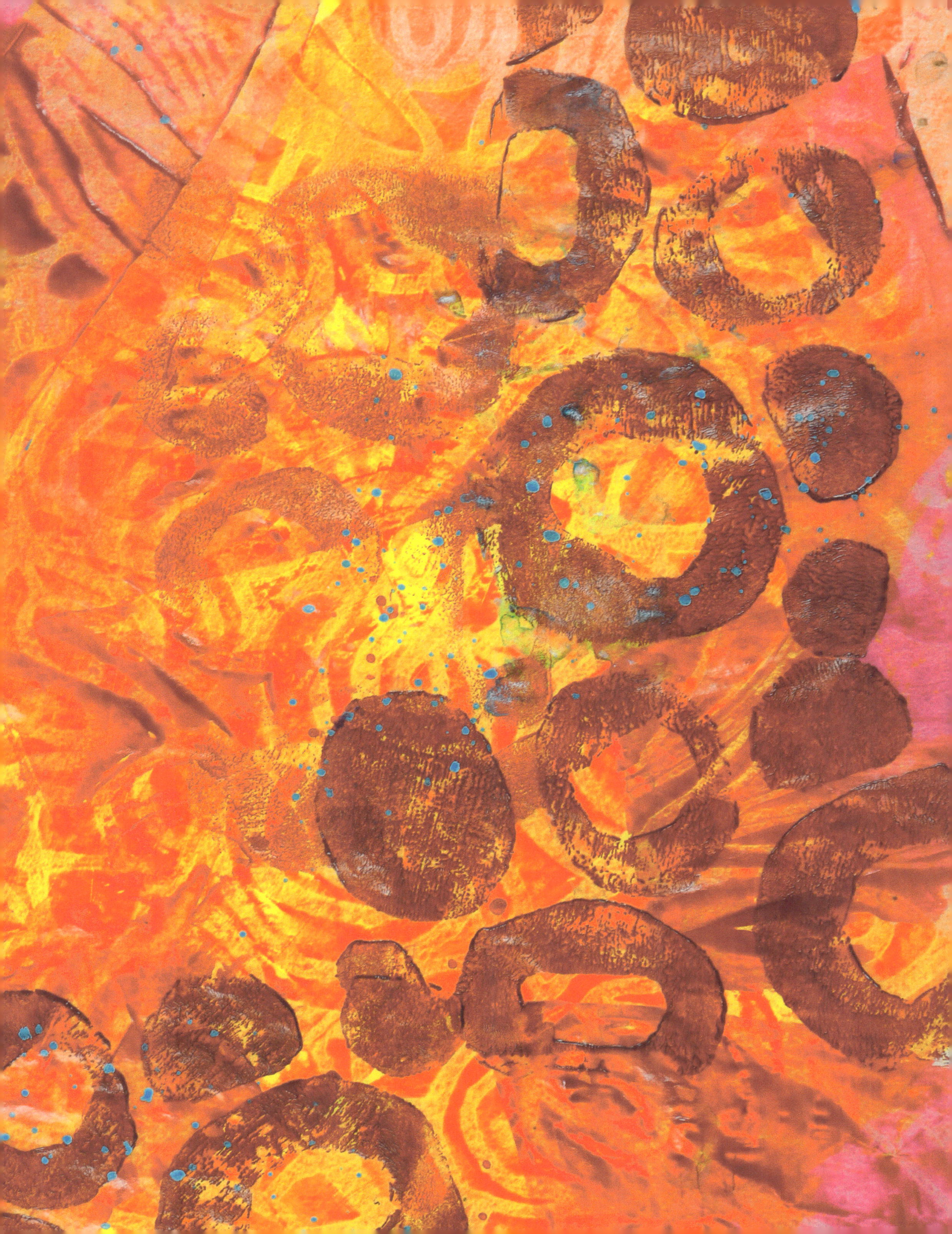

gel plate techniques

subtle subtraction

Hand-carved and commercially purchased stamps offer wonderful textures on the Gel Press printing plate. Pressing a stamp into the paint layer removes it subtly, revealing the pattern in a painterly impression. Overlapping and combining stamps with other effects offers more variety and interesting results.

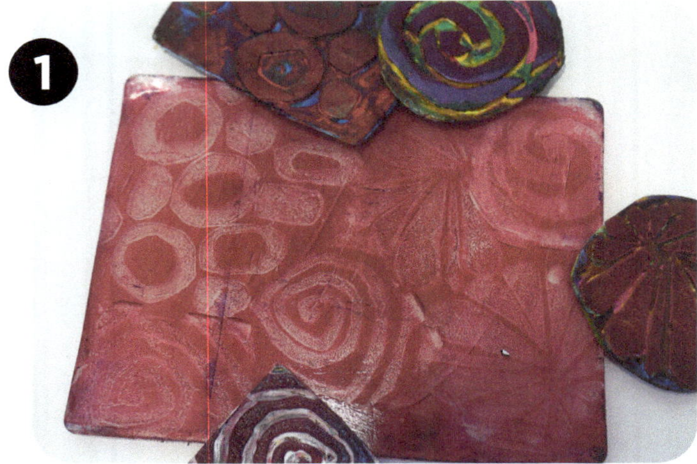

Removing paint with a clean, dry stamp pressed into it will create a subtle pattern on the plate.

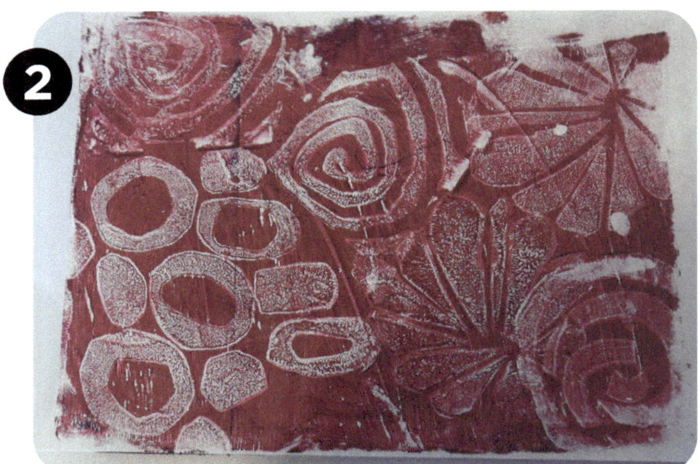

A print on white paper of the stamped plate.

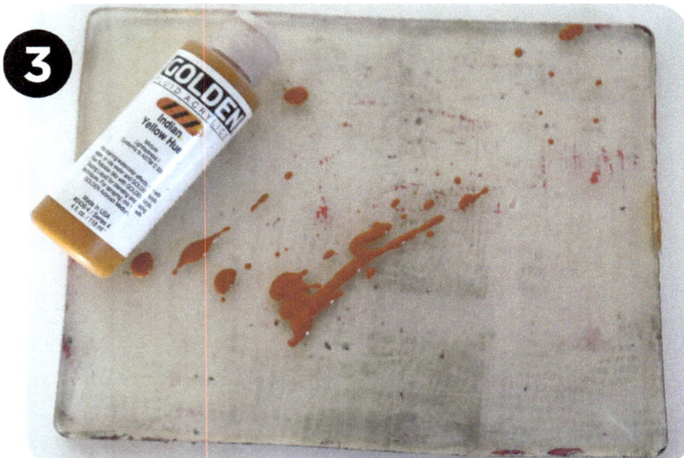

Set up the plate with a thin layer of light gold.

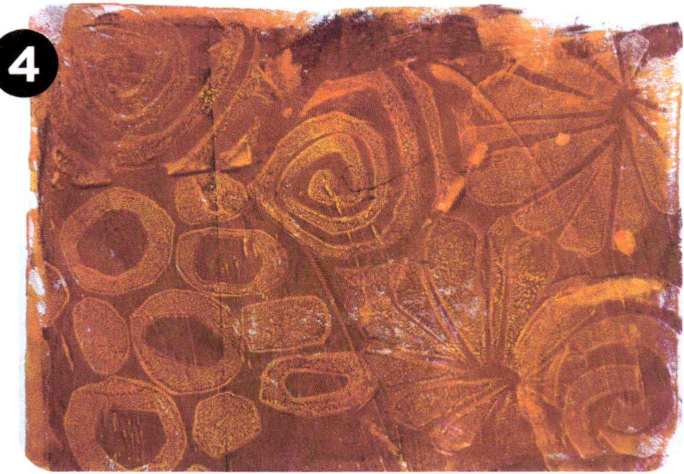

Overprint the light gold onto the pulled red print to tone down the whites.

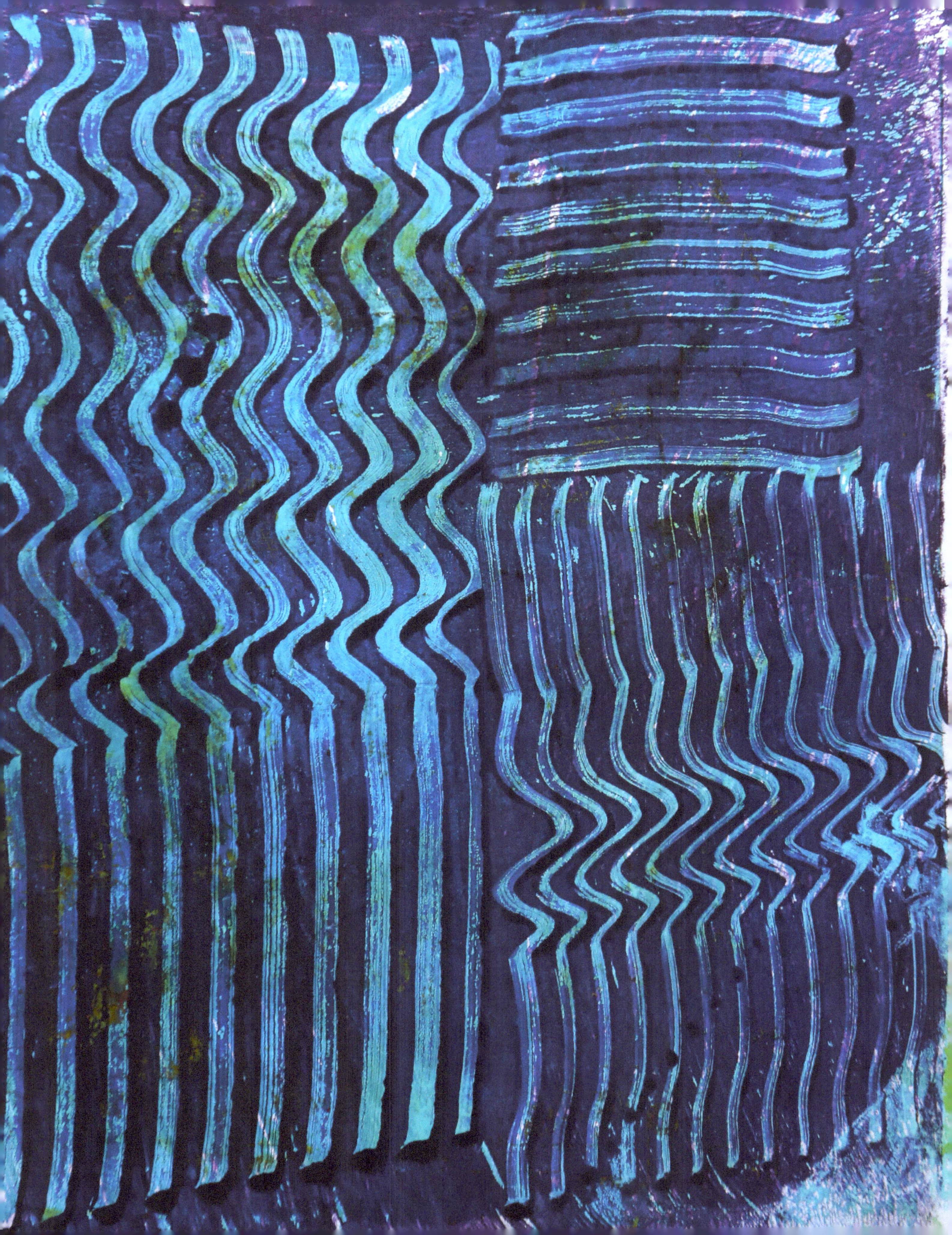

gel plate
techniques

catalyst wedges

Princeton makes a line of hand held wedge tools with teeth on two edges. They fit nicely in the palm of your hand and come in many different widths and patterns for scraping. The wedges work wonderfully on the Gel Press printing plate to scrape in straight, wiggle, zig zag or any combination of motions to create interesting patterns scraped out of (removing) the paint.

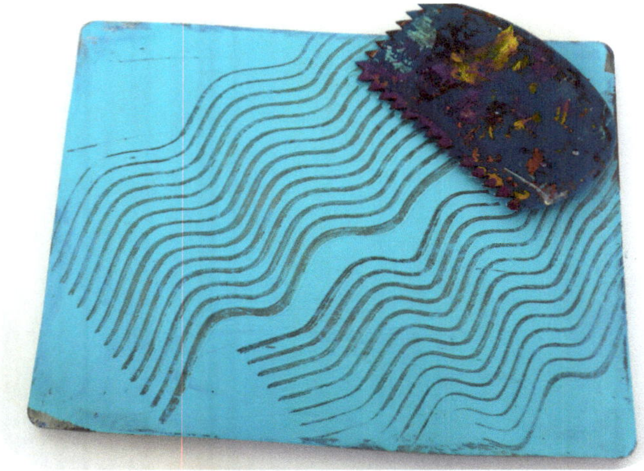

An example of removing paint from the plate with the scrapers.

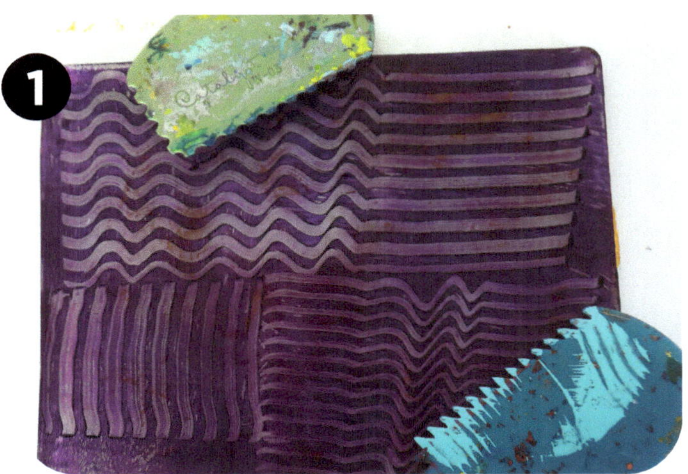

Apply a thin layer of paint with the brayer and scrape through the paint layer with the scrapers.

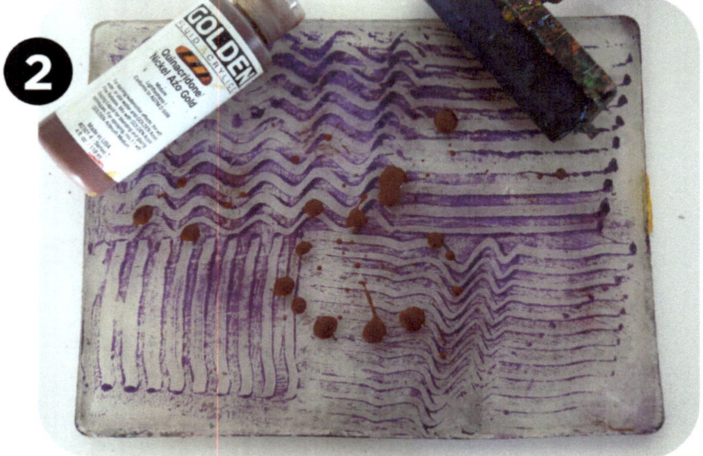

Apply a thin layer of light brown paint to the residual paint after pulling the first print.

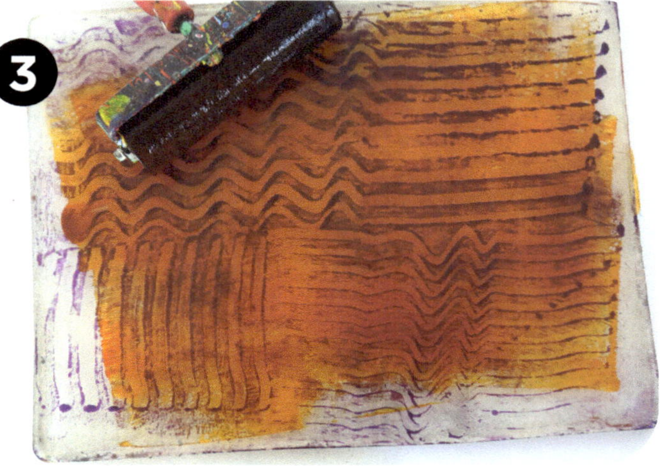

The brown paint and residual paint layer will pull off together for a subtle, painterly print.

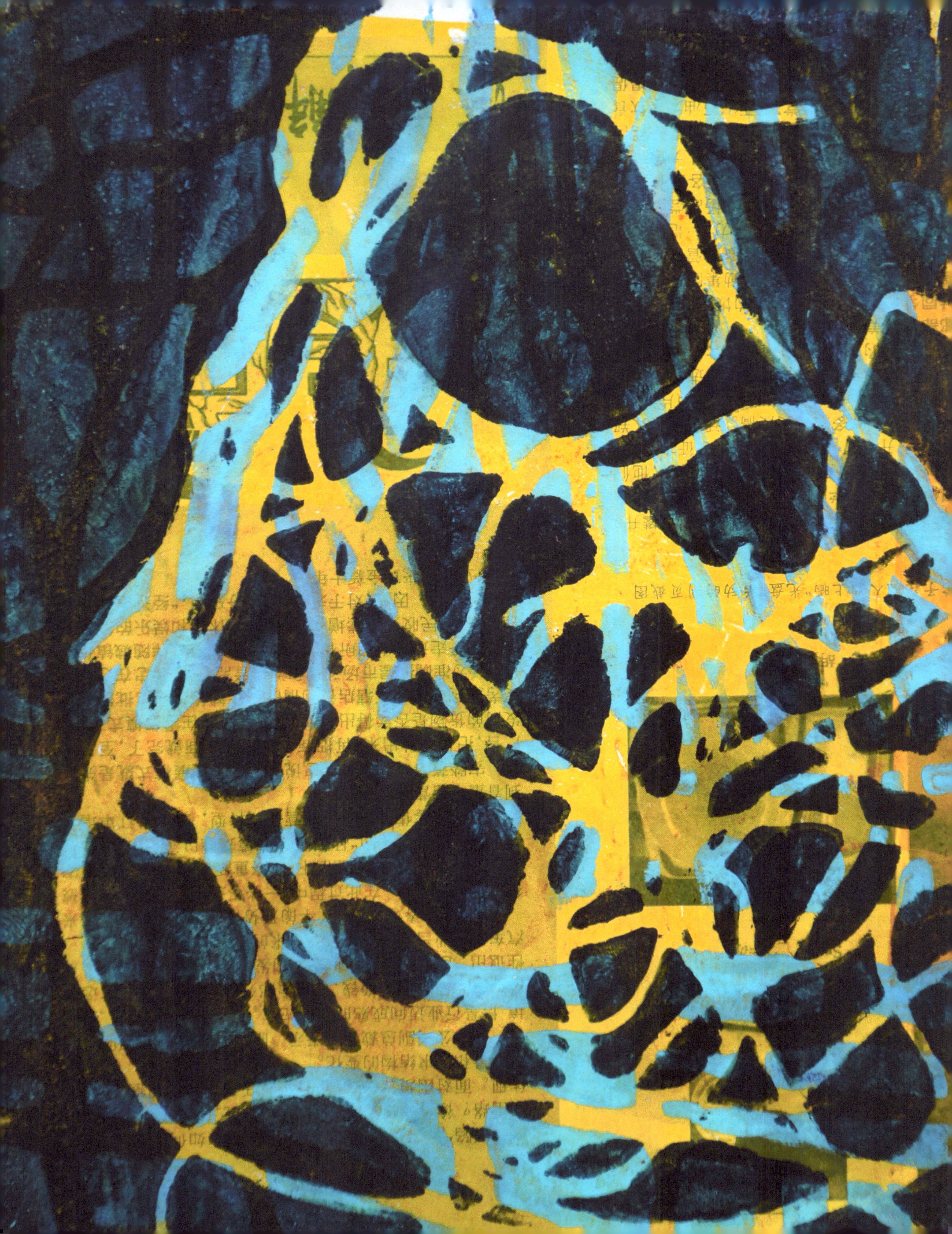

gel plate techniques

found objects

jute string and layering

A look around your home might reveal some wonderful objects for patterning on the Gel Press Plate. Here I am playing with jute string and taking advantage of adding it on top of some previous printed, lighter layers as well as using the ghost print from it to add on top of another light colored solid layer. Sometimes the most creative art materials are found outside the art supply store.

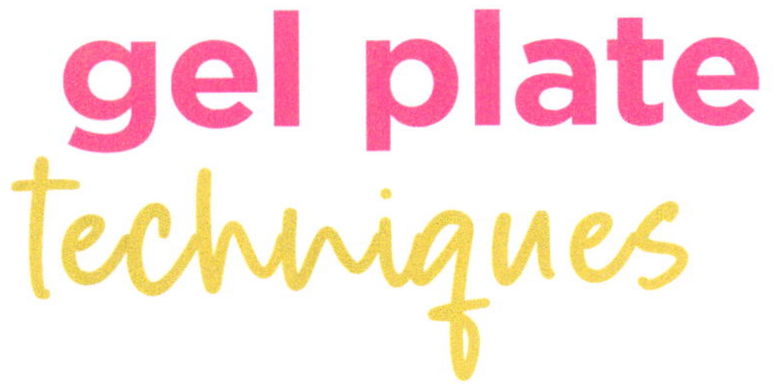

Jute string has a slightly fuzzy edge, it's thin enough to yield detailed line patterns.

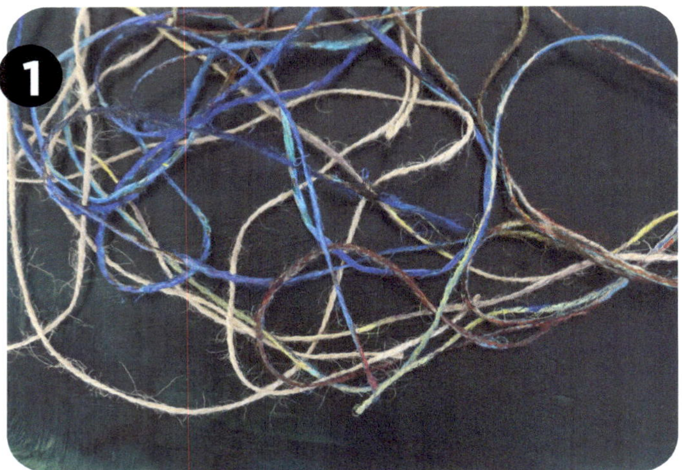

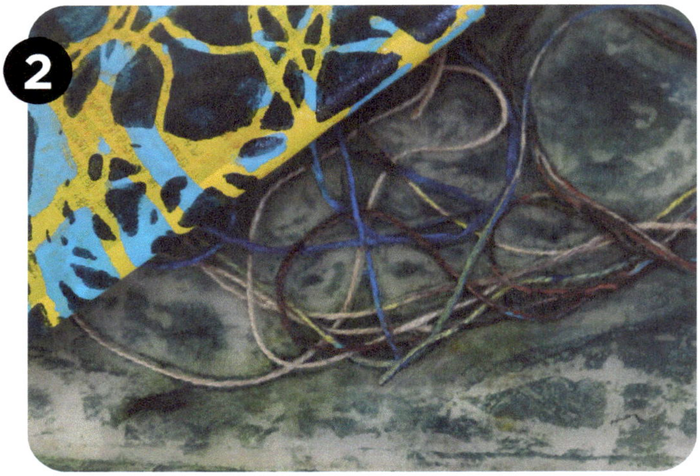

Pulling a print of the string on top of a prepared sheet.

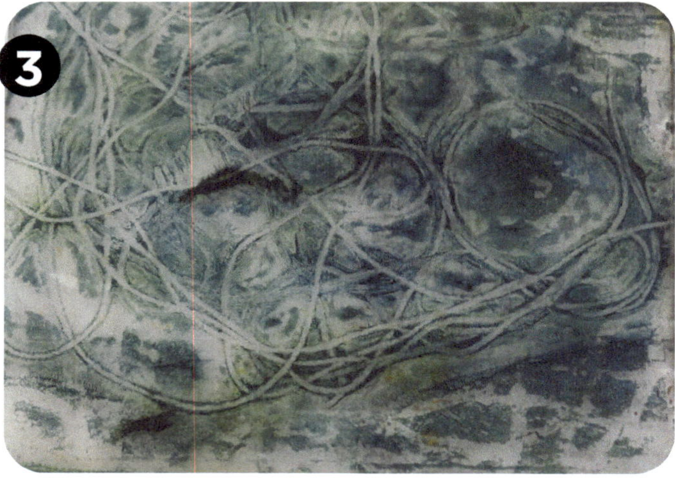

The ghost print after the first print is pulled, and the string is removed from the plate.

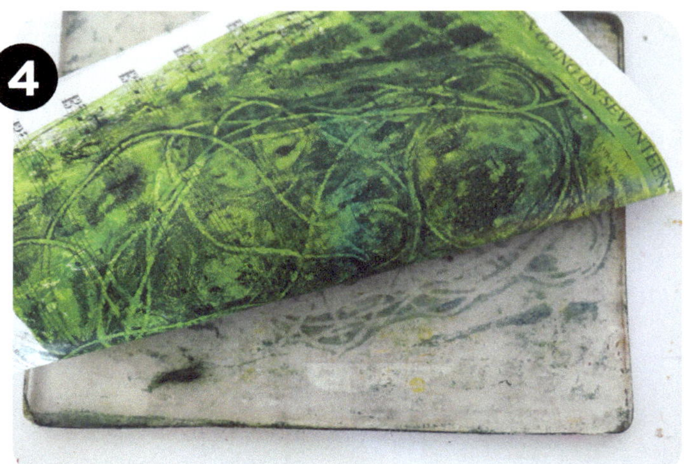

The ghost print applied over a light colored solid that was ready and waiting in the wings.

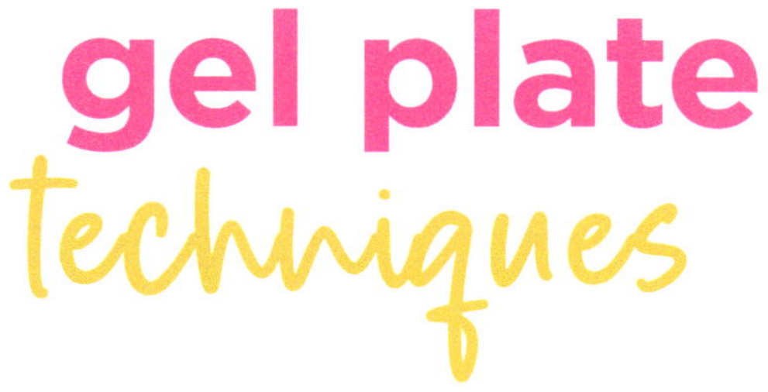

mark making and imprinting patterns

Marks can be made in the plate from any blunt object. I like to try writing with the eraser tip of a pencil, the end of my paint brush, a credit card corner, or my finger. All of the marks you make into the paint will transfer to the print when you press it into the paper, some more subtle than others. There are many interesting patterns in unusual places, like the bottom of your shoes, tile samples, jar lids, flip flops, and plastic containers. Think beyond the commercial art supply rubbing plate, the possibilities are endless!

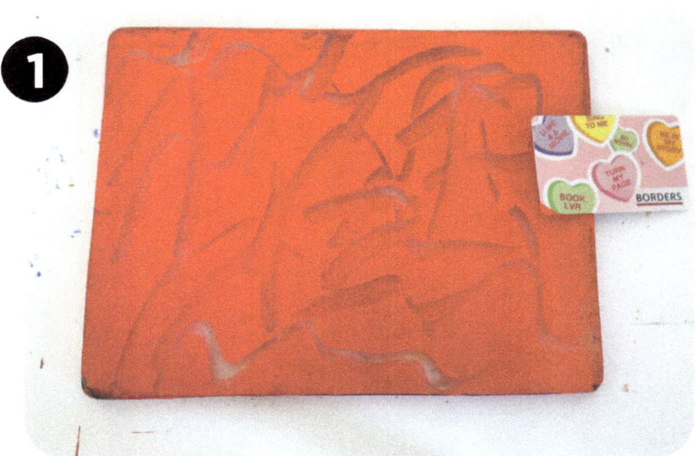

Using the corner of a gift card to make marks.

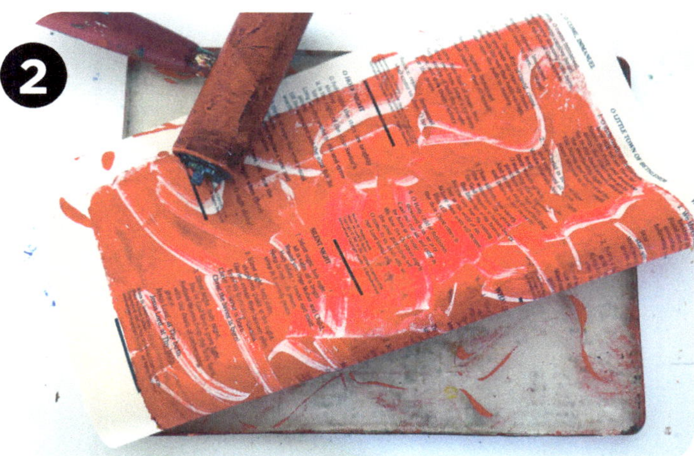

Pulling the print from the gift card pattern.

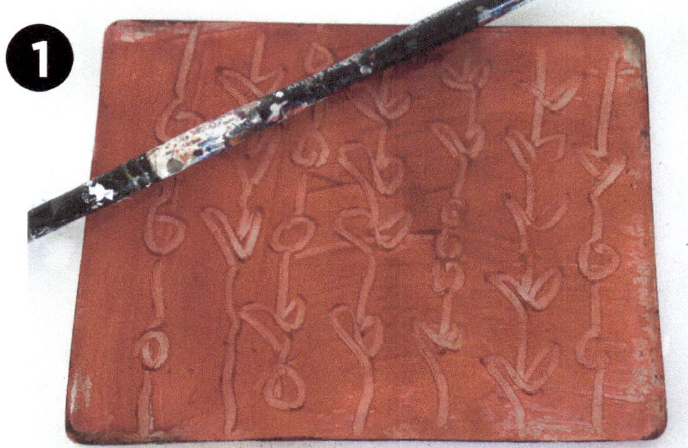

Drawing into the paint on the plate with the end of a paintbrush can yield spontaneous patterns.

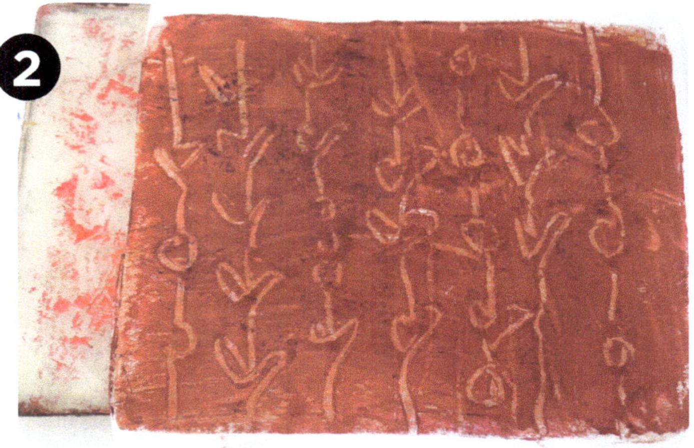

The print from the paintbrush marks. Note that the print is the mirror image of what is on the plate. Something to remember when writing letters.

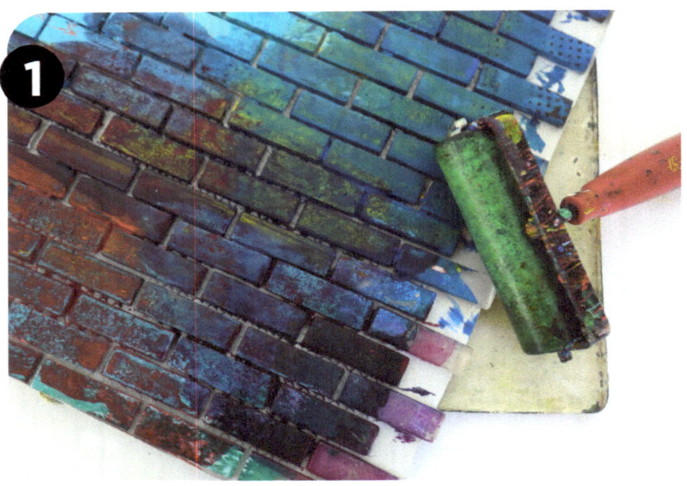

Tile samples from the hardware store in 12x12
sheets come in many different patterns.

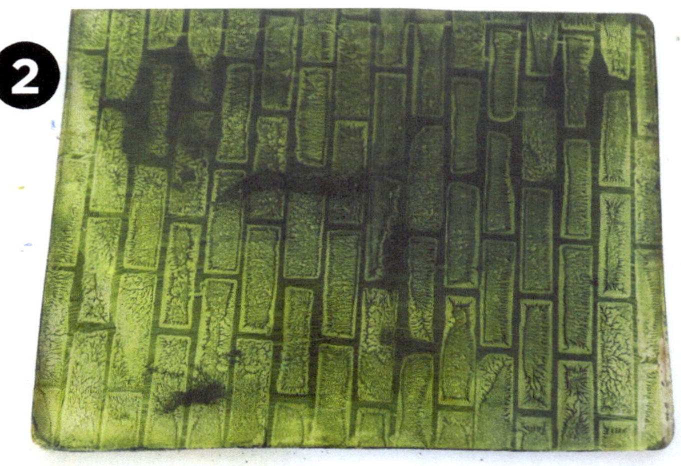

Tile can press into the paint on the plate to create
subtle patterning.

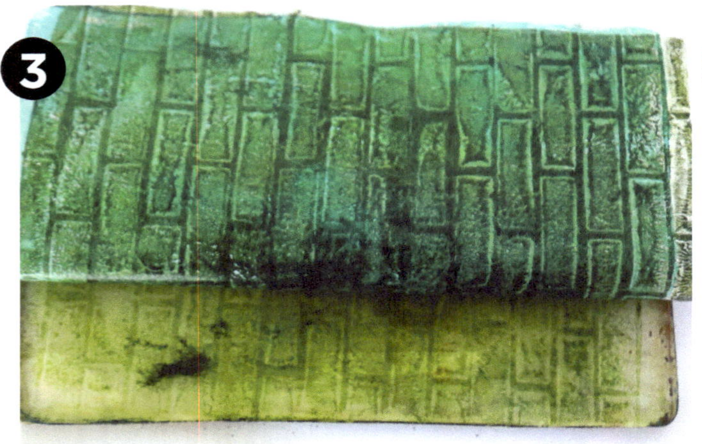

The print over a prepared light colored solid gives
a two-tone subtle tile pattern.

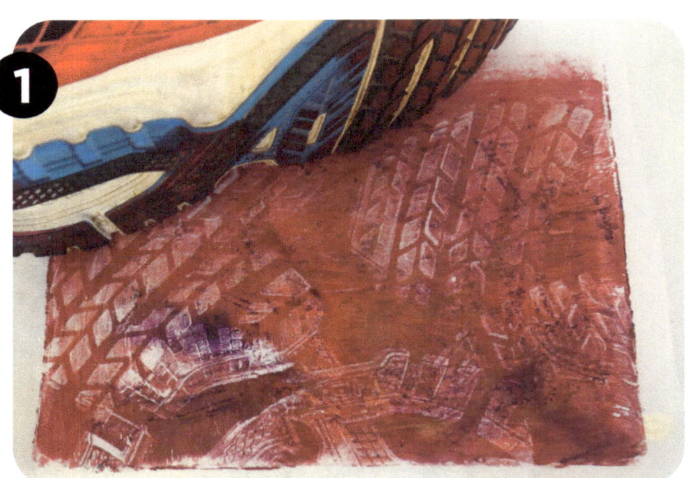

The pattern from the sole of my running shoe.

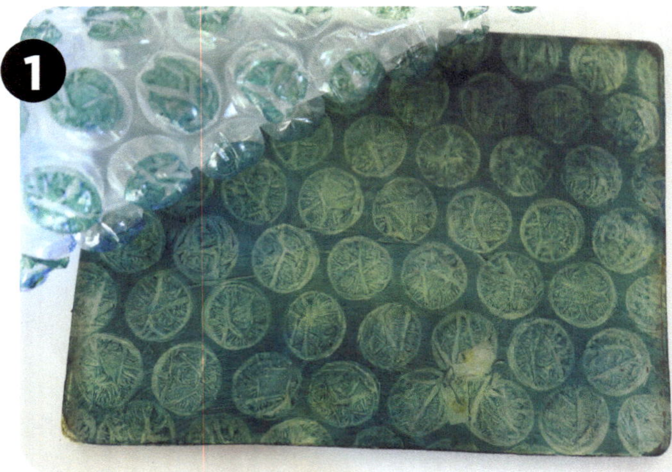

Bubble wrap from packaging comes in different sizes.

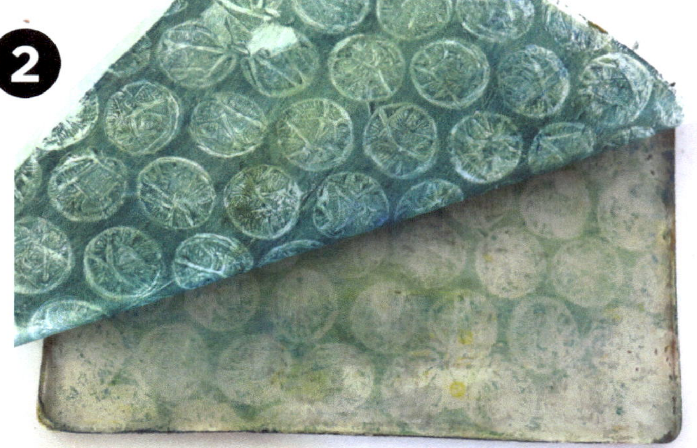

The print over a prepared light colored solid gives a two-tone subtle
bubble pattern.

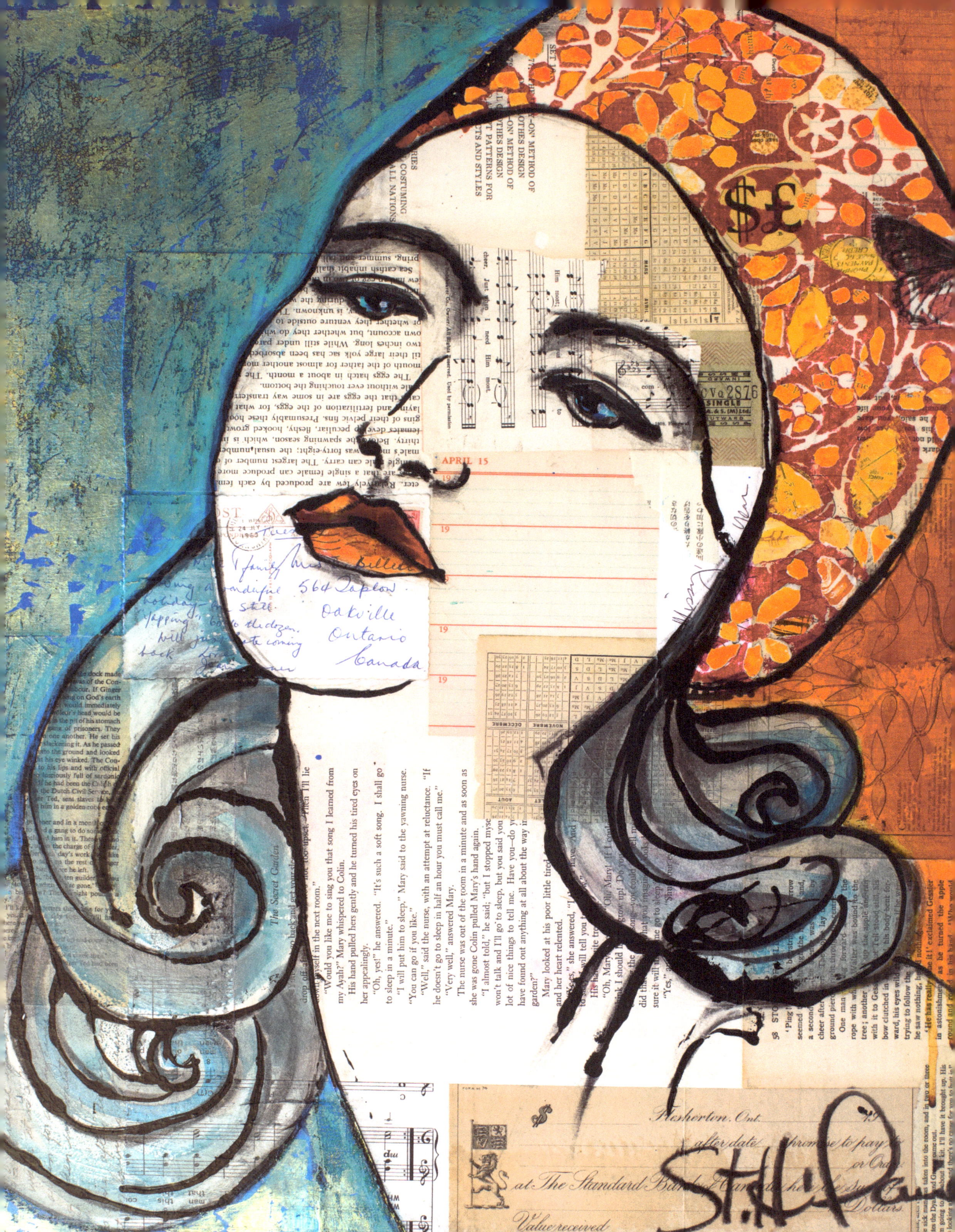

finding
EPHEMERA

ETSY shops such as **judgedbyaBOOKScover** offers vintage themed ephemera, stamps, tickets, labels, papers, collage fodder, mixed media bits, scrap pack, junk journal embellishment. I scour eBay as well as local used book stores, the Goodwill, and books sales from the local library. Also, I am lucky enough to have people gift me things they have kept or have found. If you put the word out to your friends and family, you might be surprised what people offer; post it to Facebook!

The types of materials I incorporate into my backgrounds include old books, sheet music, old letters, maps, canceled checks, card catalogue cards, library book pocket cards, playing cards, etc. If you are using anything that has been written with a pen, give it a smudge test before you glue it down. Put some water into the ink with your finger to be sure it doesn't bleed. Pencil is always good, it's archival and subtle.

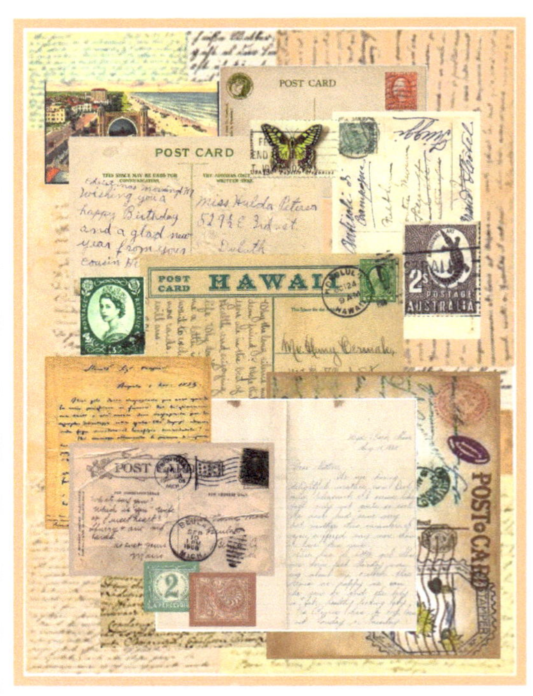

Bathing Beauty (left)
Before I found the encaustic effect I would
paint on ephemera that was not toned back at
all. You might like this more bold approach to
the background

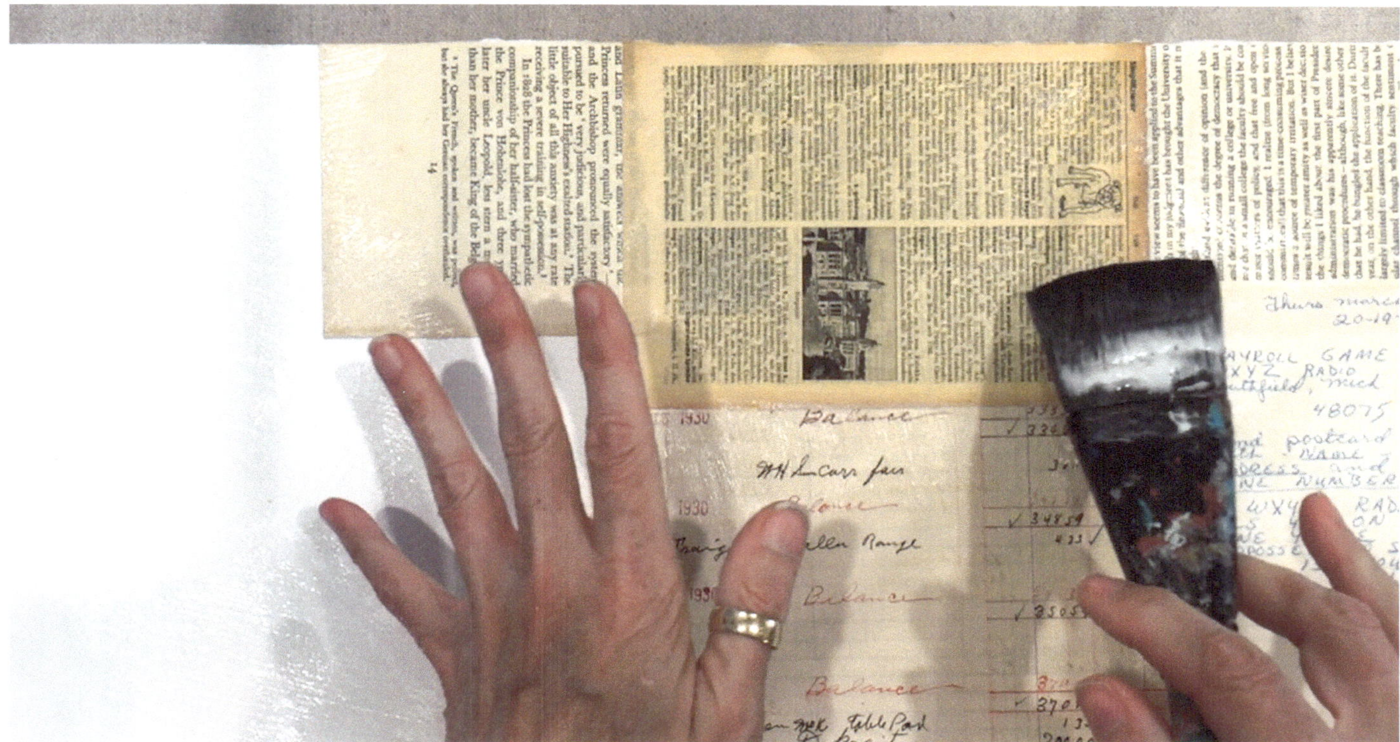

The Princeton Catalyst #20 Flat brush is my favorite for applying the ephemera

building the
BACKGROUND

Lay your ephemera papers out onto the board first in order to curate them for the best arrangement. Keep in mind where the face of your subject will fall in the composition and keep busy, dark papers out of that area. Note that any ephemera that you really want to show in the final composition should be kept out toward the edges. You may want to have your reference image sized up at this point so you can determine what areas are going to be covered by your subject.

Spread the glue generously onto the surface of your cradled wood panel with the big brush. Working quickly (the glue dries fast, you may want to apply it in sections), lay your ephemera papers, one at a time, into the glue and then brush more gel medium over the top of the paper. Use pressure from the rigid bristle Catalyst brush to smooth out all the wrinkles and press out the air bubbles, while applying more glue on top.

Go through these steps until you cover your whole board, wrapping around the edges. For the sides of a cradled wood panel, take a paper from the front and fold it down over the edge, adhering it in the same manor. Do your best to smooth everything down flat, the layer of glue over the top will help your papers continue to flatten as they dry overnight.

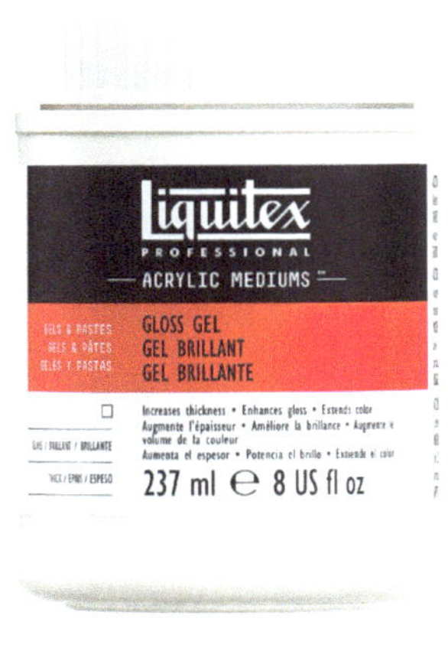

fashion plate **PORTRAITS**

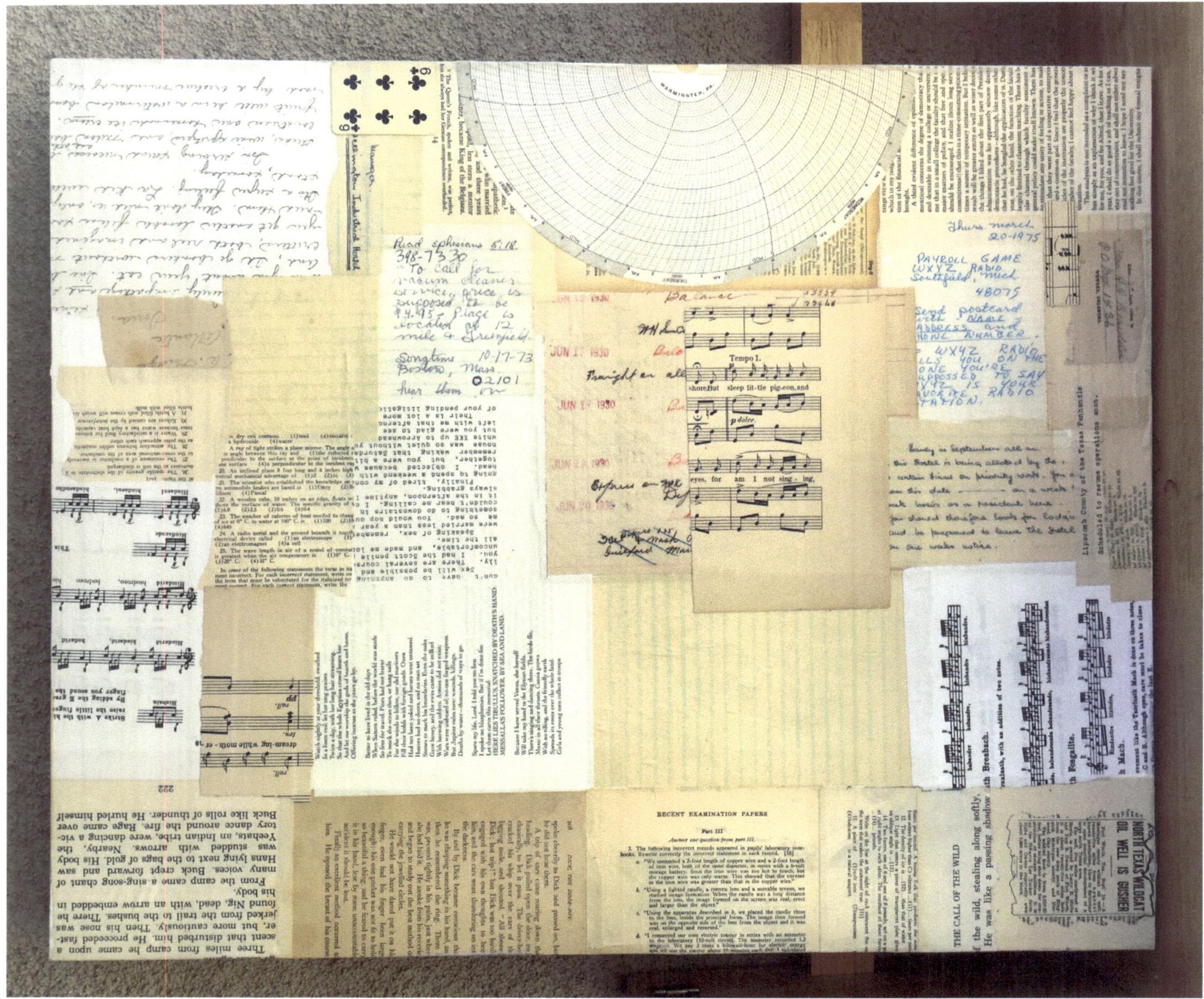

A 20x24x2-deep wood panel covered with ephemera

My preferred brush for applying the ephemera background is the Princeton Catalyst #20 Flat. This brush is BIG and has very rigid bristles, which makes it a great tool for pressing the papers flat.

I do not recommend any matte products be used for collage glue. It is important to use gloss gel medium in such applications in order to maintain the intensity of your colors. Matting solids, the particles of silicates that lower the sheen, can obscure underlying paints, especially when used in a thick application. The thicker the film and the more matting solids in the film, the more opaque it will appear.

Maintaining clarity and intensity of color is critical, and therefore it is always better to use gloss gels. You can always apply a satin or matte varnish over your artwork at the end to tone back the gloss finish. One thin layer of matte or satin varnish at the end will reduce the overall glare on the surface of your artwork, but will have much better translucency than thick layers of matte gel. My preferred collage glue is Liquitex Gloss Gel Medium, we use the same product to glue down the ephemera background.

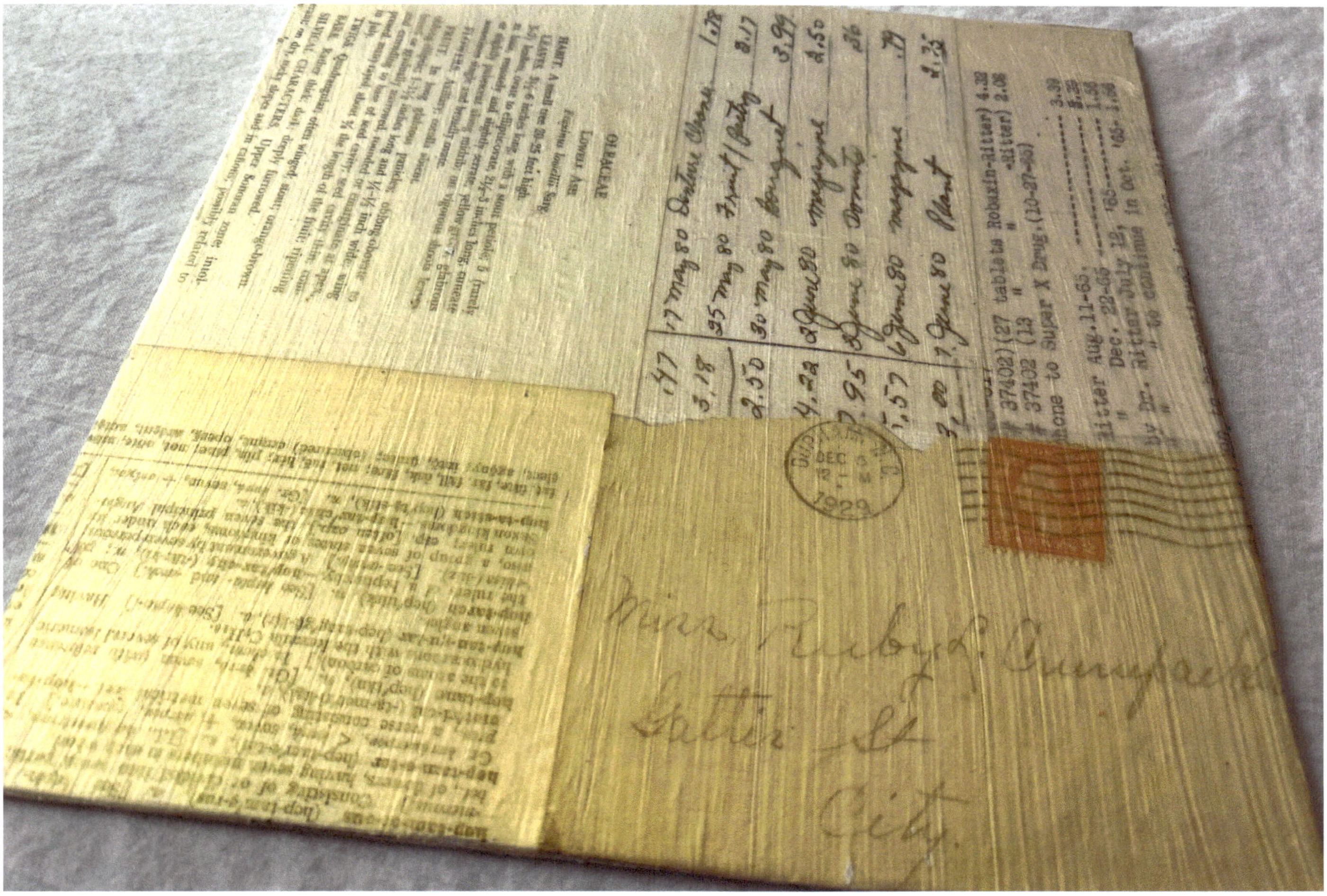

Adding the Gold Interference Fluid Acrylic lends a beeswax-like color to the Extra Heavy Gel Matte

the encaustic
EFFECT

Golden Extra Heavy Gel Matte is the thickest of Golden's gels and it dries to a wax-like finish. This is the product that gives the background the look of encaustic.

Golden Interference Acrylic Colors offer a unique metallic gold effect when viewed from different angles. From one angle the color appears highly reflective and golden, from another angle it's effect is very subtle. This is the product that adds a beeswax-like coloring to the gel medium.

NOTE: Regular gold paint will not give the same effect as the Interference Fluid Acrylic.

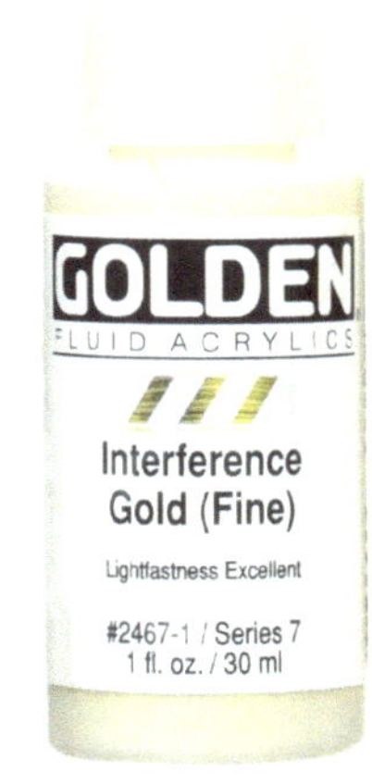

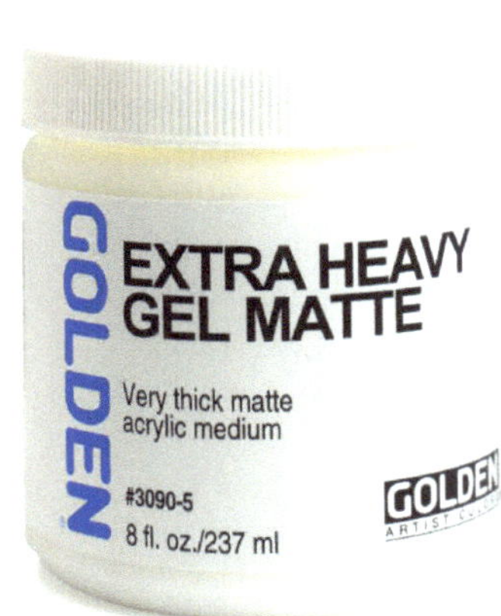

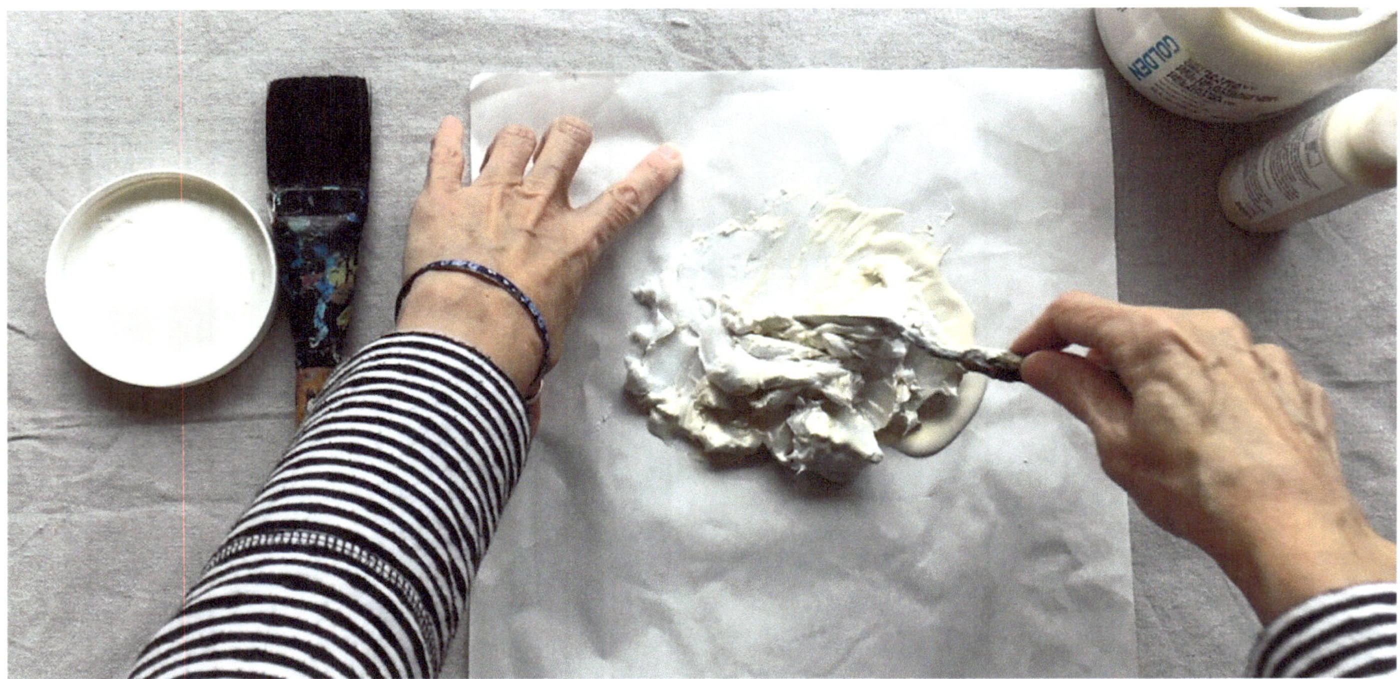

Blend the mixture thoroughly with a palette knife on a sheet of waxed palette paper

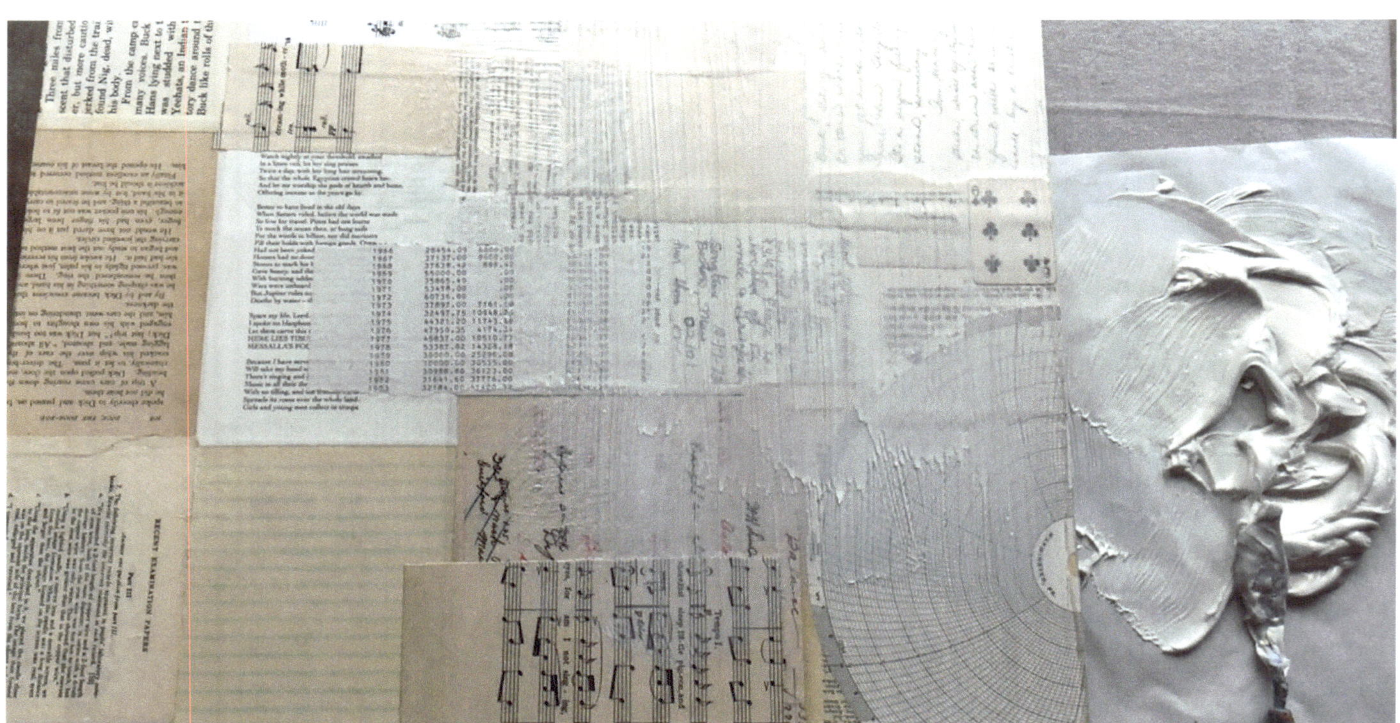

Spread the encaustic mixture over the ephemera background

Mix about one cup of Extra Heavy Gel Matte with three tablespoons of Interference Gold Fluid Acrylic paint. The amount of gold is a personal preference, you may decide that you want more or less than my formula after some practice.

Blend the mixture together thoroughly with a palette knife on a sheet of waxed palette paper. Once blended, spread the encaustic mixture over the entire surface of your board (sides included) about 1/16 inch thick, using the same Catalyst #20 Flat brush you used to glue down the ephemera. Take care to make the surface as smooth as possible, checking for ridges and uneven areas. A smooth application takes practice. Return any unused portion of the mixture to an air tight container for a future use. Allow your project to dry overnight.

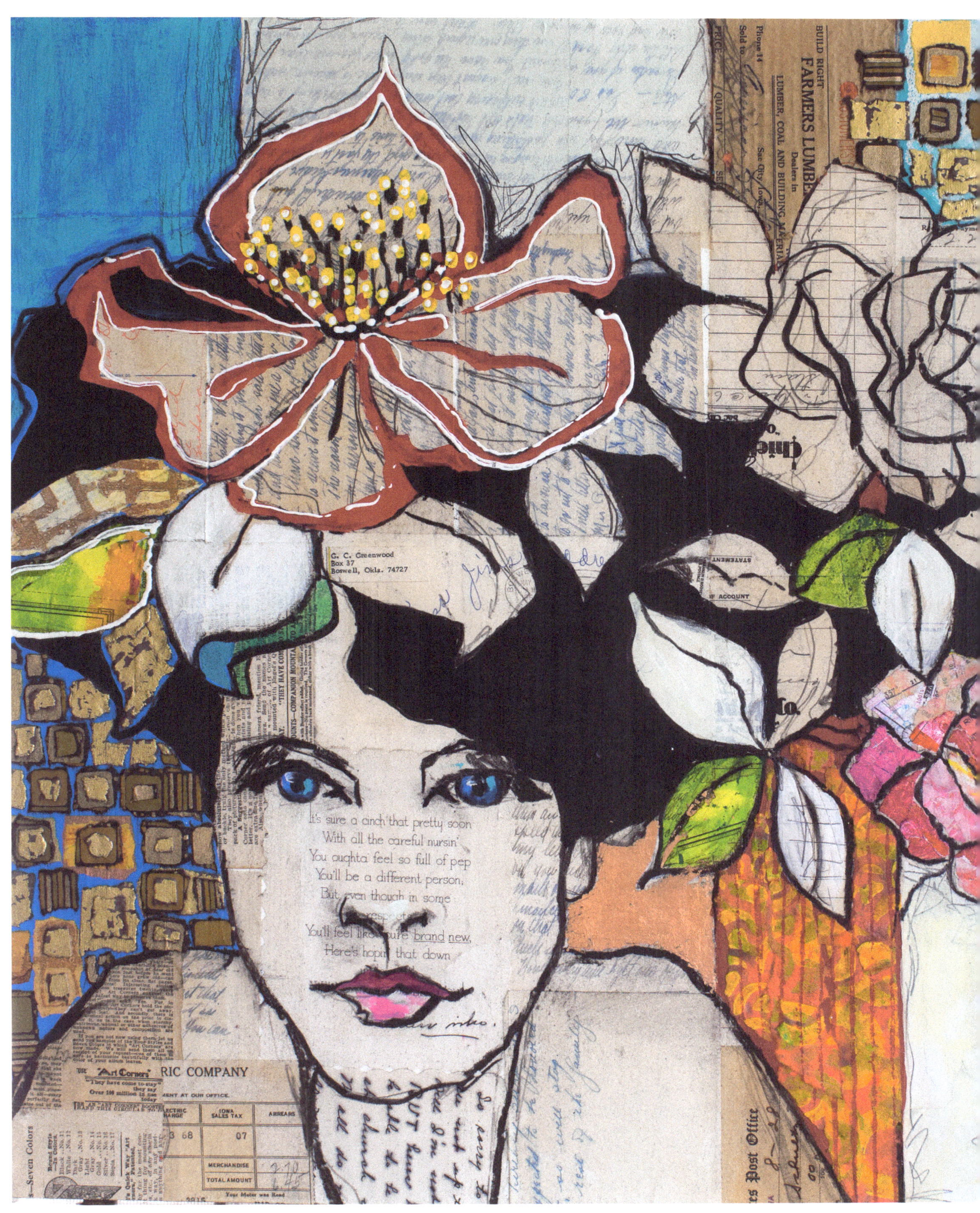

FARMERS LUMBER
LUMBER, COAL AND BUILDING
C. C. Greenwood
Box 37
Boswell, Okla. 74727
It's sure a cinch that pretty soon
With all the careful nursin'
You oughta feel so full of pep
You'll be a different person.
But even though in some
You'll feel like you're brand new,
Here's hopin' that down
RIC COMPANY

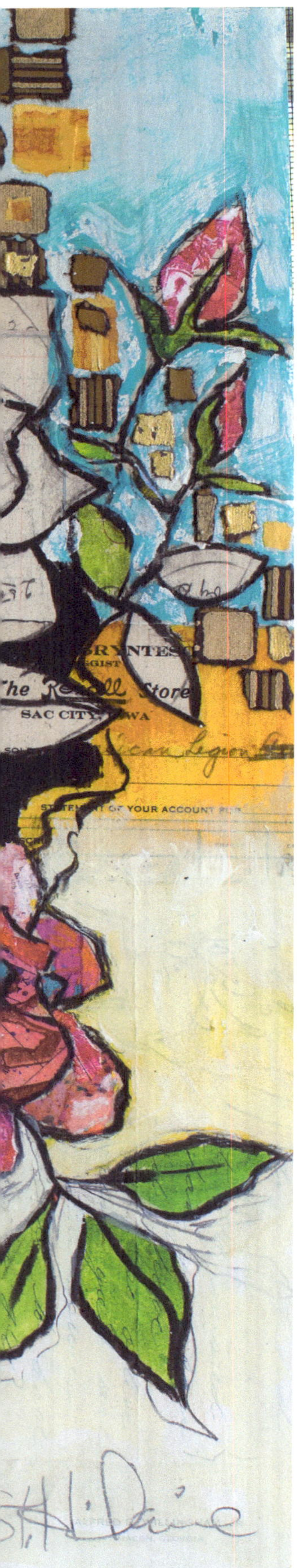

Different Person (left) *utilizes white Posca Paint Pen on the red flower and graphite pencil on some of the other flowers, stems, and leaves.*

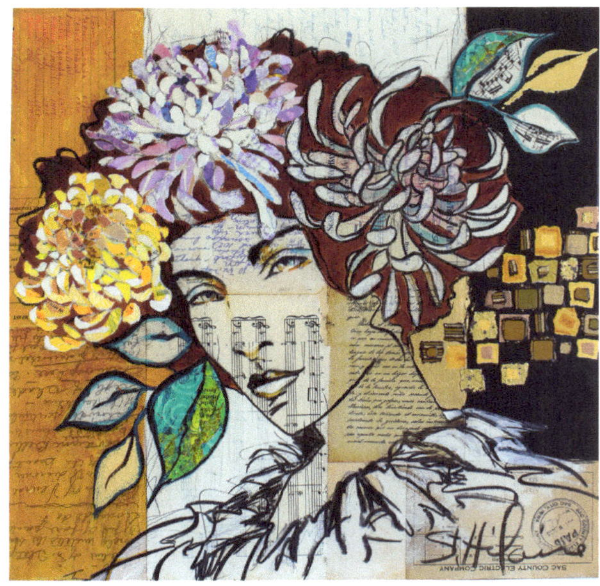

Autumn *utilizes a similar sectioned background effect*

embellish the
BACK GROUND

Oftentimes I leave the entire background ephemera (with or without the encaustic effect), but for some pieces I am inclined to embellish sections of the background with paint, collage paper, gold leaf, etc. You can see in the piece to the left *Different Person*, that the ephemera background remains in the face and flowers of the subject, but I have embellished behind her.

The blue section is paint, the letter to the right of that has a layer of watered-down gesso that allows the writing to be further subdued. I've added collage elements in the upper right corner, on top of paint; this same effect can also be seen in the lower left. To the immediate right of her ear, there is a small section of copper metallic leaf, then a strip of collage paper. The lower right utilizes a thicker layer of gesso which allowed me to draw on top and sign my name with pencil–gesso adds tooth and is opaque enough to block out the printed material below it.

NOTE: the two examples on this page do not have the encaustic effect over the ephemera, you can see how much more bold the printed material appears without it.

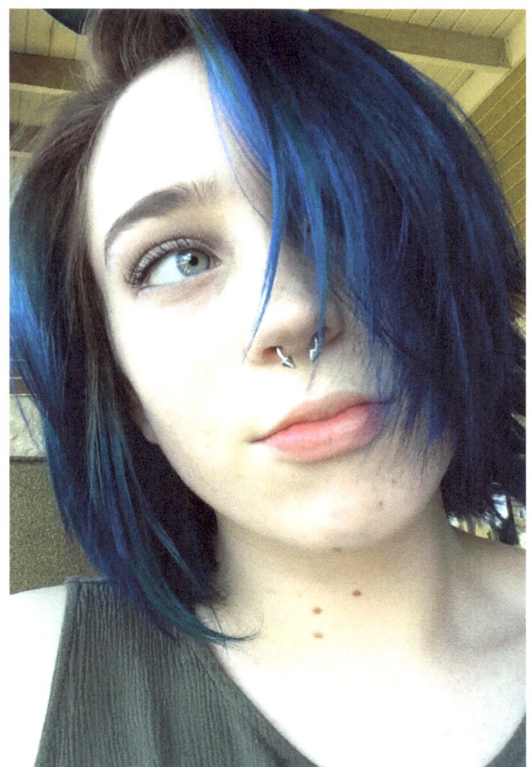
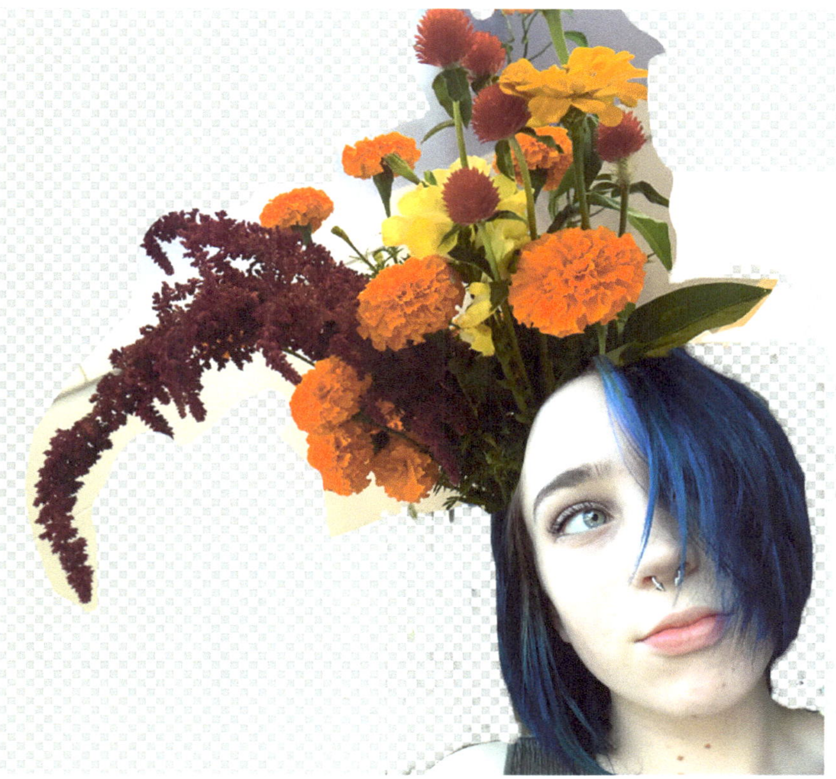

My Muse took this photo of herself while we were having coffee outside of Starbucks.

manipulating PHOTOS

Emilie has provided me with endless iPhone selfies which I save to a folder on my computer. I am pretty tech savvy and utilized Adobe Photoshop to combine her selfie with a photo reference of a flower arrangement from my sister's garden. If you are not tech savvy, you can have your images enlarged and printed out so that you can take scissors to them—crop, cut, and arrange your image by hand.

You can also consider taking images from magazines or books, cutting them up and putting them together to form a fun fashion composition that you can then photograph with your iPhone and enlarge to the size of your substrate. When using the graphite transfer paper it's important that your image is enlarged to the same size as the board that you are working on.

NOTE: You'll want your large print-out to be on regular copy paper, not thick photo paper in order to have the best results with the graphite transfer paper process.

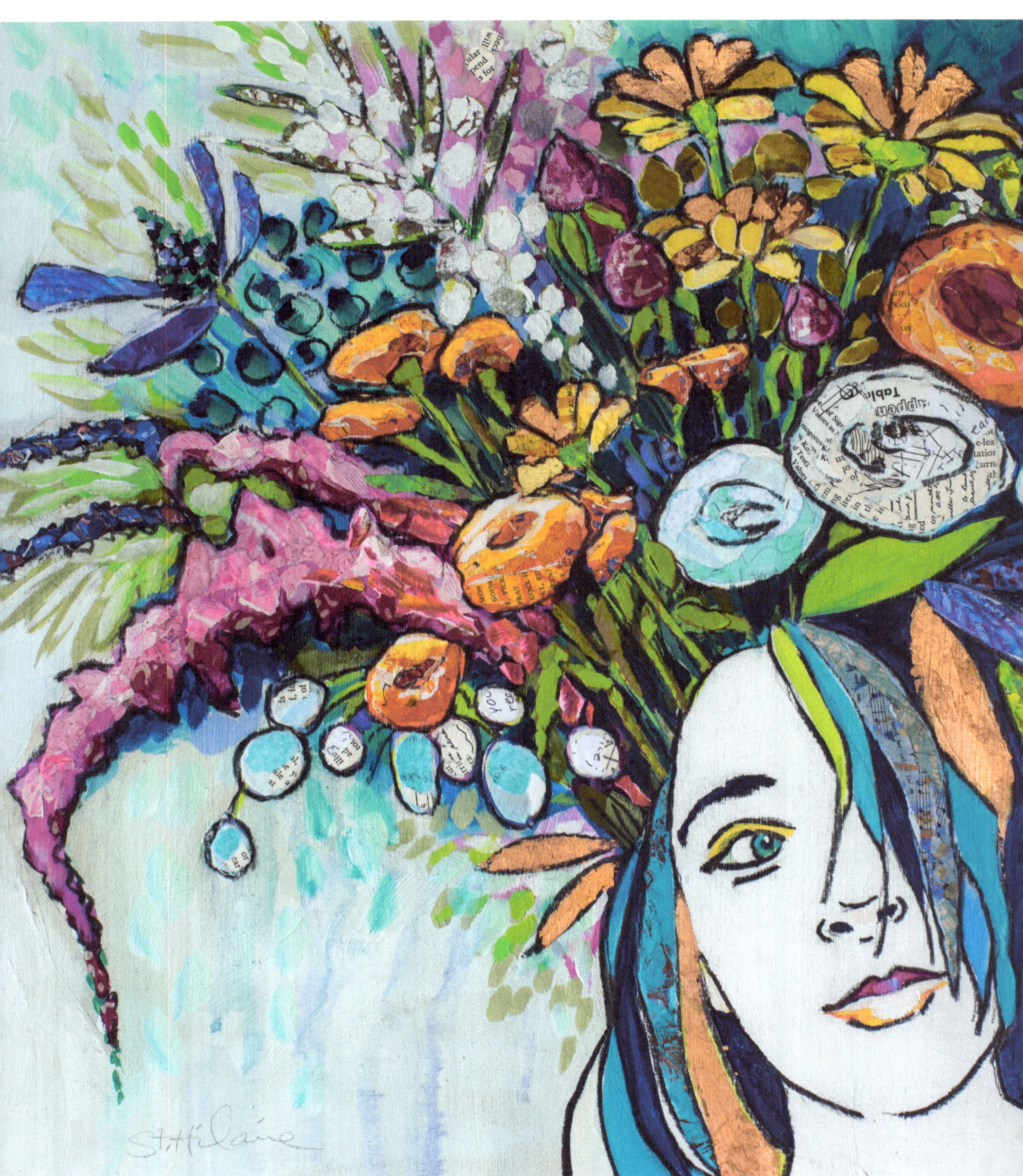

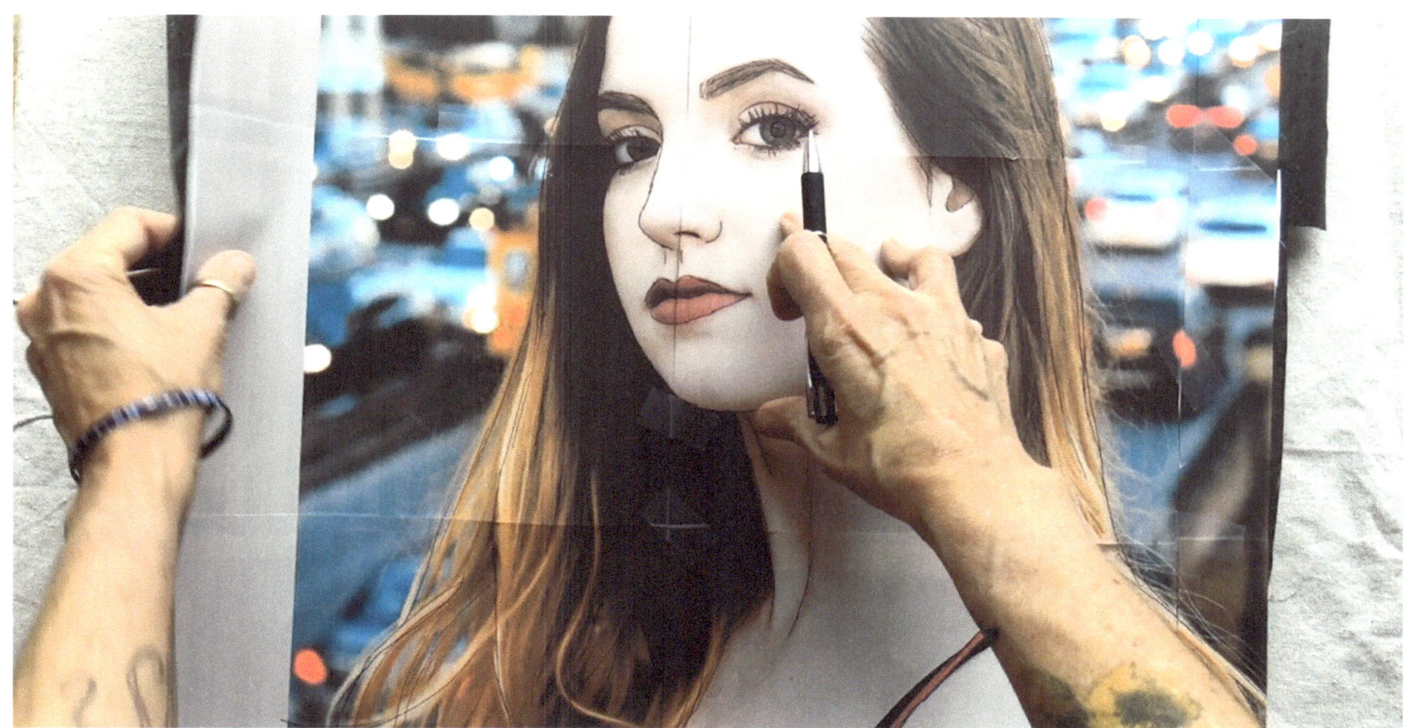

Use a ballpoint pen for the transfer .

START
with a sketch

graphite transfer paper

I always start with a pencil sketch before I begin painting. If you are not confident in your drawing skills you may use graphite transfer paper (shiny side down) underneath your sized-up reference image and basically *trace* your photo with a ball point pen. The graphite transfer paper works like old fashioned carbon paper... It transfers graphite to the substrate from the pressure of your pen! These marks can be erased and edited if needed.

Secure the reference image and the transfer paper with tape at the top so that it does not shift out of alignment. Lift the corner every now and then, to be sure you have not missed any areas of your sketch. My sketch (right) gives me all the info I need to make a good painting.

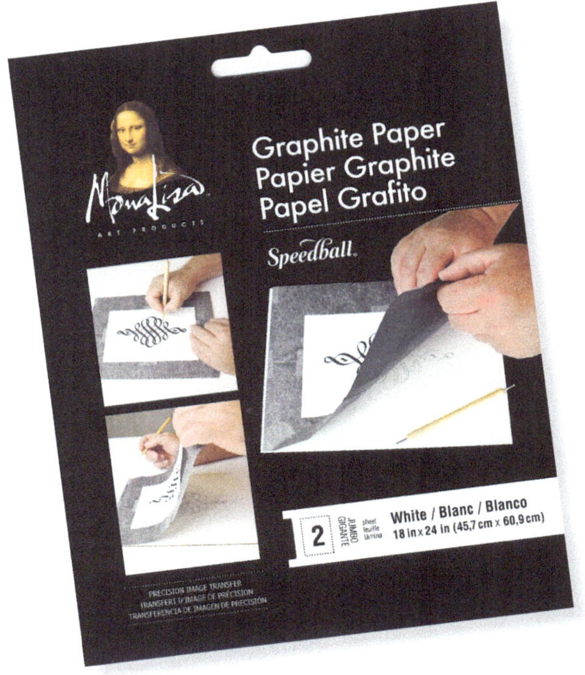

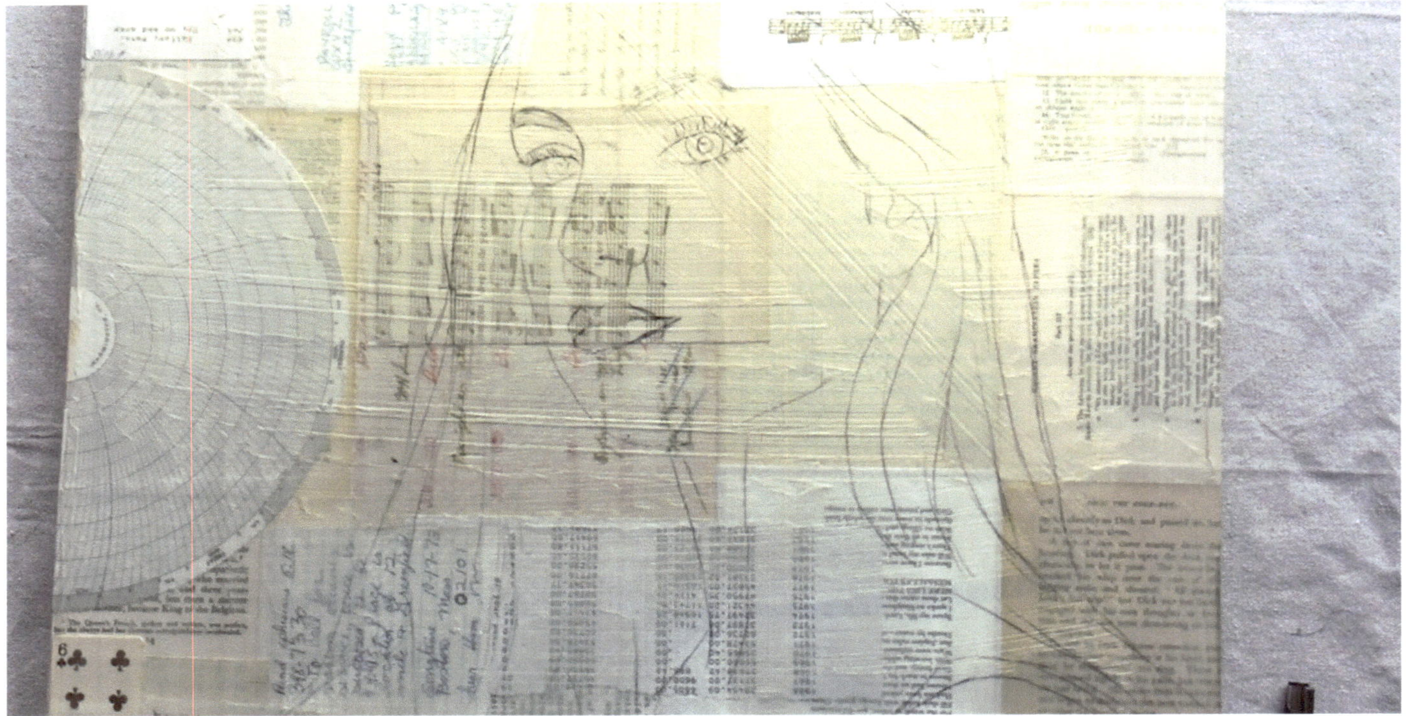

Be sure all your details are transferred before you dismount the reference image.

adding your personal touch

When you choose to embellish with fashion elements such as jewelry, hats, scarves, etc you can print them out separately to size and then transfer them to your portrait, OR you can draw them in freehand, make them up, and just have fun with it! Remember that these elements are where you have the opportunity for collage and mark making/embellishing.

Mia's photo (right) was cropped to a head and shoulders portrait at 20x24. I added a necklace, earrings, and a floral headpiece which I drew freehand after I transferred her likeness. I loved the way Mia's hair waved and curled at the bottom, so I embellished that in my portrait.

Some of my students have added birds with a nest and big fashion hats into their portraits, I love this! Get creative, don't restrict yourself to the reference image.

NOTE: Clean up your graphite transfer image with a Pink Pearl eraser for the best results. I use a drafting brush to remove eraser crumbs without smudging.

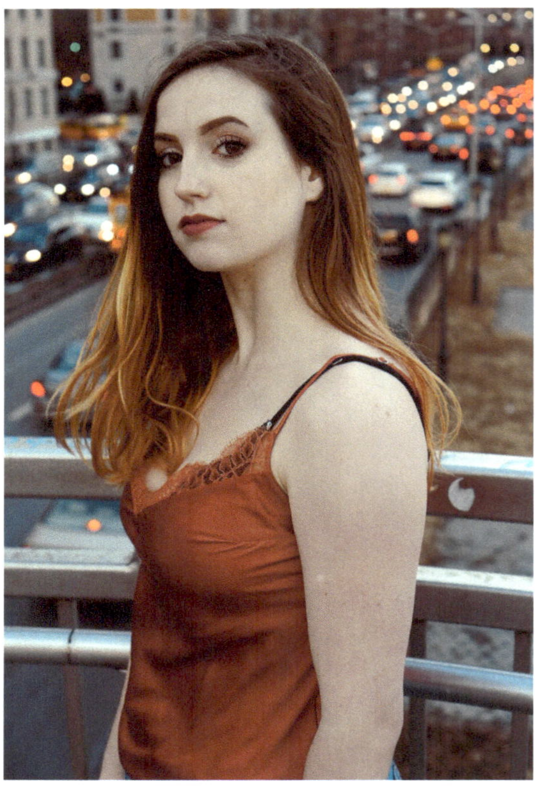

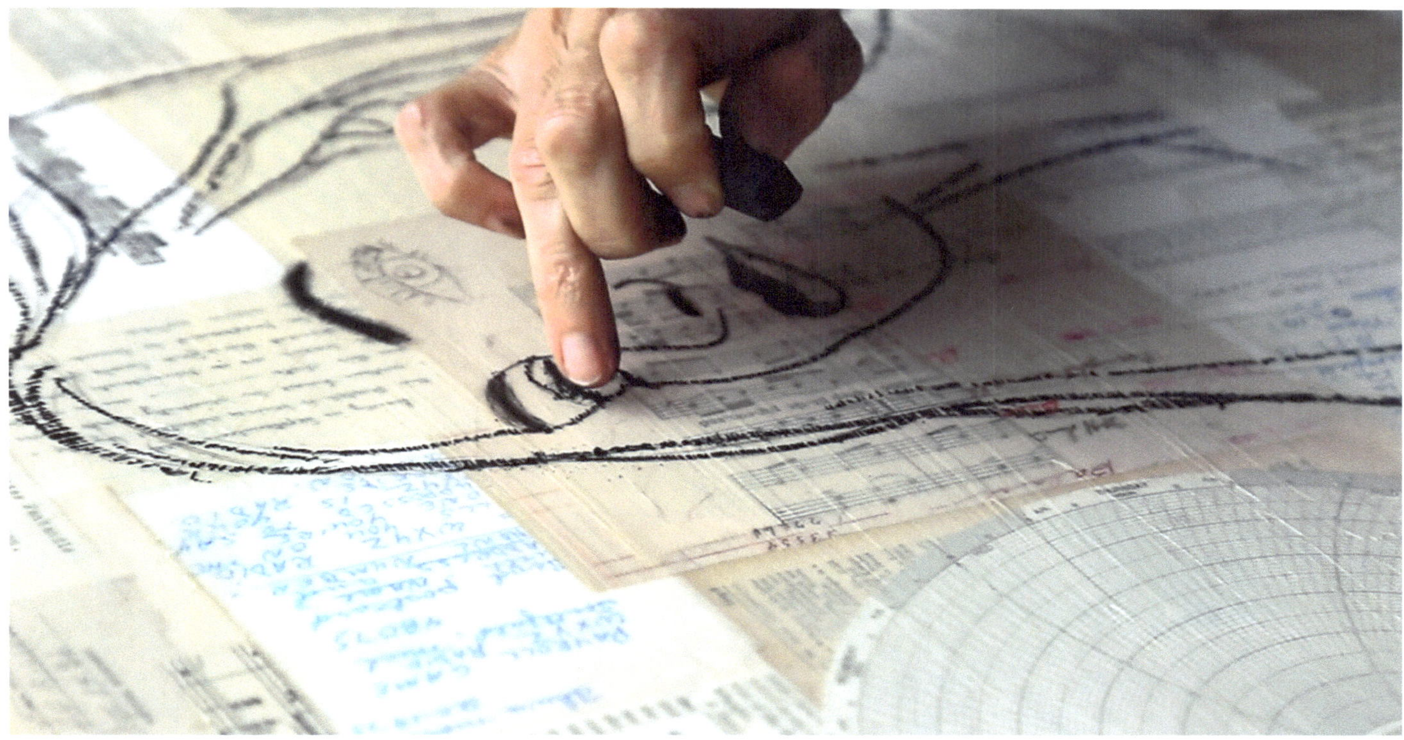

Smudge with your finger or a blending stump for pastel

pastel smudge
SKETCH

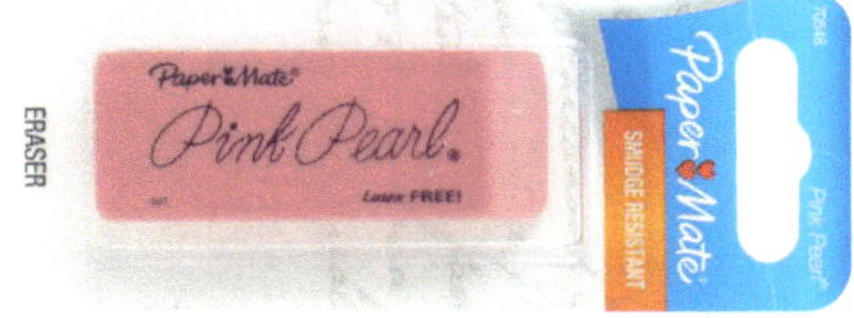

creating a drawing

Using soft black square pastel sticks on their sharp corner, carefully draw over the pencil sketch. When the sharp corner gets dull, rotate the stick to another edge and then crack it in half in order to create more sharp corners. When you are finished, gently smudge the drawing with your finger OR use a blending stump if your fingers are too big for fine details. Rub your finger over the surface to create shading with the black pastel buildup. Be careful not to make shading too dark in the face, fashion portraits typically utilize lighting that produces very little shading–always go lighter than you think!

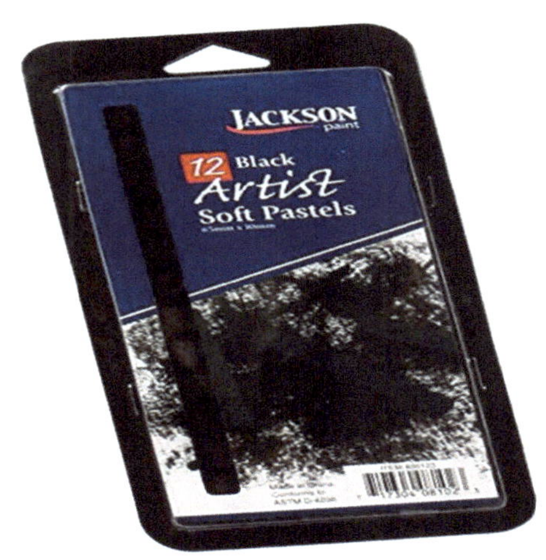

Use your Pink Pearl eraser to edit the pastel. You can pull highlights out by erasing. Note the bottom lip and the light strands of hair to the right, they were created by erasing. Thoroughly clean your eraser (and your fingers) periodically with soap and water for best results. Use a drafting brush to gently remove dirty eraser crumbs from the surface of your artwork so as to avoid black streaking.

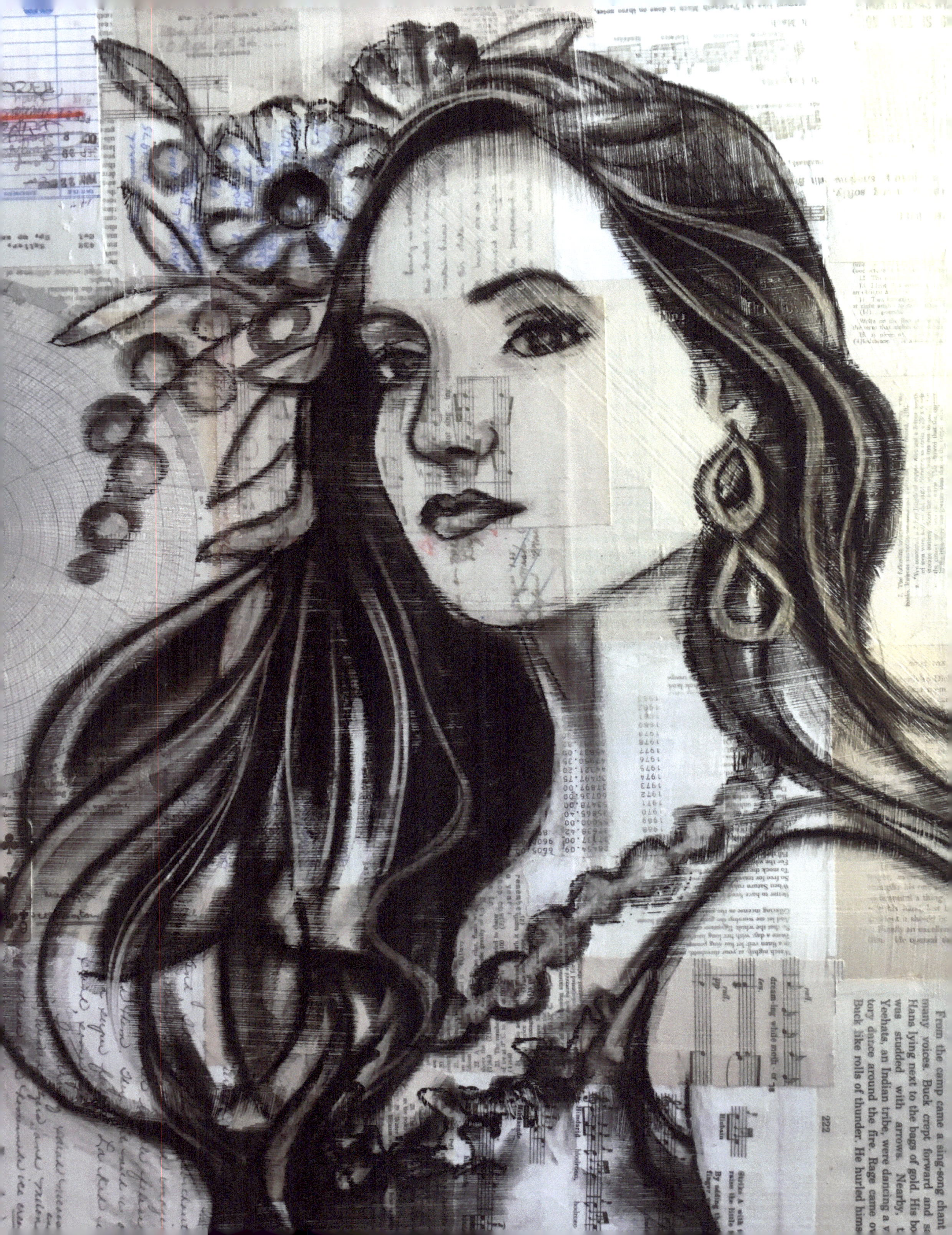

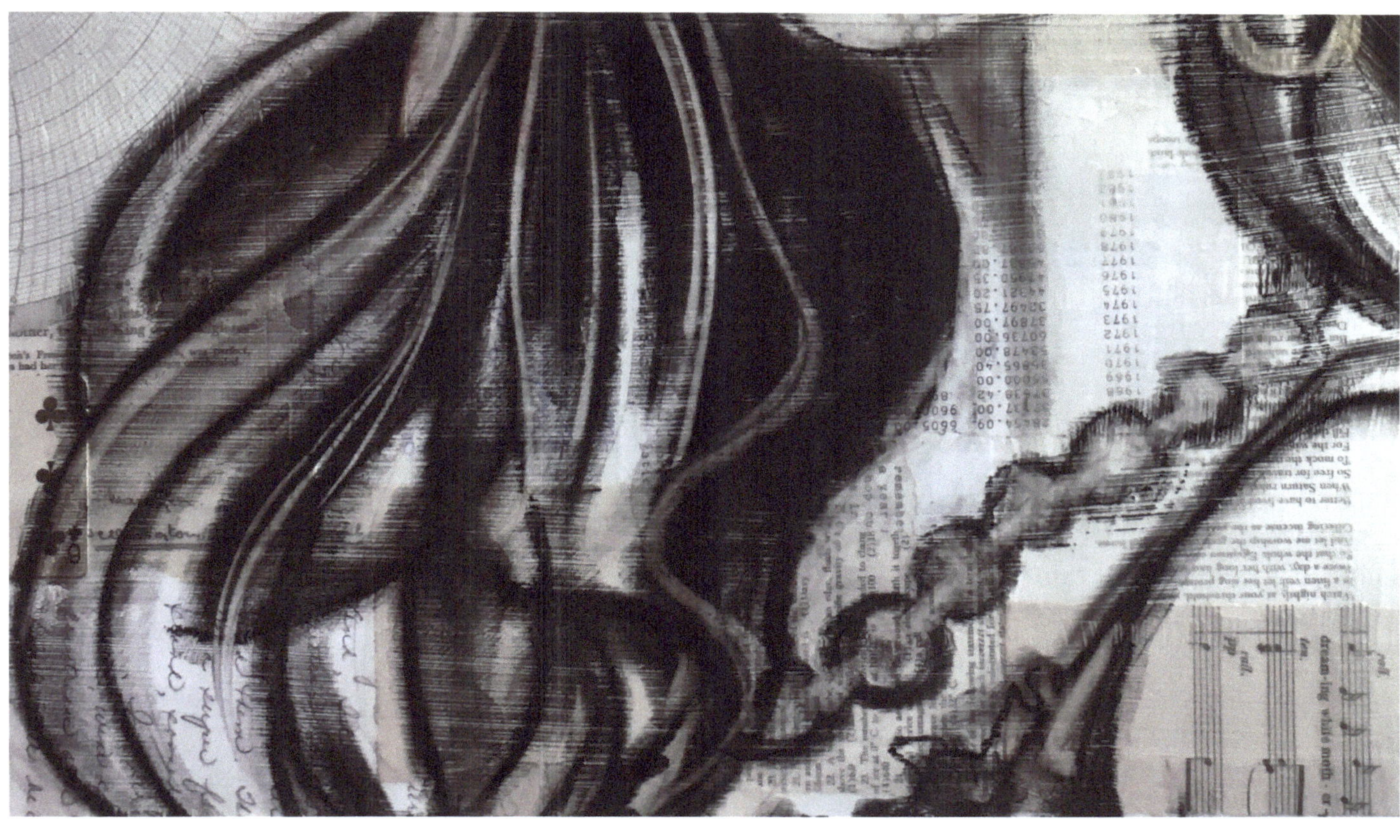

Areas with heavy pastel coverage will need several coats of varnish

sealing the
DRAWING

spray varnish

A spray varnish coat seals the pastel from smudging so that you can move on to the next step. The major benefit of this step is that aerosol varnish can be applied without touching the artwork surface. In addition to the pastel layer, you will also use spray varnish to seal your Stabilo Woodies and Posca Paint Pens used for mark making before you apply a final layer of brush varnish. My preferred product for this step is Krylon Satin Finish. I like satin because it gives us a little bit of tooth for painting.

Before you seal your piece, be absolutely sure that there are no smudges or errant marks that you do not want in your final piece–once you varnish there is no more erasing or editing!

Shake can thoroughly for at least two minutes to ensure that all material that has settled over time in the can is thoroughly mixed. It's important not to skimp on this step because you don't want settled material clogging the can or clouding the finish of your artwork. Additionally, a well shaken can will apply more evenly, giving you a better finish.

Spray in an area separate from your studio. Sometimes it takes a while for odors from drying varnishes to dissipate, so it's better if you can leave the artwork to dry in another area.

position of artwork

Artwork should be kept in a fairly upright position. Do not place your artwork flat because the varnish or fixative will not apply evenly.

ideal spraying conditions

Use aerosol products in good weather, ideally when temperatures are 50°F to 90°F, and relative humidity is below 85%.

• Do not spray in high humidity. This can cause bloom, a white cloudy haze that remains under the varnish where moisture is trapped.

• Always spray in a well ventilated area, preferably outside. When spraying indoors, open windows and doors and use a fan to keep air circulating.

application

For varnishes, several thin coats will be needed to provide the best protection against smudging. Wait a minute or so for any solvents to evaporate off the surface, and then spray the next coat in a vertical, up and down motion instead of side to side. Alternate directions with each coat for an even finish.

• Be sure that you have blown off any excess pastel dust from the surface of the drawing.

• Take your time. Always use thin, multiple coats instead of one thick coat, and move the can at a slow, consistent pace.

• Hold the can of varnish or fixative parallel to the surface at the distance recommended on the label to ensure the product sprays evenly. Maintain this distance continuously while spraying.

• Always begin and finish spraying off the artwork to ensure that the entire surface, including the edges when you are working on cradled panel, have an even application of varnish or fixative.

• Begin at a far top corner just off of the artwork, and spray horizontally across the surface using an even motion continuing off the other side of the artwork. Then spray back across again, continuing in an even, side to side motion.

• With each pass, try to slightly overlap the area you just sprayed by about one-third until you've covered the entire surface.

• Do the smudge test to see if your pastel is sealed, rub your baby finger into the darkest area and see if there is any transfer. If you get black on your finger, you need additional coats of varnish.

• Repeat these steps after you use any smudgy mark making mixed media materials and before the final brush varnish coat is applied. When in doubt, give it a coat of spray varnish before brushing.

after use

Clean the spray valve after use by turning the can upside down and spraying for five seconds until only clear gas comes out of the valve. This helps prevent the spray tip from clogging.

Source: Krylon.com

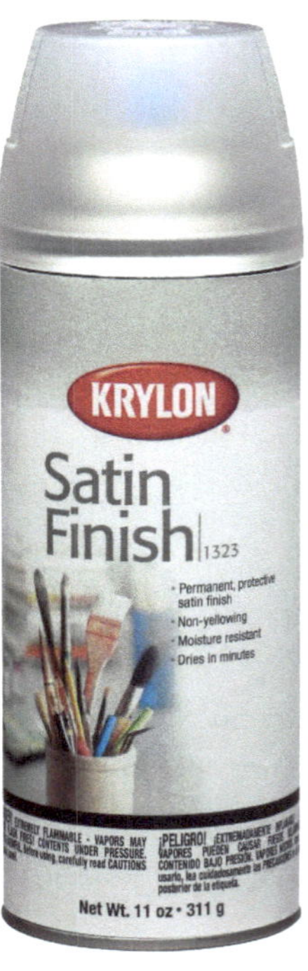

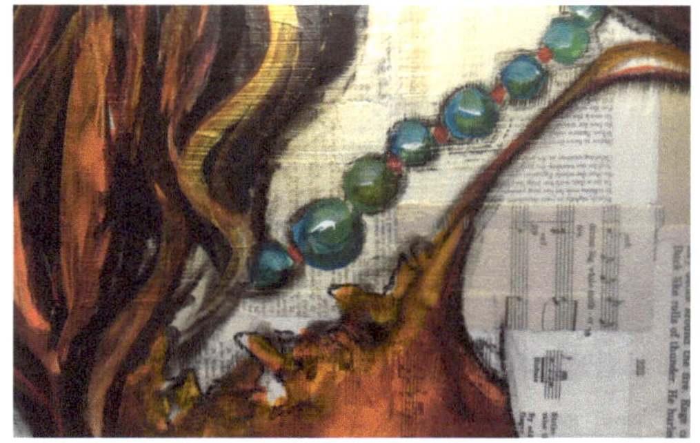 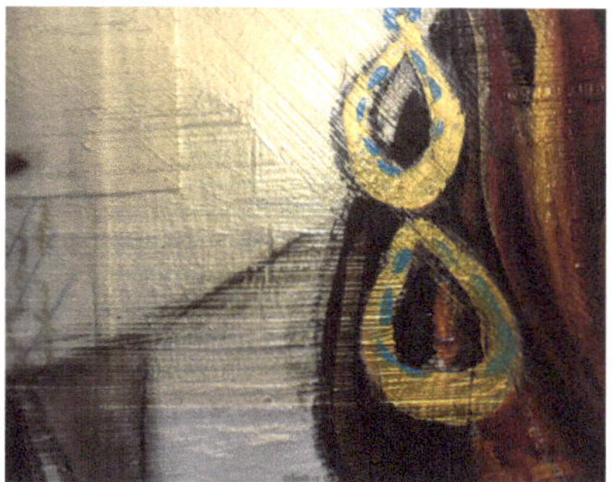 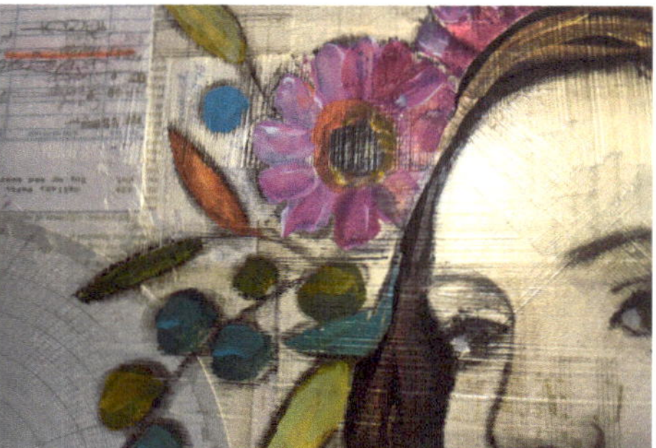

Paint everything BUT the skin, including iris of the eyes and lipstick.

PAINT
your drawing

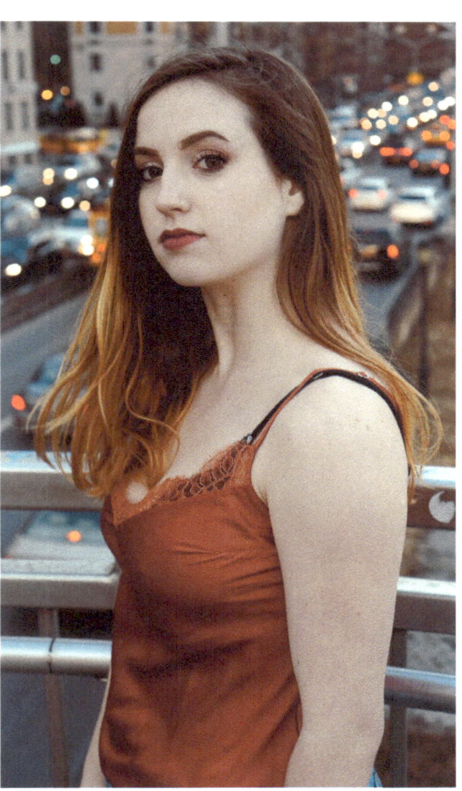

After the sealed sketch comes the under painting. I use the under painting process to block in all my colors so that when I work in the collage sections, I have a road map for the color and value. It is in the under painting process that I work out my values, the light, dark, and medium tones. I also establish my colors (sometimes I deviate from the photo reference) and determine what areas I will leave painted at this stage. It's much easier and quicker to work out these solutions with paint first than to have to work and rework the collage application.

Pay close attention to your photo reference in terms of value; what is dark and what is light? There are highlights and shadows in the hair, the floral headpiece, the earrings, the necklace, and the clothing that need to be carefully painted. We have already established the shading in the portrait by smudging the pastel. I do not paint the face of the portrait, I allow the ephemera to be the skin tone and the face to be a drawing. Once I get the values and colors to my liking and close to the photo reference I allow the painting dry completely.

In a mixed media portrait, I leave sections painted, without collage application. In the portrait to the right, what remains painted is the hair, the lips and the iris of the eyes. I do not paint in the white of the eyes generally, I leave them to ephemera background color. When you are adding fashion elements to your portrait, these are the areas that you will likely collage, be sure to consider this when painting your composition. Make room for collage!

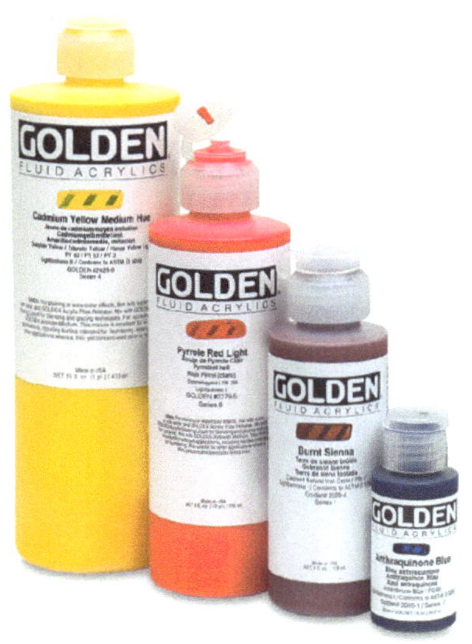

fashion plate **PORTRAITS**

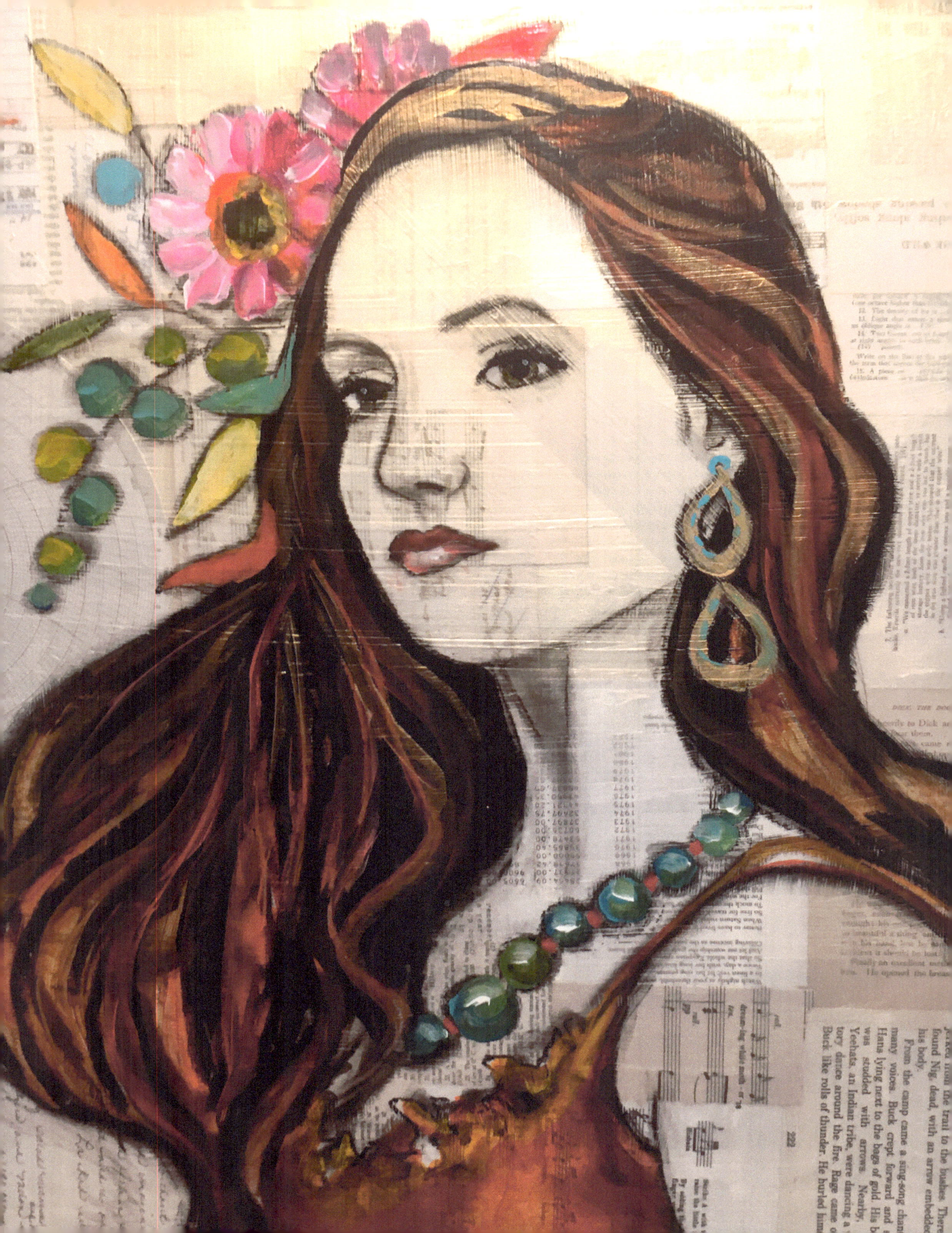

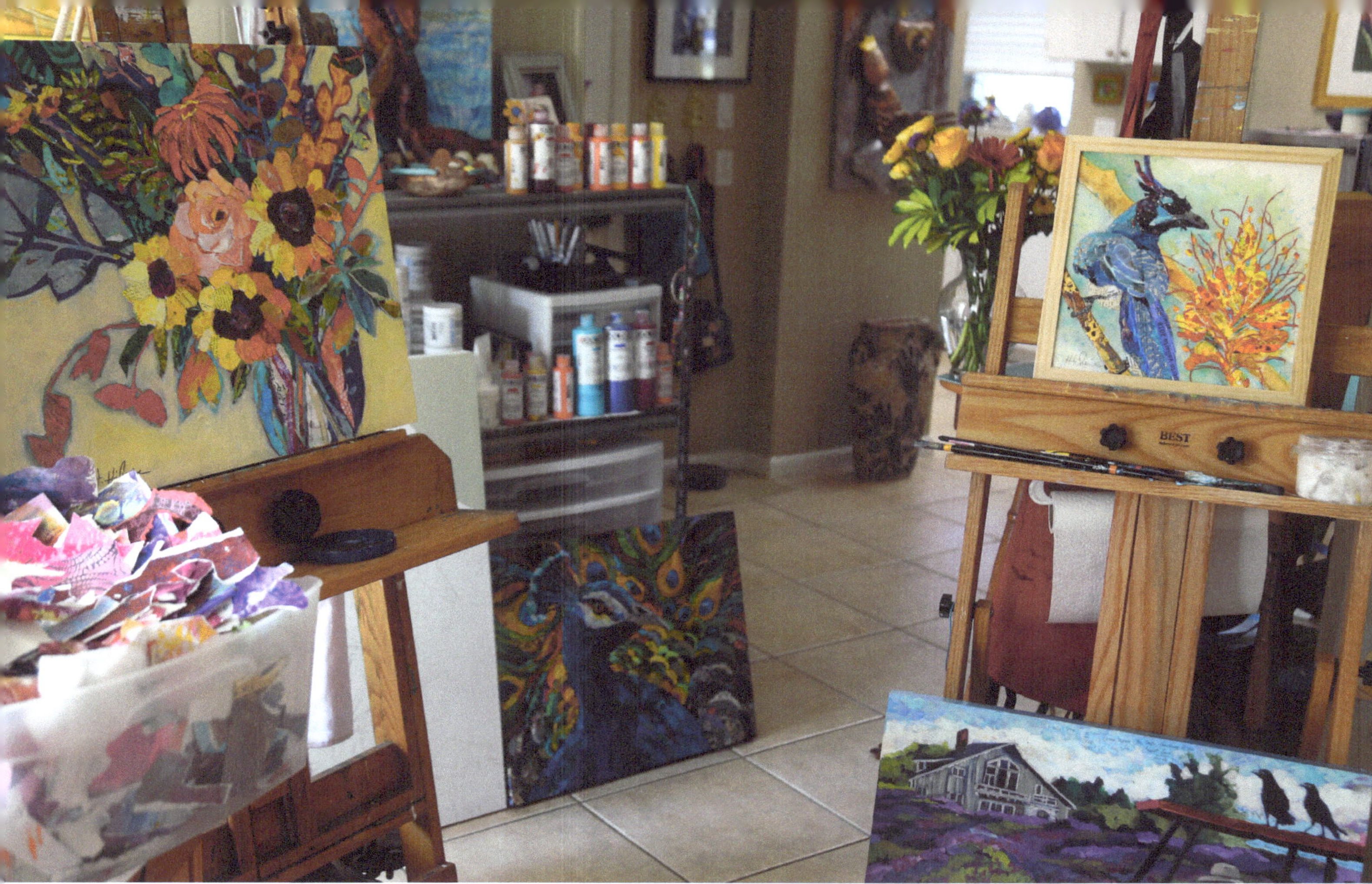

I use Golden Fluid Acrylics exclusively for painting my collage papers and my under paintings.

gesso and
PAINT

fluid acrylics

I use Golden Fluid Acrylics for the under painting. Since I have the colors on hand for painting my papers, it makes sense to use the same paints for the under-painting process. I add a bit of white gesso to lighten colors or to make them a bit more opaque. Avoid lots of white, however, as it can give your colors a chalky look. All the white areas on my portrait of Emilie Flöge (right) are white gesso and not white paint. I use gesso for my white because it's more opaque than paint and it has a tooth, which made a nice surface for the mark making I applied on top, bringing the black pastel back in at the end.

black gesso

Much like black pastel, black gesso is deeper, darker, richer, and denser than black paint. The bulk of Emilie's hair is black gesso as are the deepest shadows in her dress (right). In Mia's portrait, (previous page) much of her hair is also black gesso, but with red highlghs

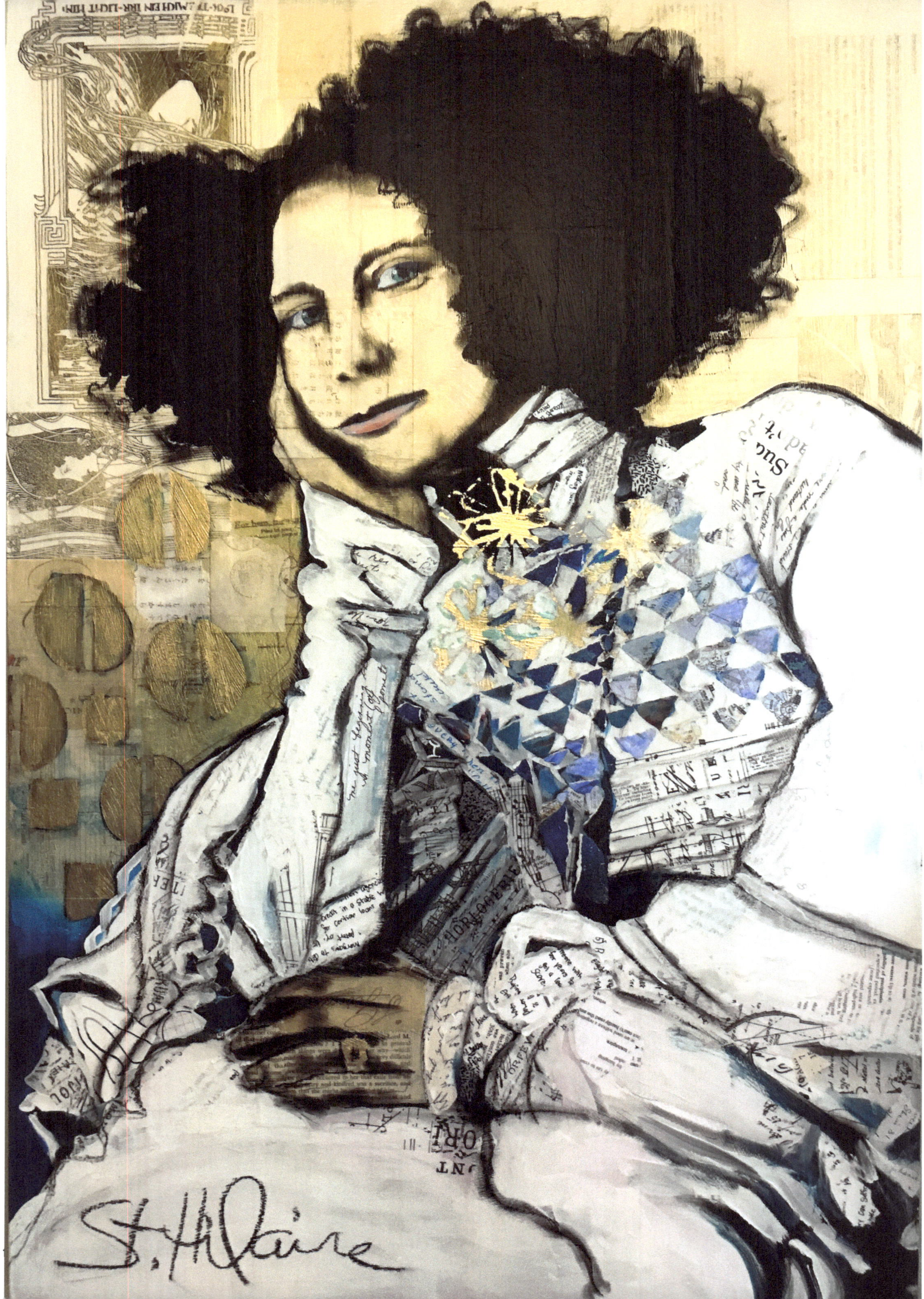

St. Hilaire

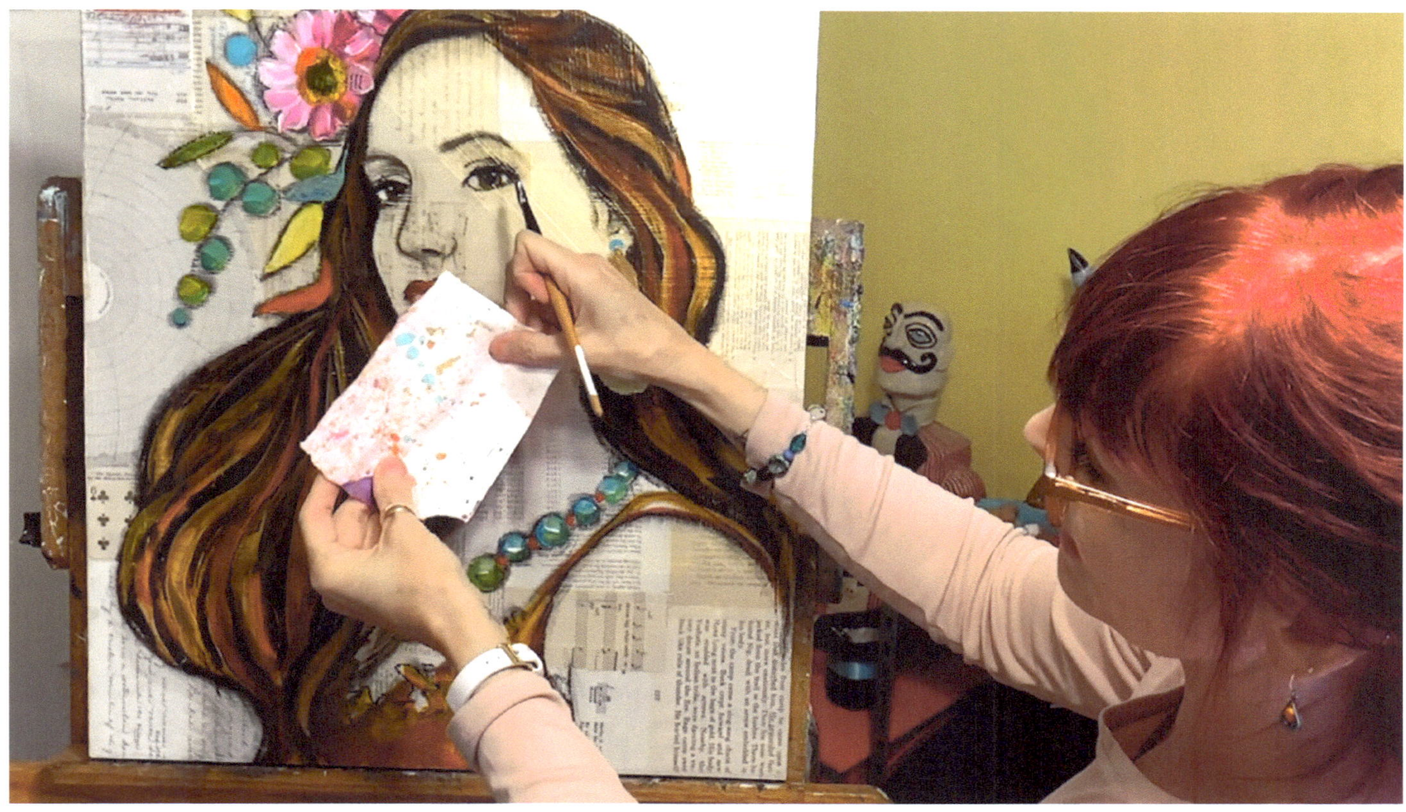

Auditioning the collage paper, hold it up to the under painting and see if it's the right color and value.

applying
COLLAGE

My pieces of paper are torn, I never cut with scissors. I treat each piece of paper as a *brush stroke*, therefore I do not want any hard edges.

Consider making your shapes end organically, rather than having them cut off abruptly like a piece of tape. An organic end that trails off naturally will visually flow into the next piece—just like a brush mark. We are painting with paper, so you want to follow the shapes, sizes, and direction of marks that you intuitively created in your under painting.

I apply the glue to the board, place the torn paper into the glue, and apply more glue over top with pressure from the brush to make the paper lay down nice and flat.

Follow your under-painting in color and value, hold up your papers and be sure they are the right match before tearing and gluing them down, I call this *auditioning*. Once you start auditioning, you may find that you do not have enough colors or values in your paper palette, because someone once said…"*You can never have enough paper!*"

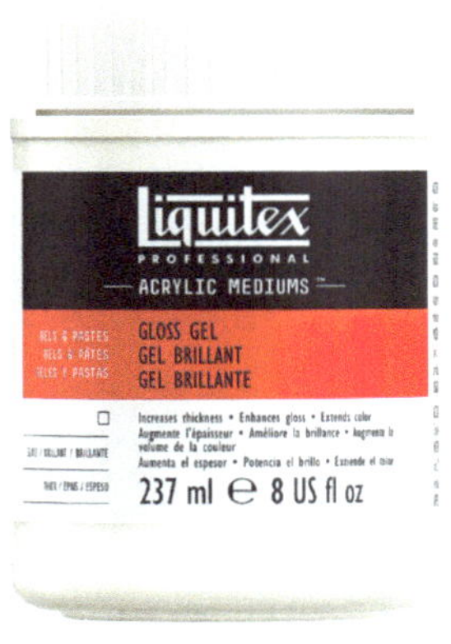

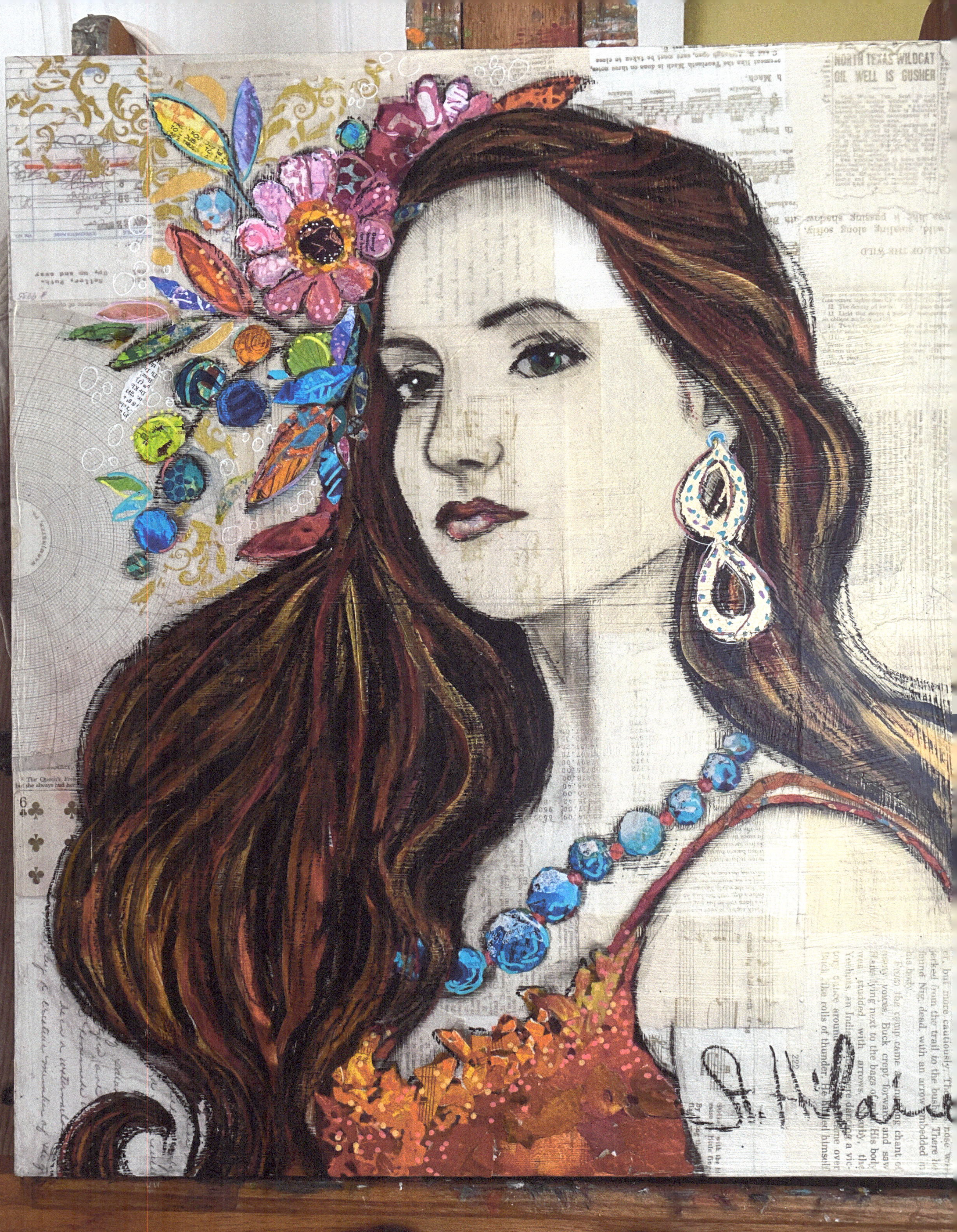

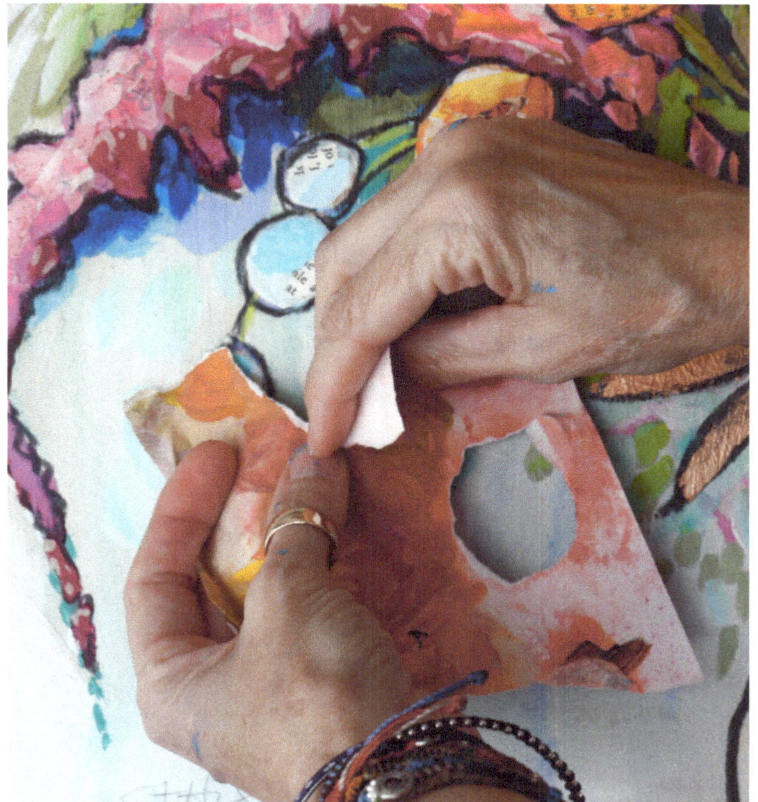

Eliminating and embracing white edges with tearing techniques takes a little bit of practice. Pulling the paper up toward yourself with your dominant hand eliminates white edges.

working back to front

Evaluate your composition and determine what is farthest back and what is closest to the front. Start with what's furthest back and work your way forward. Apply collage in that hierarchy, working from back to front.

using arbitrary color

Don't be afraid to deviate from your reference photo and add some spice with colors that are not necessarily present in nature! This gives you the opportunity to infuse more color into your composition and WE LOVE COLOR!

following the form

You intuitively followed the form of your subject with your brush marks when you painted. In other words, you would not paint a round object with straight horizontal strokes, you'd paint it with curved marks. Think of your torn paper as paper brush marks and glue them down in the same direction and in similar shapes.

directional patterning

1 Sheet music lines need to follow the form of the subject

2 Type and text needs to follow the form of the subject

3 Patterns need to follow the form of the subject

simple shapes

Suggesting vs Precisely Rendering

Breaking down forms into simple shapes is the best way to work in an impressionistic medium. Simple shapes give the subject enough information to make the visual connection, you don't need to render every petal of the floral element or every strand of hair. Simplify the shapes and edit out some of the complex details of fashion elements such as jewelry.

eliminating white edges

1 Pull up, with your dominant hand, toward you to create the shape that you want

2 The white edges will be left on piece of paper in your non dominant hand

embracing white edges

1 Consider using the white edge of a paper for a highlighted edge

2 Consider using the white edge of a paper to help separate overlapping beads in jewelry

3. To achieve a white edge, turn your paper colored side down and follow the same steps from above

no scissors!

Every tear of paper represents a brush stroke in a Paper Painting, for this reason, we do not use scissors which would create hard edges that are not consistent with a painterly effect

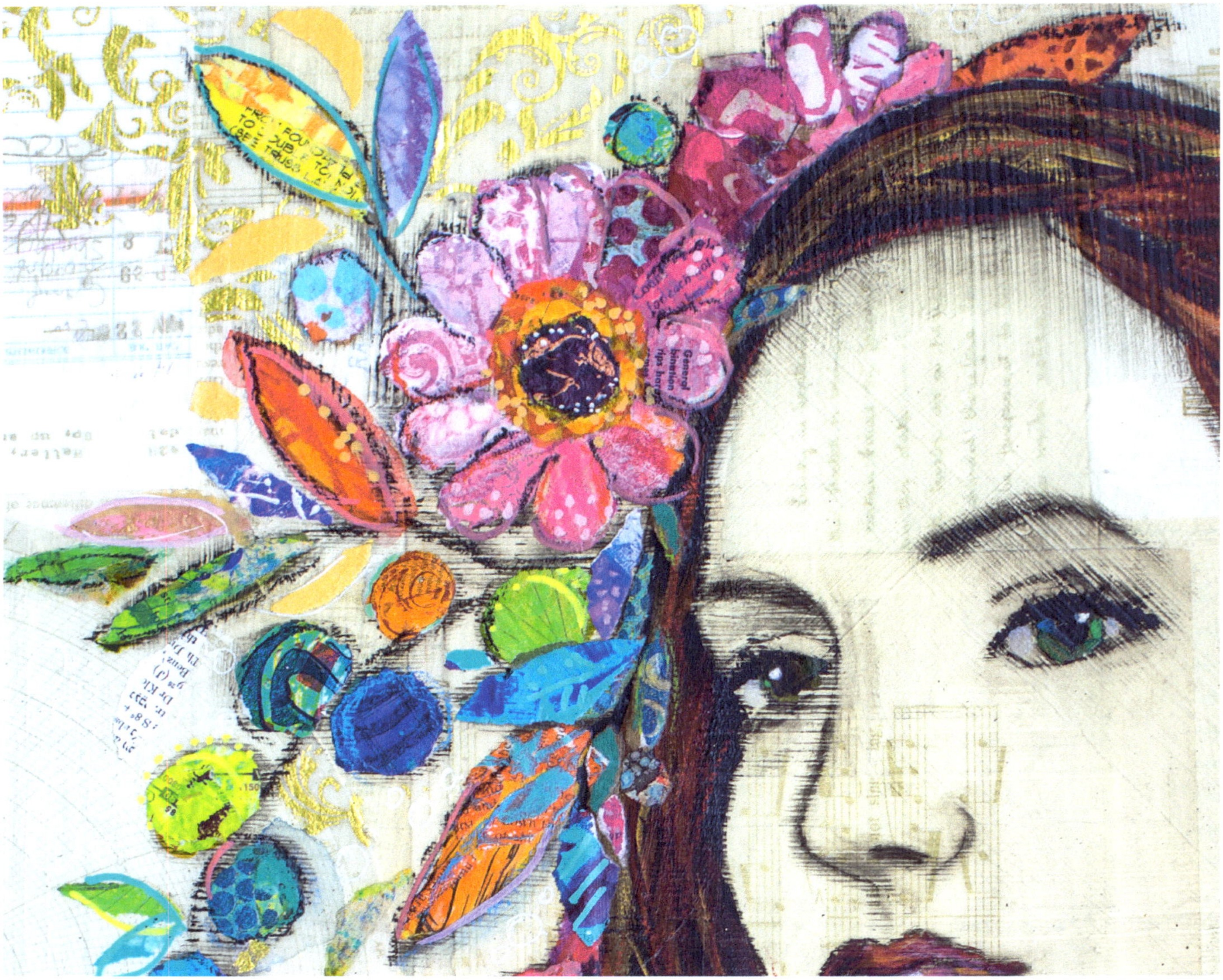

The added floral elements give me the opportunity to incorporate color and collage.

I prefer the Princeton Catalyst short handle #8 Filbert Polytip Bristle brush

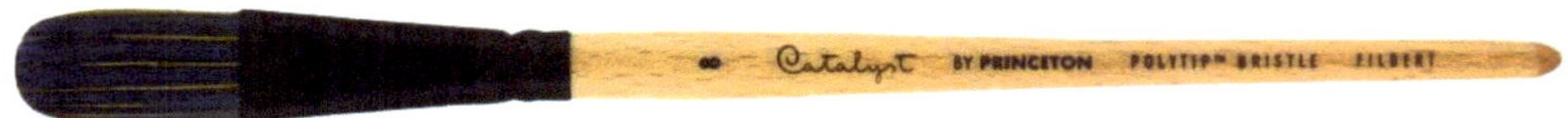

applying the glue

1 Apply a thin layer of gloss gel medium to the board with a 1-inch filbert style rigid bristle brush

2 Place paper, one piece at a time into the glue

3 Press the paper down with the glue brush, applying enough pressure to get the paper to lie flat, and applying a thin layer of glue over the paper at the same time

4 Bring the glue in from all sides of the piece of paper, making sure there are no loose edges

5 Examine the art as you work to be sure there are no erroneous lumps of glue, it dries hard and is not removable

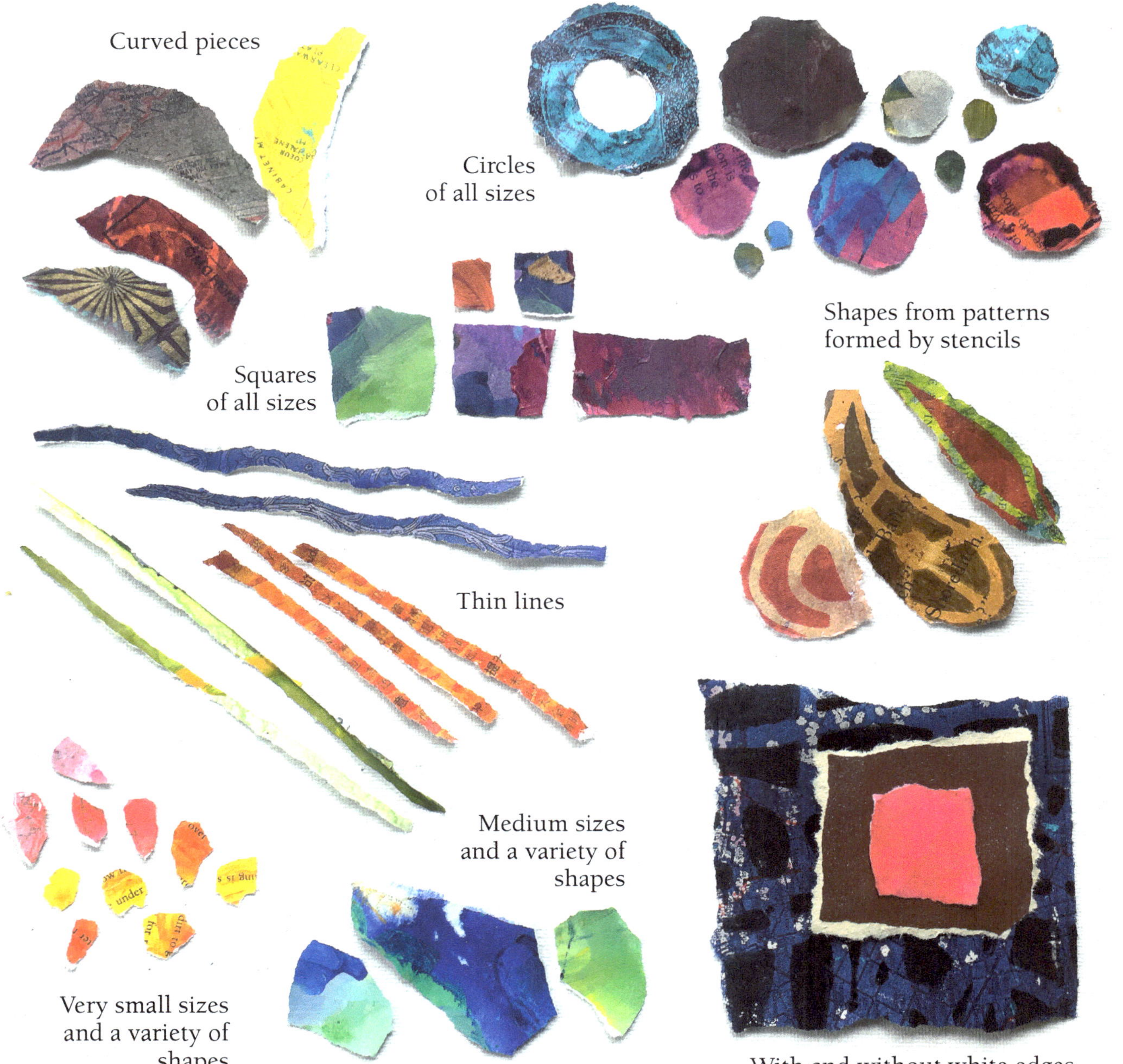

directional ripping

Directional ripping is basically following the form of an object with pieces of collage paper that have been torn into shapes that follow the direction of the brush marks from your under-painting. Practice tearing your paper brush marks in a variety of shapes and sizes.

Once you get a feeling for following the form with directional ripping and shading you will realize that this style of collage is much like traditional painting.

more white edges

Eliminating white edges requires pulling the paper UP while ripping– as you pull in an upward motion, the white edge is left behind. Practice pulling UP while ripping and rotating the paper so that you are always tearing in an upward motion. This takes a bit of getting used to–I suggest practicing on some scrap papers to get the hang of it.

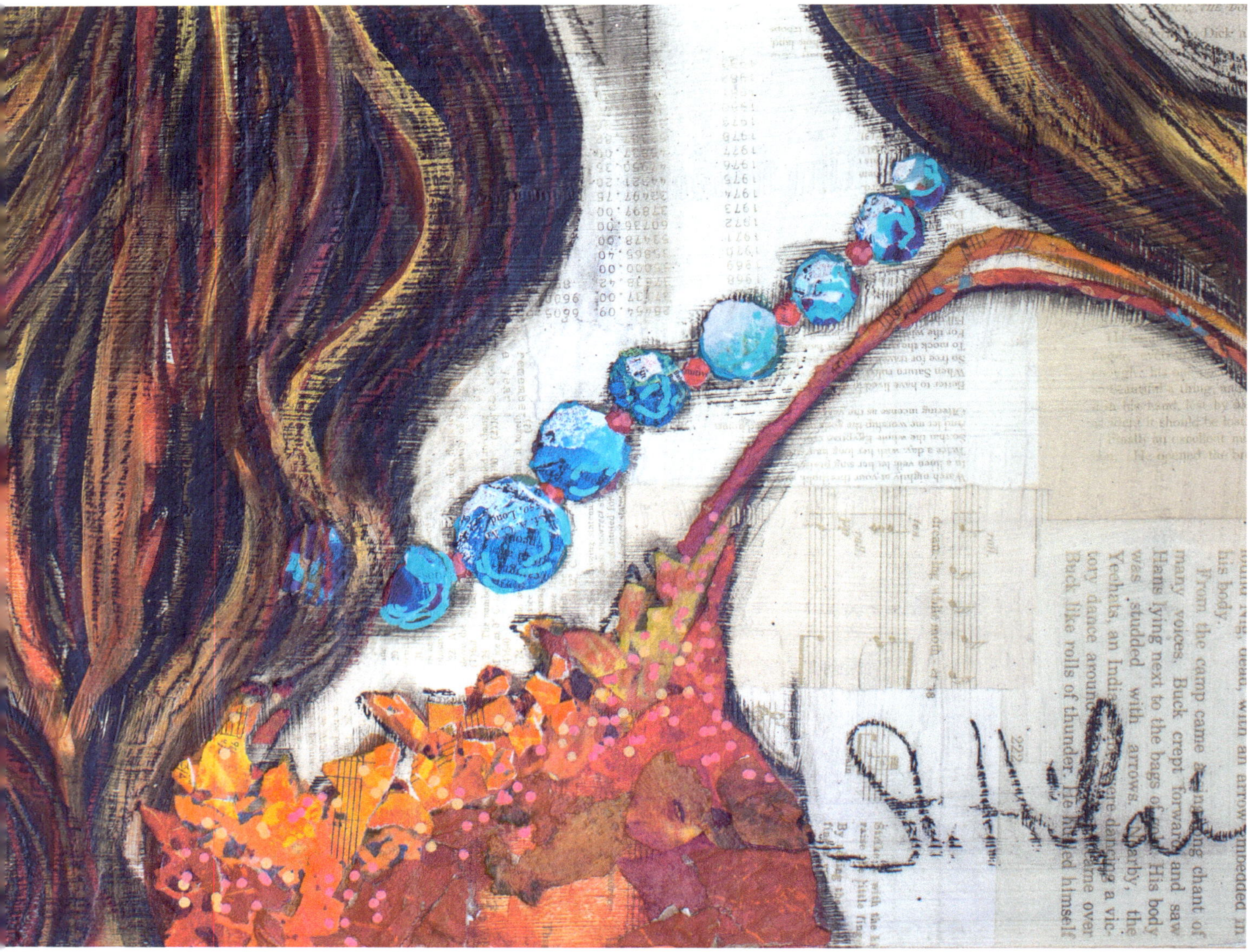

Note that the sheet music lines change direction to suggest the ruffled edge of Mia's blouse

applying paper brush marks

Note how the torn paper curves around the roses, following the form, the paper brush marks swoop around to give the feeling of circular stacked petals. See how the orange flower petals in the upper right are laid down in a direction that follows the form of the flowers, outward and straight from their center? The stems in the vase are created from long skinny tears, as are the leaves in the top right corner.

Painting with paper is just like painting with a brush, you must carefully tear each piece of paper, allow it to end in an organic shape, and apply it in a way that follows the form and volume of the subject in the same way you used your paint brush in the under-painting.

Paper brush marks should be torn to end organically vs. with straight edges like tape.

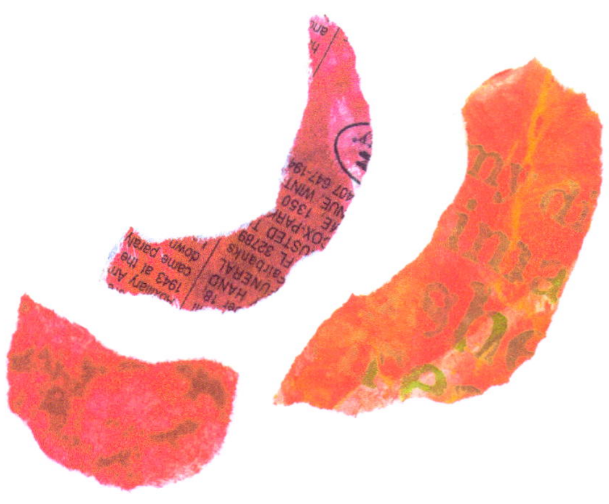

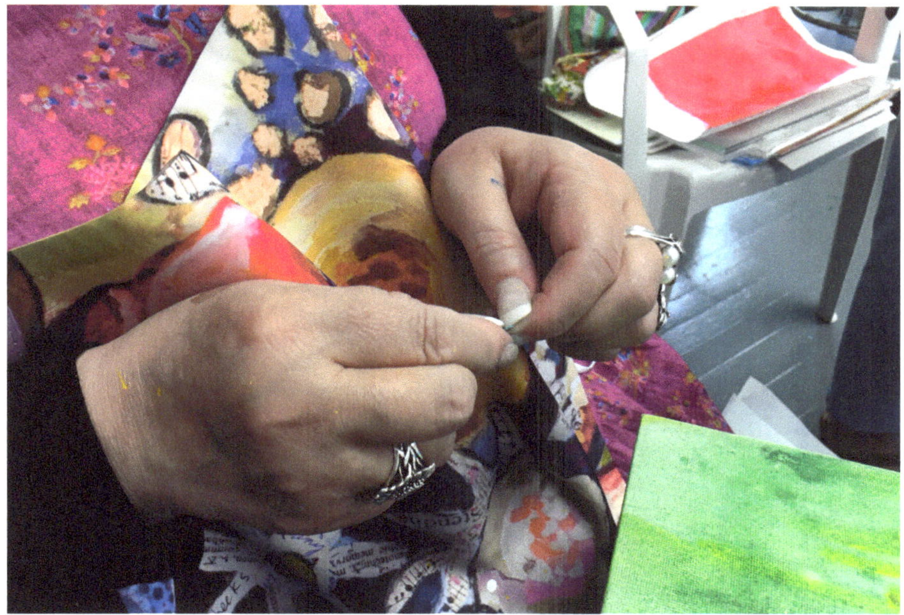

Students in the classroo learn to tear paper brush marks

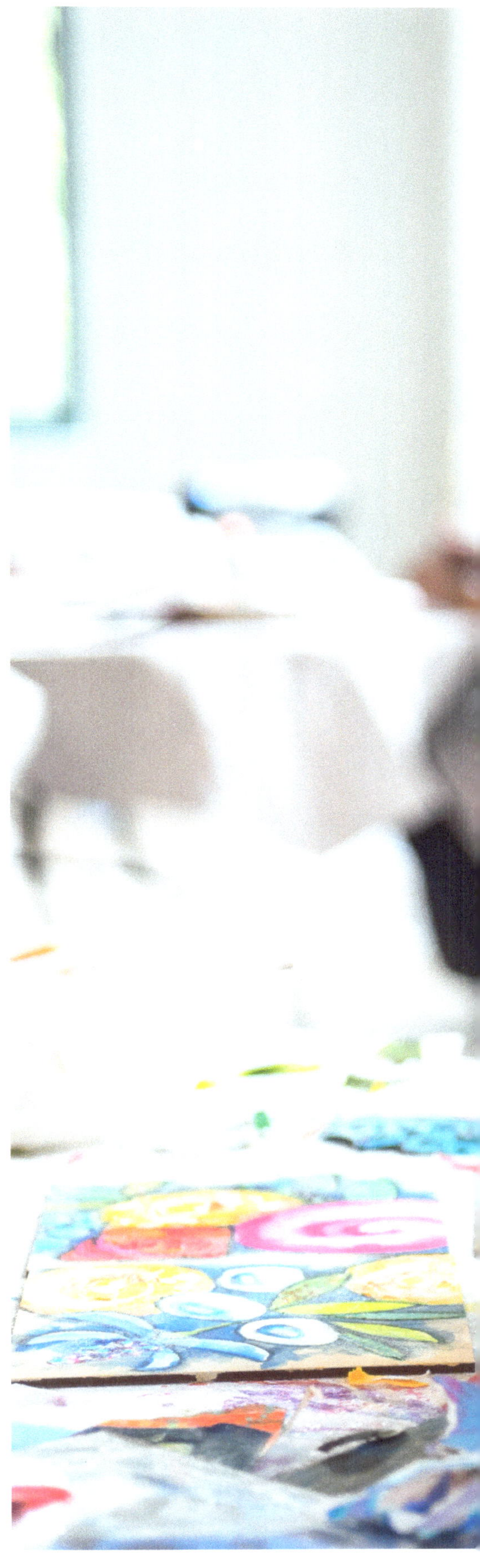

mixed
MEDIA

anything goes–almost

Mixed media is an artwork in which more than one medium or material has been employed. Collage is a good example of an art form that combines different materials including paper, paint, found materials and mark making on top.

In the next pages I'll talk about some of my favorite mixed media materials but do not let my choices prevent you from experimenting with what you may have in your studio.

Just remember that our surface does not have much of a tooth for drawing tools, which is why I have chosen some that do not require it. BUT experiment and see what you can come up with, there are not many rules other than to stay in acrylic based products vs. oil based and to keep with things that can be coated with varnish in the end.

In addition to the mark making tools, I will also re-work and possibly add more black pastel at this stage. If I find that some lines are not as dark as I would like, or that I just feel like I need more, now is the time to bring out the pastel again as we apply the finishing touches.

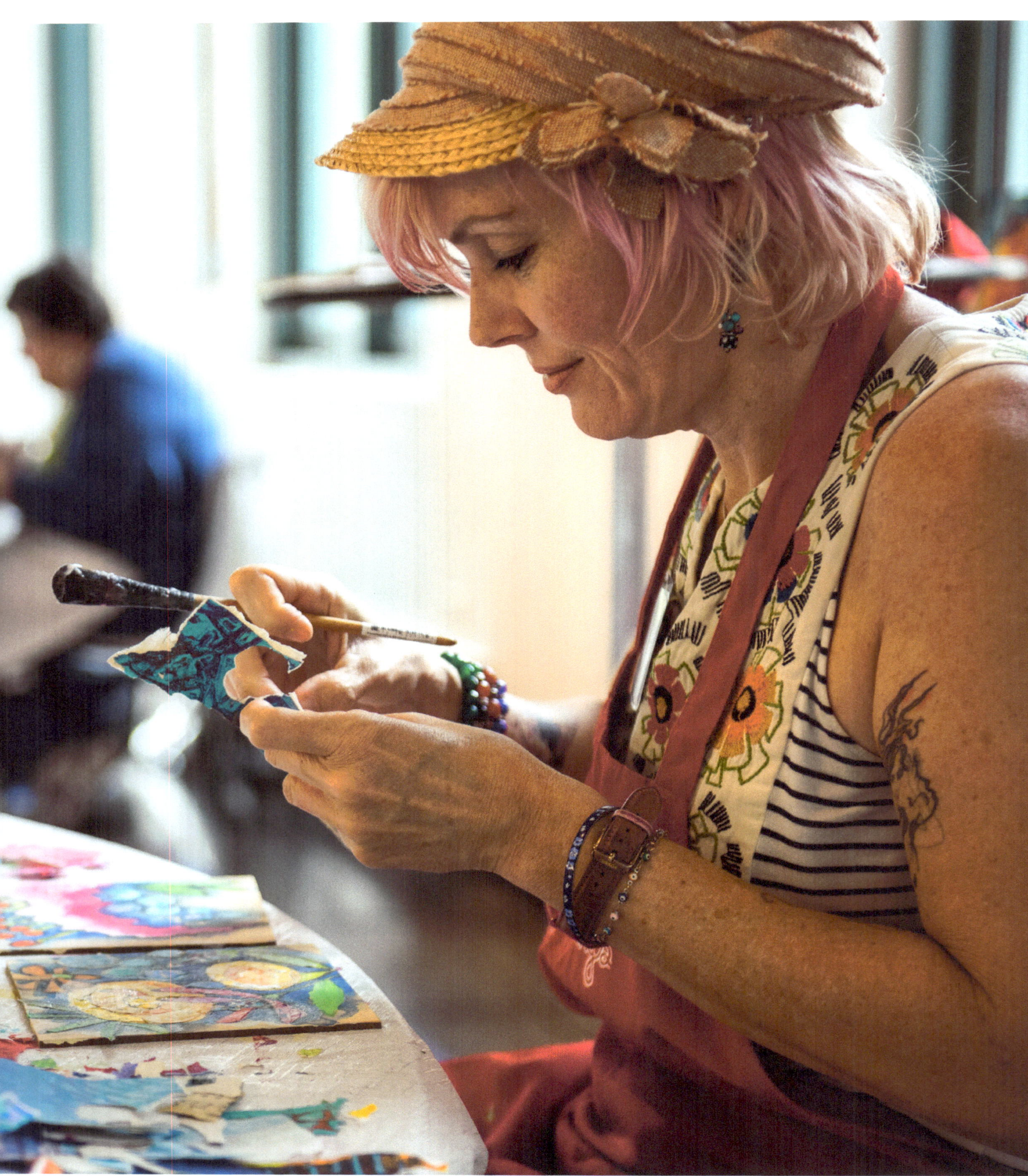

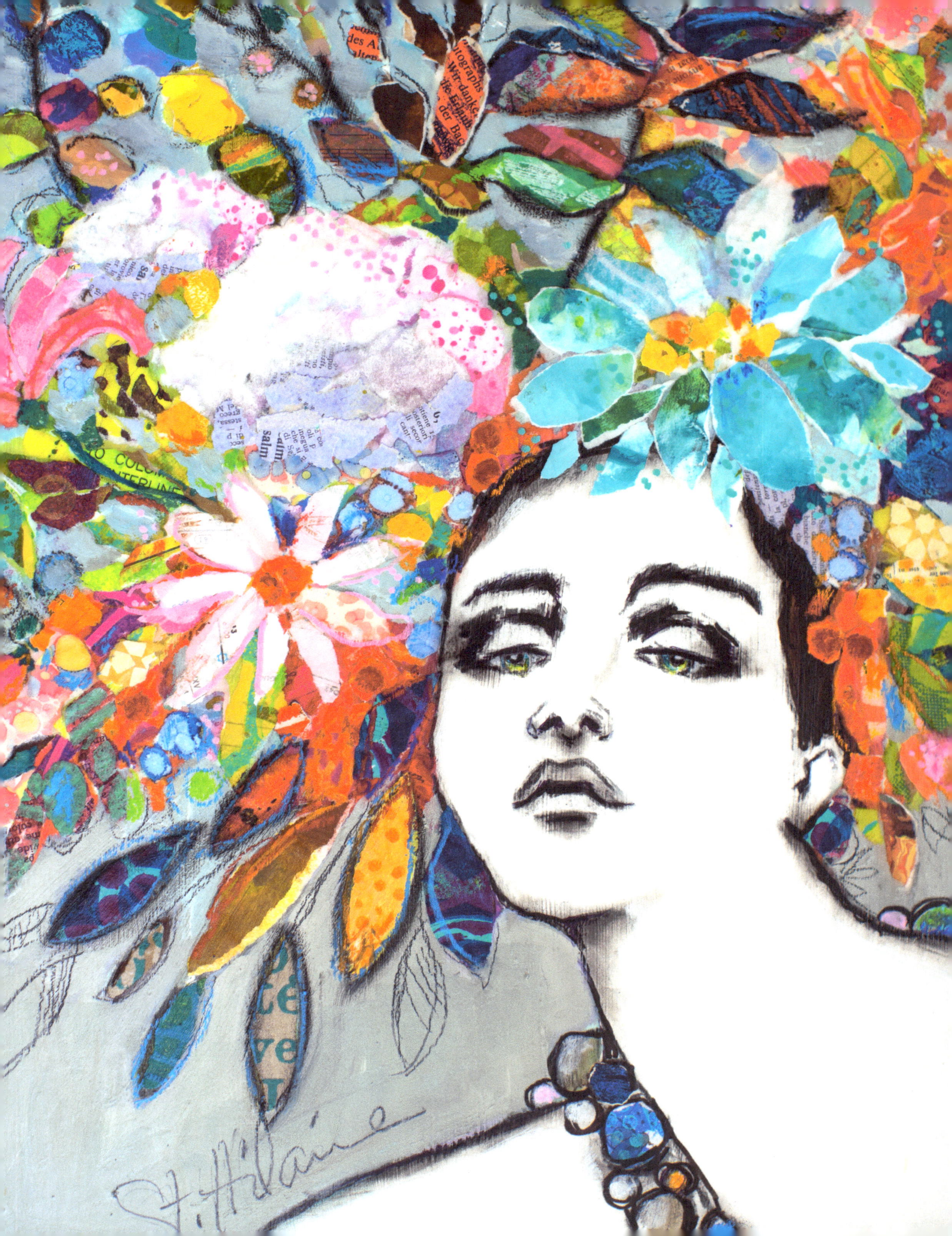

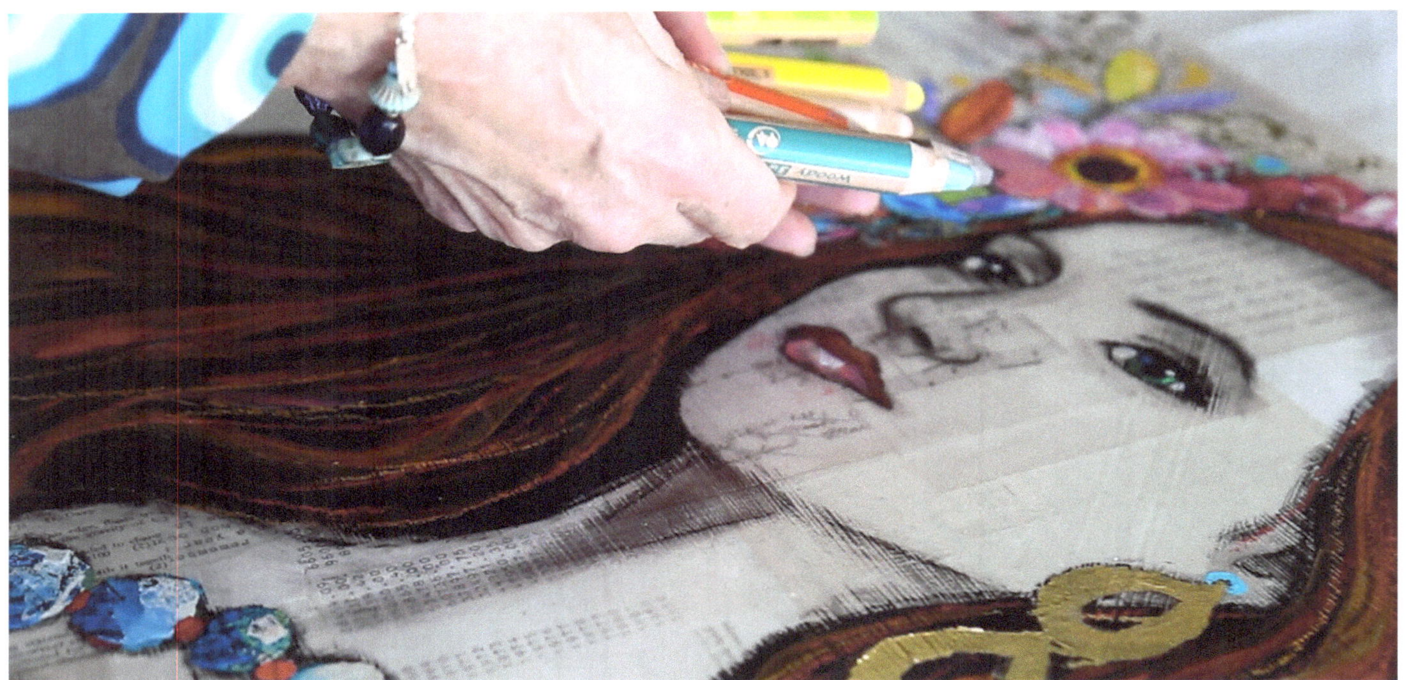

Stabilo Woodies do not require any tooth, they will work on top of glue!

Mixed
MEDIA

stabilo woodies

I enjoy adding marks on top of my collage work.
My current favorite mark-making tool is Stabilo Woodies. These fun sticks are colored pencil, watercolor, and wax crayon all in one! Woodies are available in 18 rich colors, they go on like crayon and blend with water.

Woodies require NO TOOTH, they will adhere over collage glue without a problem (they will even write on glass). Woodies feature high opacity and color intensity, even over dark paper. Their thickness makes them perfect for large areas, the break-proof lead is a diameter of 10 mm. so they are good for heavy lines.

NOTE: If you add mark-making with Woodies on top of your collage work, you will need to seal it with spray varnish.

I have embelished some of the flower petals in this portrait (left) with colorful Woodie outlines.

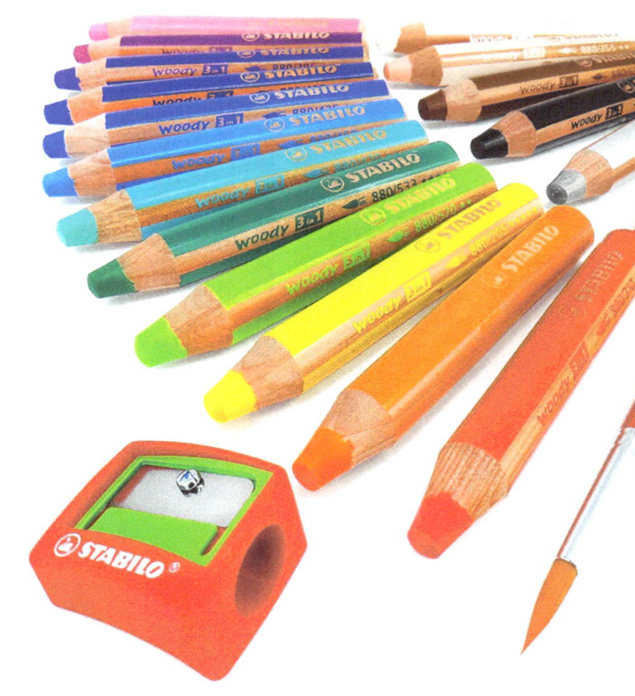

Fashion Plate Floral (left)
Before I found the encaustic effect I would paint on simple white gesso. You might like this more simple approach to the background

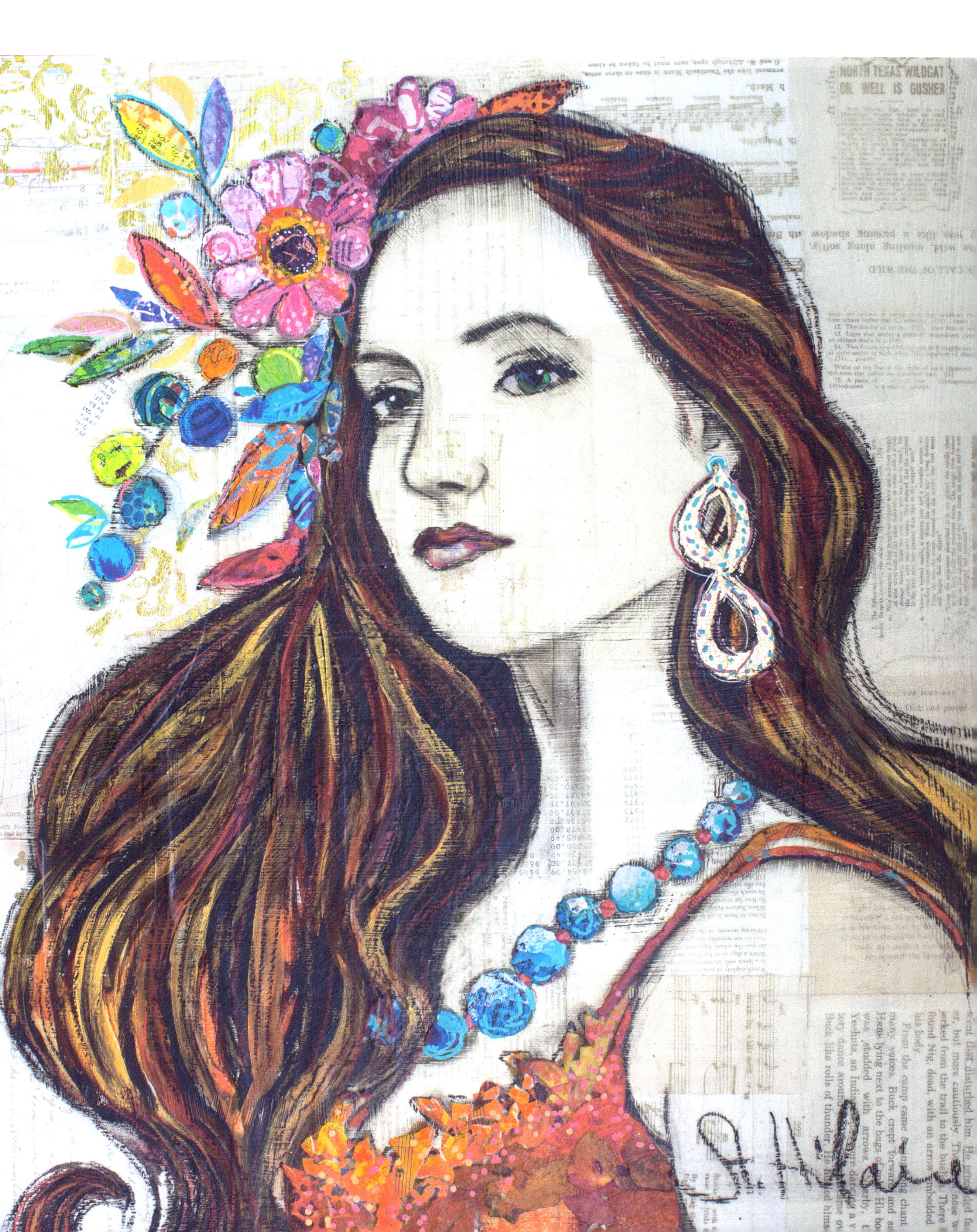

NORTH TEXAS WILDCAT
OIL WELL IS GUSHER

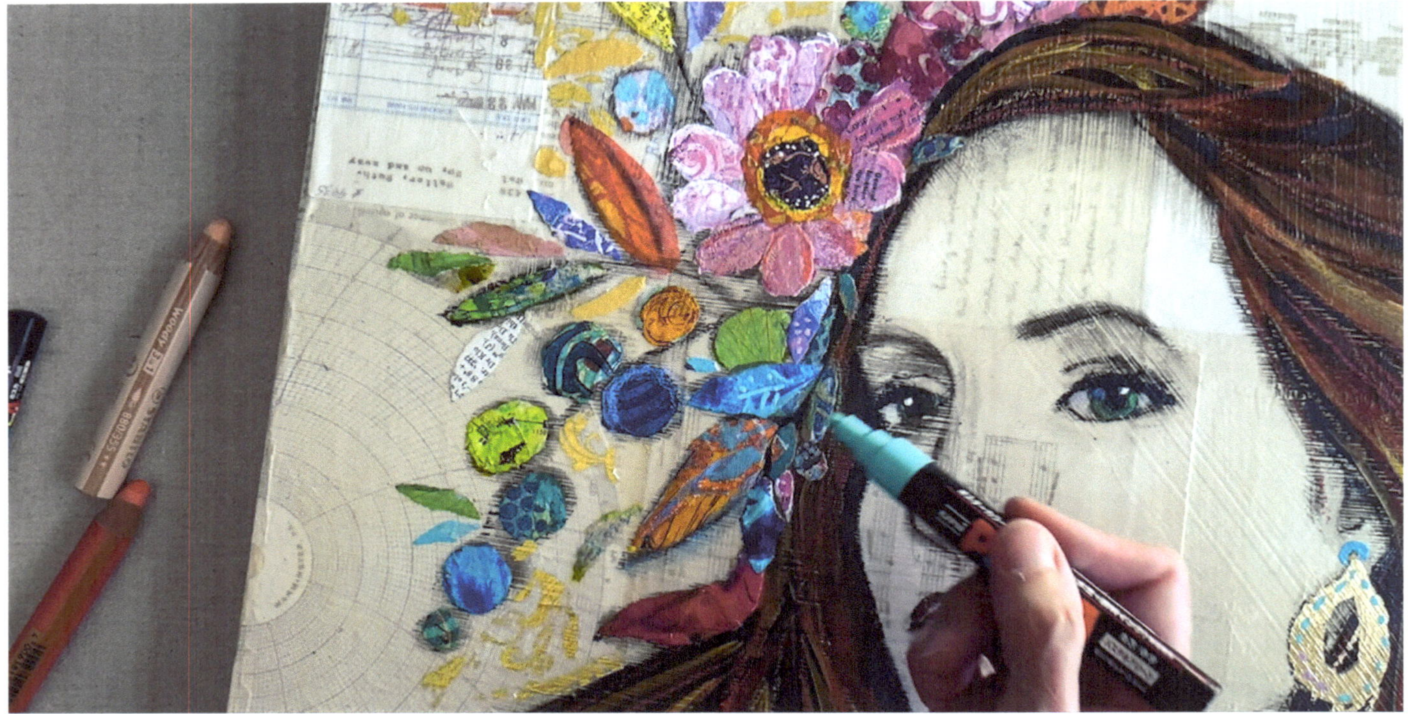

Using Posca Pens to embellish on top of the collage paper and the metallic leaf.

Mixed
MEDIA

posca paint pens

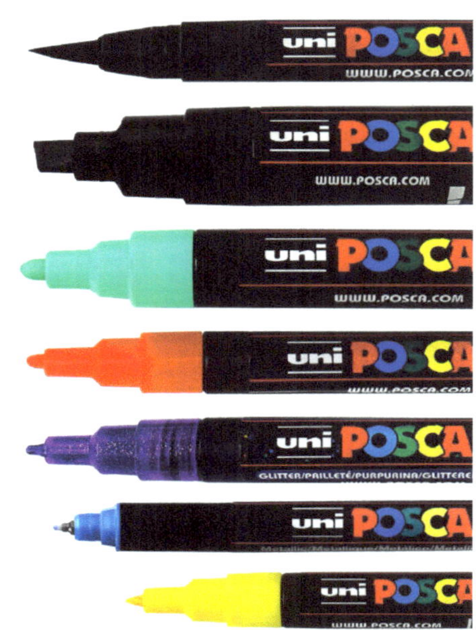

I enjoy adding marks on top of my collage work. Another of my favorite tools for this is Posca paint pens. The opaque, water-based ink in Uni Posca markers dries to a matte finish on both porous and non-porous surfaces. Odorless, fade proof, and bleed-proof, the markers are great for marking on top of your work! Use them on paper, wood, metal, plastic, vinyl, glass, and more.

There are a wide range of tips on these markers from extra fine to very broad, it all depends on how you will use them and on what size piece of artwork. I find the broad markers are better for larger works.

I have embellished Mia's necklace with light blue Posca lines as well as the top of her blouse with yellow and orange dots. I have added blue cross hatching lines to the leaves and white dots in the flower center of her floral headpiece.

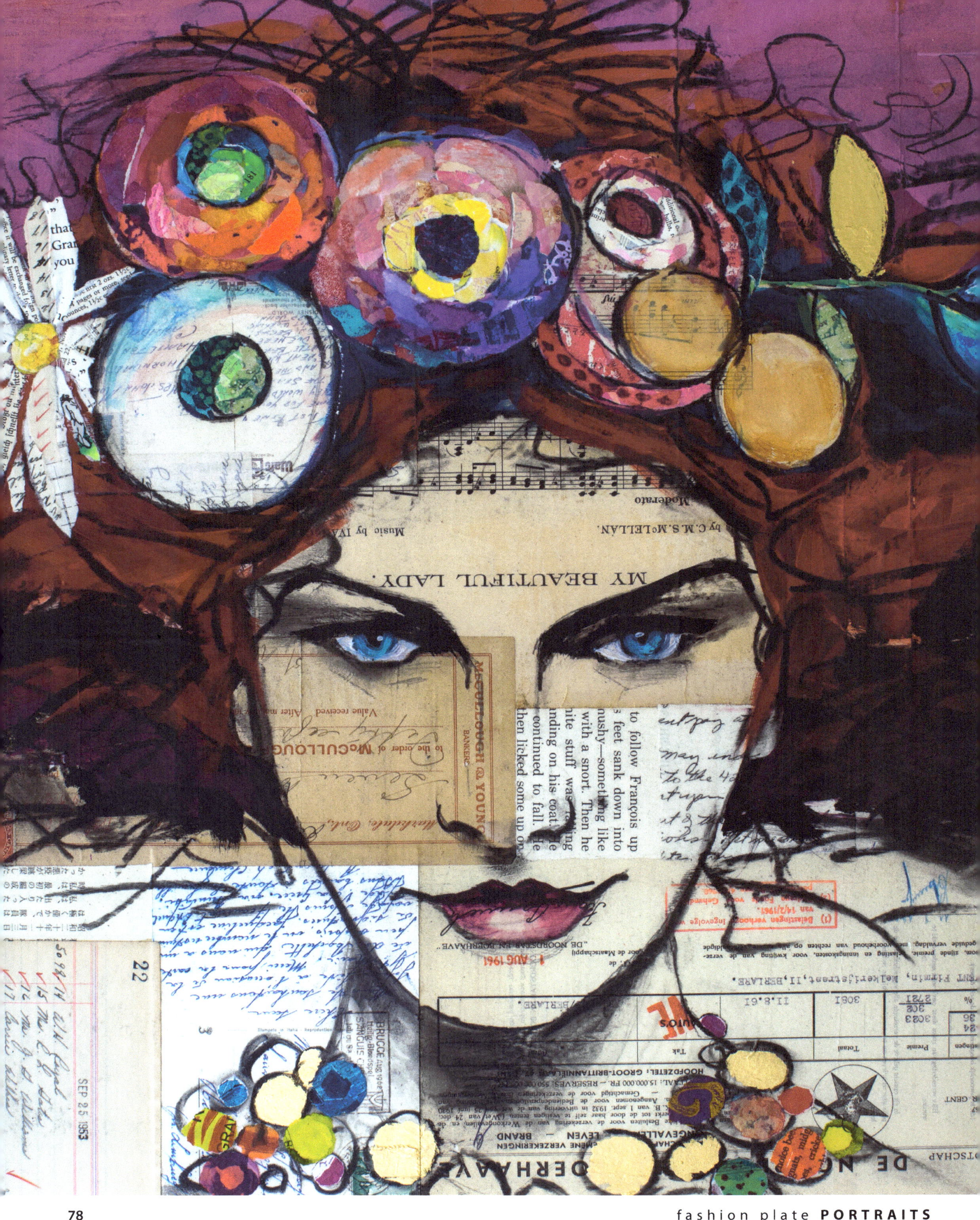

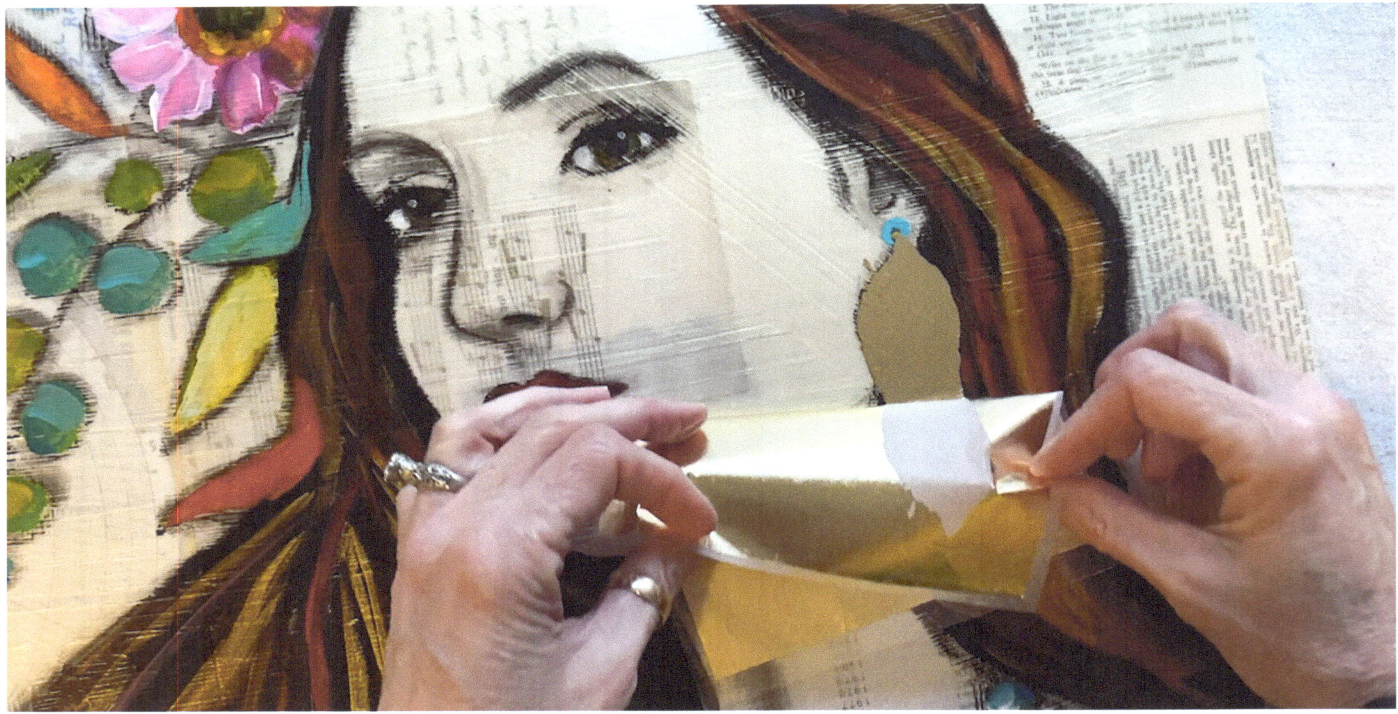

Applying metallic leaf to the earrings (above) and to the necklace (left).

Mixed
MEDIA

simple metallic leaf

Be sure to purchase the adhesive that is specifically made for simple leaf. The leaf I prefer comes with transfer papers, making it easy to handle and to apply.

Follow the product directions for the adhesive, spread it on thinly with a paint brush in the areas that you want to use the leaf and wait for it to dry until it feels tacky to the touch. Once the adhesive reaches this state, take the transfer paper and press the shiny side down into the adhesive. Rub and burnish with the back of your fingernails or a spoon, and then pull back the transfer paper. Gently rub/brush away any excess leaf that releases from the paper but is not adhered.

NOTE: Coat your finished metal leaf with a layer of gloss gel medium before applying varnish, which tends to tarnish the shine.

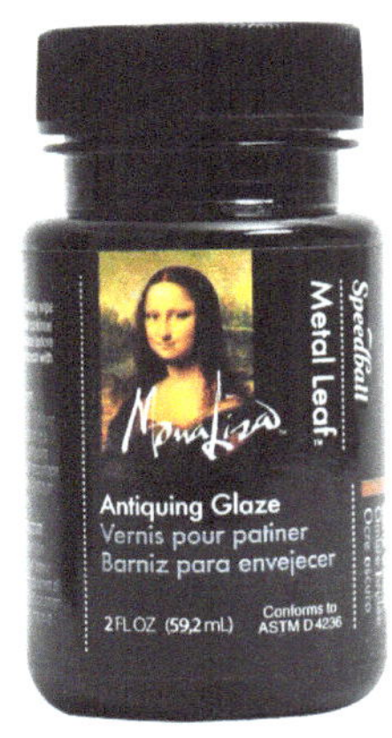

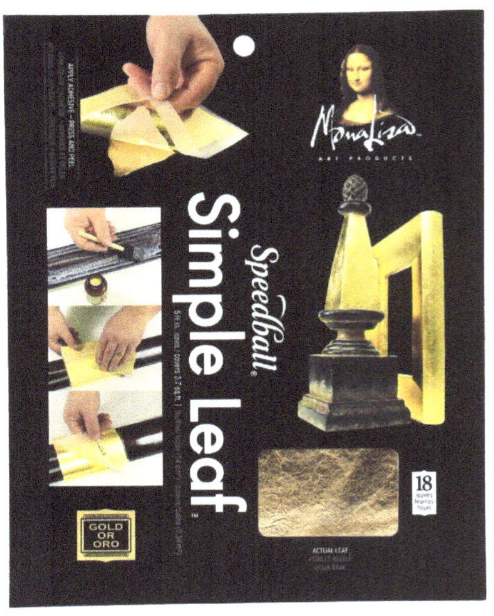

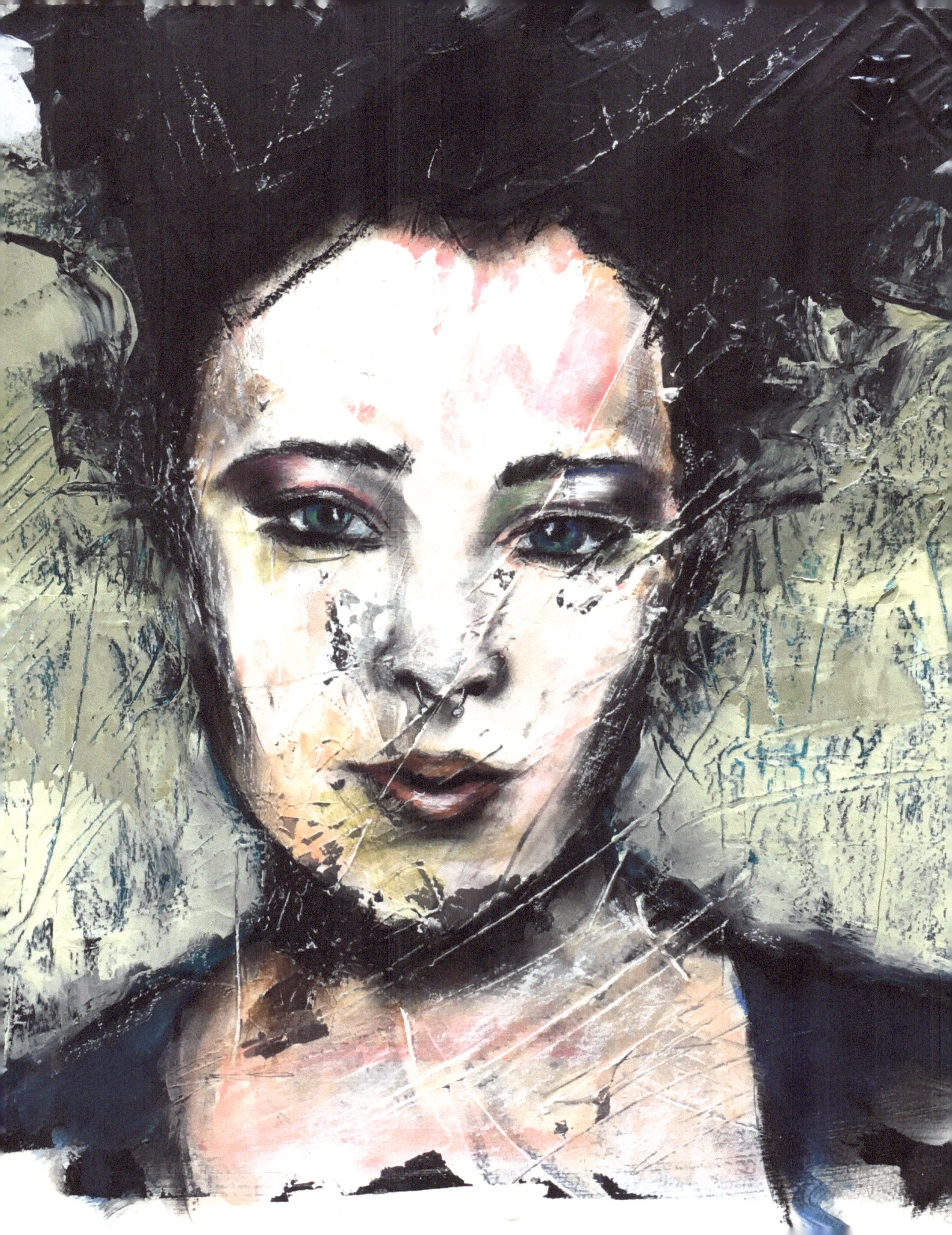

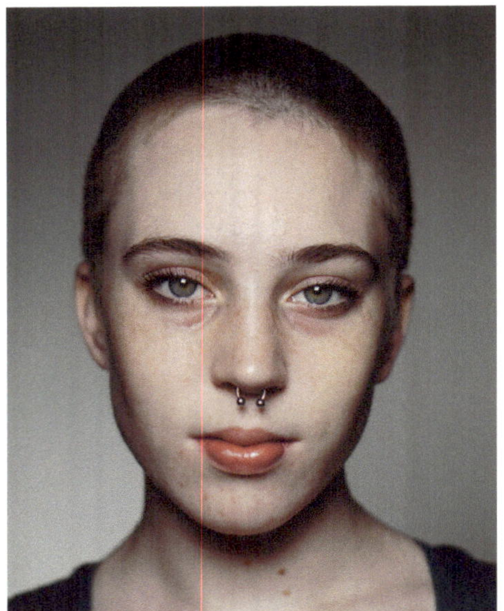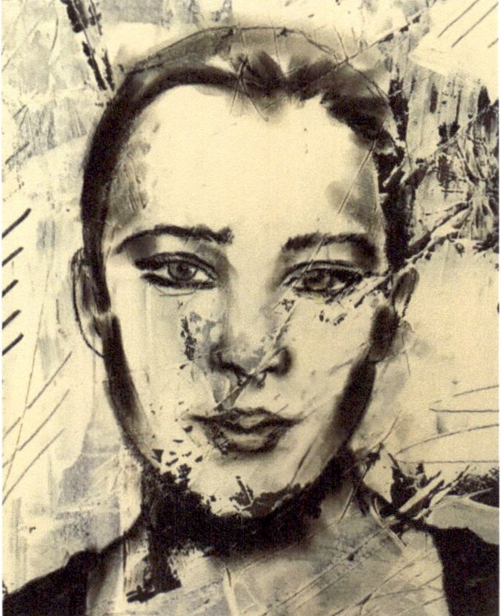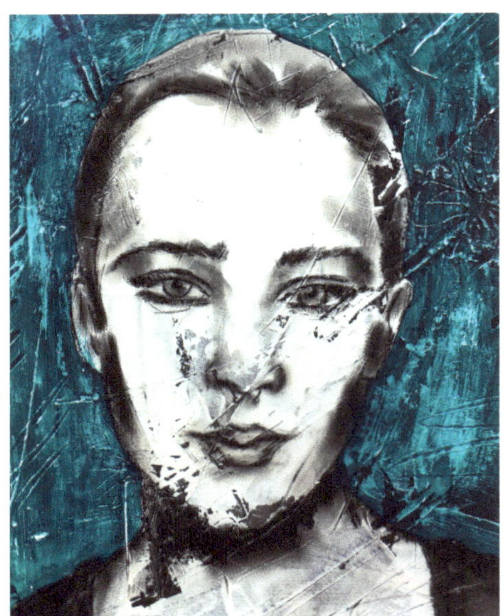

Stages of the process: Reference Image / Pastel smudge drawing / Painting the portrait.

mixed
MEDIA

alternate background

I love texture in my work, lately I have been experimenting with Utrecht gesso because it's super thick, it holds peaks and you can carve down through it with a pencil to create etched lines.

In this piece, extra thick white gesso was spread (with a credit card) over the top of a dry, dark background color. I then scraped marks and texture through the white gesso layer while it was, revealing the color underneath. Much like our ephemera background, this background was created first, and then the drawing was added on top.

After establishing the pencil drawing, i went over it with the pastel smudge technique, sealed it, and painted the portrait colors on top. I used the black pastel to really soften the edge lines of the silhouette.

NOTE: have a wet paper towel on hand to wipe excess gesso build-up off the tools you use as you are making your marks.

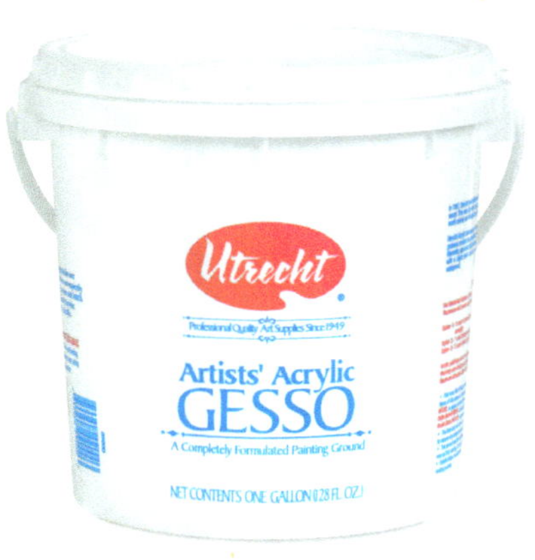

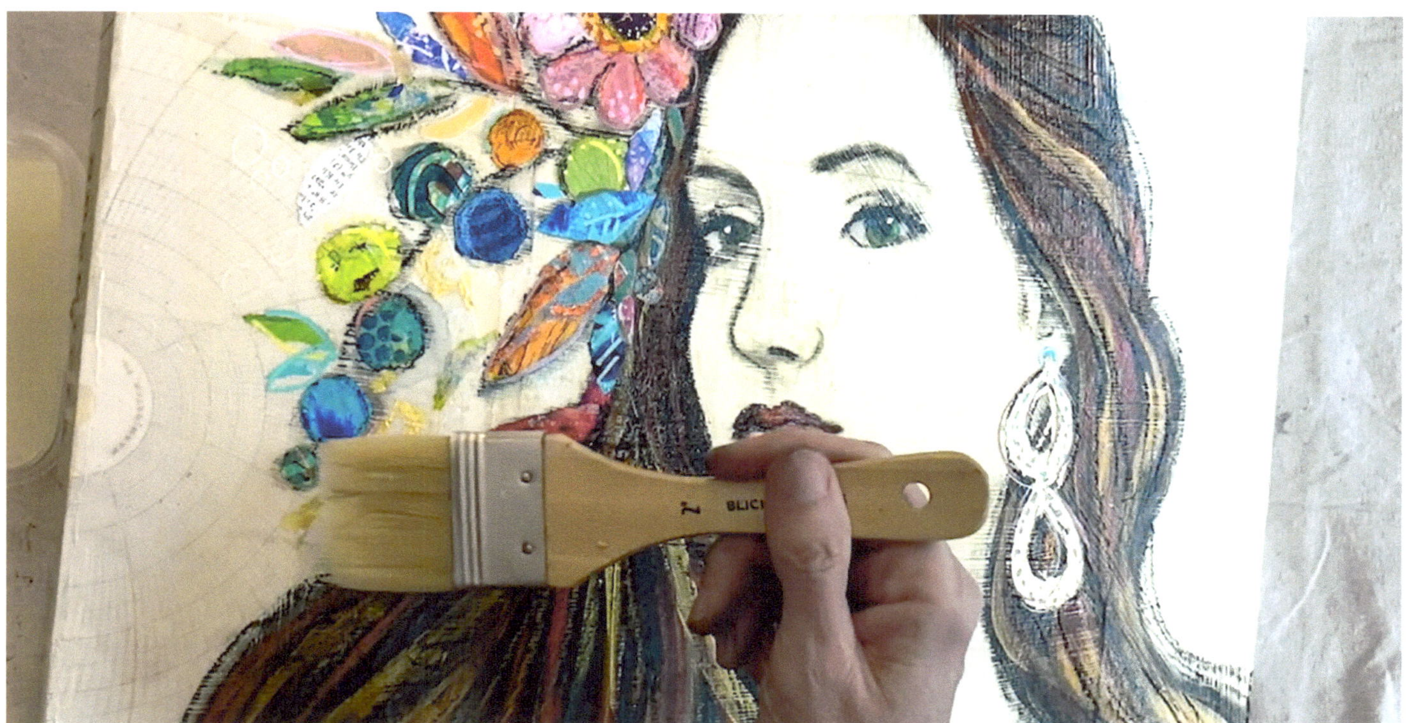

Tip your art slightly to the side in order to look for missed spots

Applying Final
VARNISH

I use Golden Paints brand varnish with UVLS to protect my work. Polymer Varnish with UVLS (Ultra Violet Light Stabilizers) is a waterborne acrylic varnish that dries to a protective, flexible, dust resistant surface over acrylic paint. It is removable with ammonia, and available in Gloss, Satin and Matte.

I typically use a satin finish (personal preference) and only two coats with several hours of drying time in between. Allow your project to dry overnight before applying the final varnish coat. I find that a desk fan can speed the dry time of varnish by circulating room temperature air across the surface; never use heat to attempt to speed dry your varnish, this causes a dry surface with dampness underneath.

Source: GoldenPaints.com

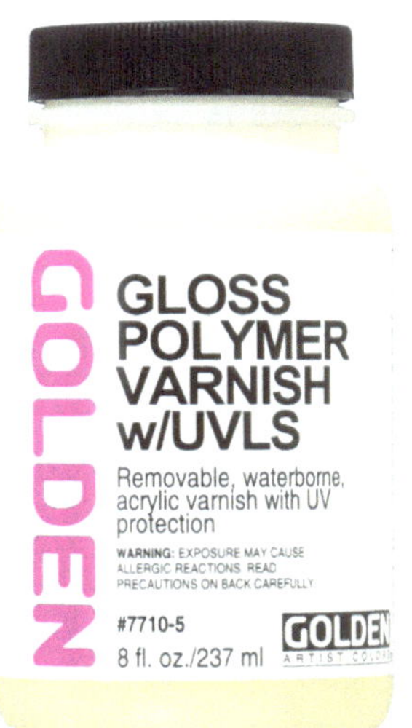

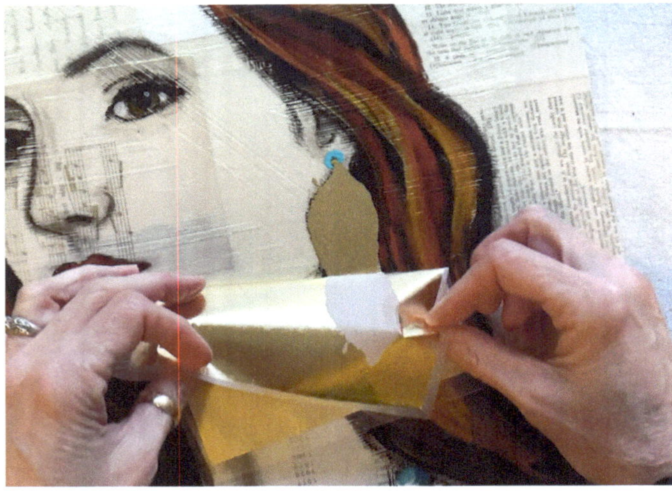

Varnish can cause your simple metallic leaf to tarnish. To avoid this, seal/coat your metallic leaf with a layer of gloss gel medium (collage glue) before applying the final varnish coat.

thinning varnish

This reduces the film thickness applied and the chance of uneven application. If applied in a thick state, the varnishes may show brush strokes and trap foam bubbles. The varnishes are thicker for the purpose of maintaining an even suspension of the solids within the varnish. Even slight settling of varnish solids during storage may result in streaking within the dried varnish film.

surface consideration

Take into account the ambient conditions of the work area. Ideally, the temperature should be above 65° F and below 75° F, while the relative humidity is between 50% and 75%. Excessive humidity or cool temperature may result in bloom, a whiteness or opacity resulting from moisture trapped between the varnish and paint layers. If the surface of the piece being varnished is warmer than the varnish applied, the varnish will become thinner in viscosity upon application. This may result in unexpected dripping or sagging, particularly if working vertically. Likewise, if the varnish and surface are relatively cool, but warm significantly shortly after application, the varnish may drip or sag.

brush application

Use a high quality bristle brush, such as a wide thin flat color-wash brush. Work from a shallow container to help control brush loading. The varnish solution should wet only the lower 25-30% of the length of the bristles. It is always best to apply the varnish on a horizontal surface in order to minimize running or sagging. Apply two or three thin coats with sufficient drying time in between, rather than one thick coat of varnish. The latter will take longer to cure, staying soft for some time, and could result in drips or a cloudy film. Apply the varnish in a manner which allows it to be brushed out to the most uniform, thinnest film possible.

two coats

When applying a satin or matte varnish, never apply more than two coats. A thick film of these reduced sheen varnishes will result in film cloudiness, dulling of color intensity, and loss of clarity.

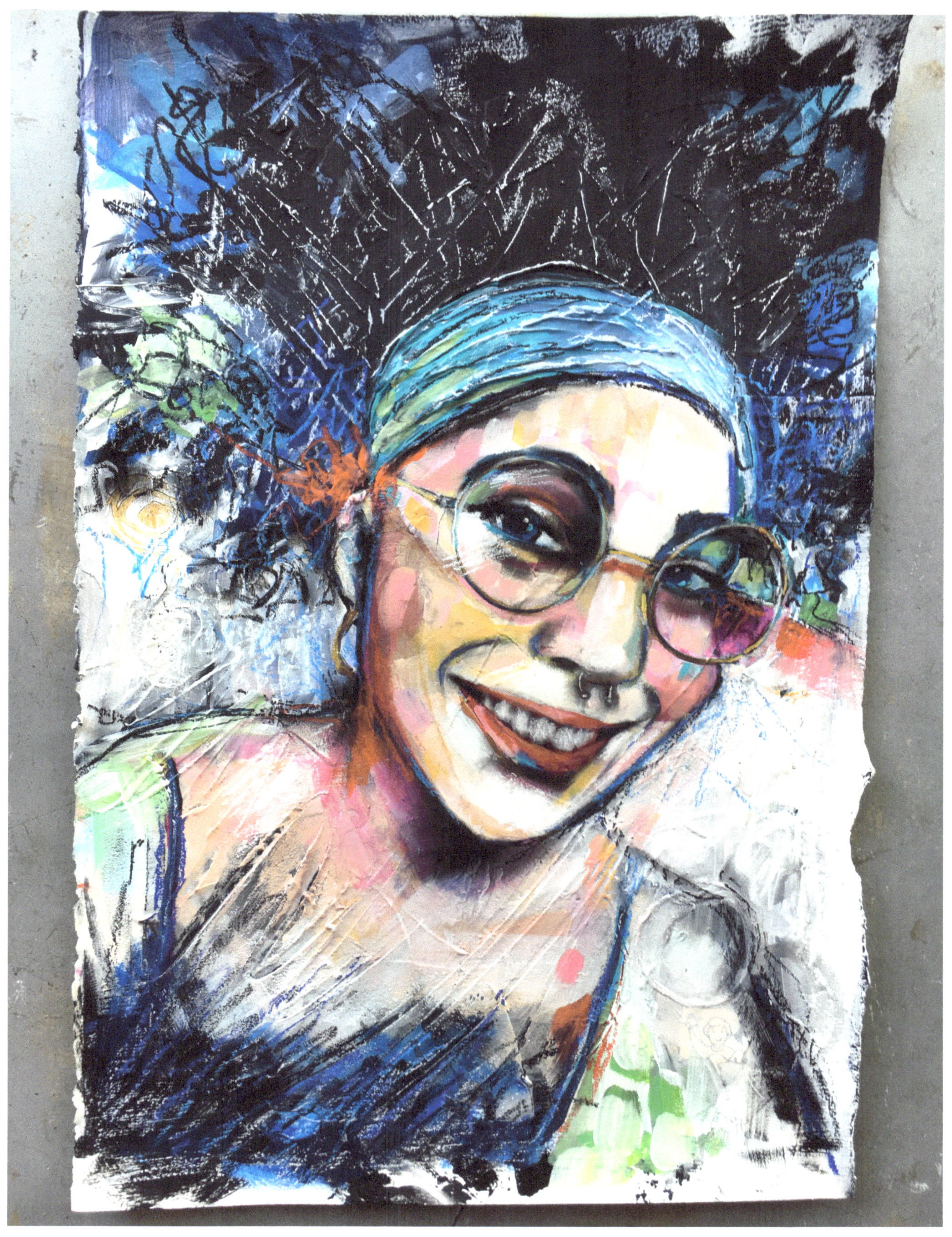

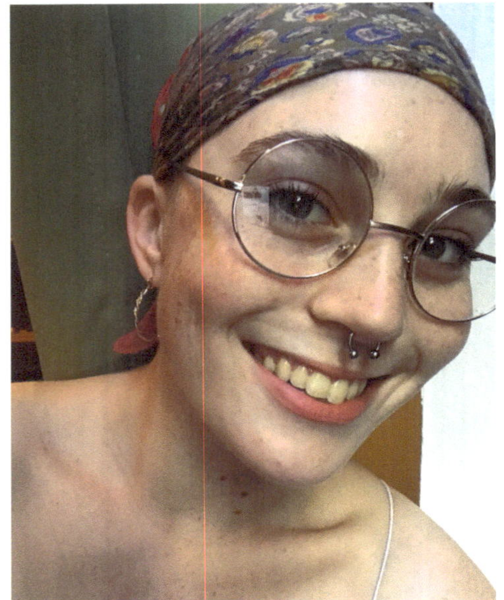

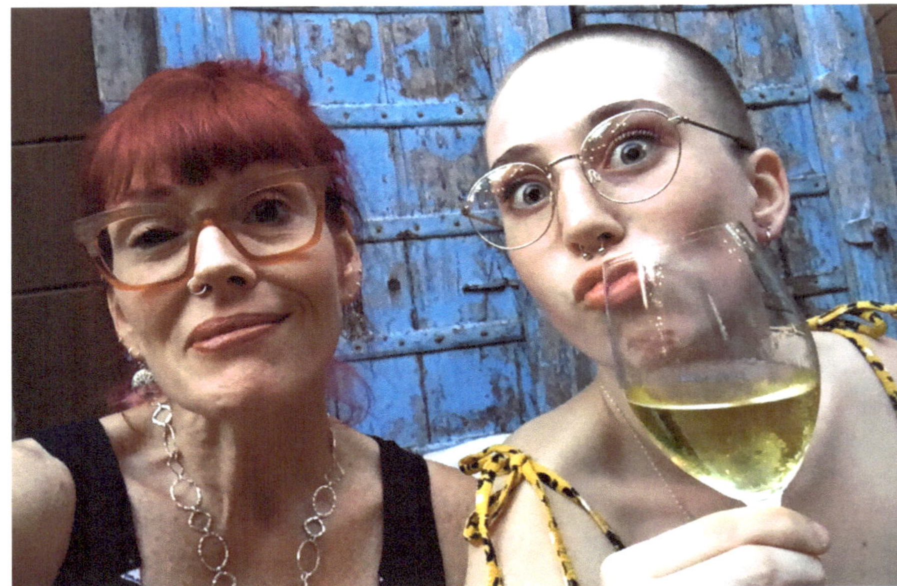

Left: Another example of the gesso textured background (based on the selfie above) as described on page 81.

ABOUT THE AUTHOR

What sets the collage work of Elizabeth St. Hilaire apart is her use of unique, one-of-a-kind papers. Her signature collage style utilizes papers colored by hand, in every hue and texture needed to provide a complete paper palette.

View a full portfolio of the artists work at
PaperPaintings.com

Contact the artist via email at
Elizabeth@PaperPaintings.com

The Facebook studio page offers work in progress and workshop info
Facebook.com/PaperPaintingsCollageArtwork

Follow her Tutorial Tidbits via the blog at
PaperPaintings.com

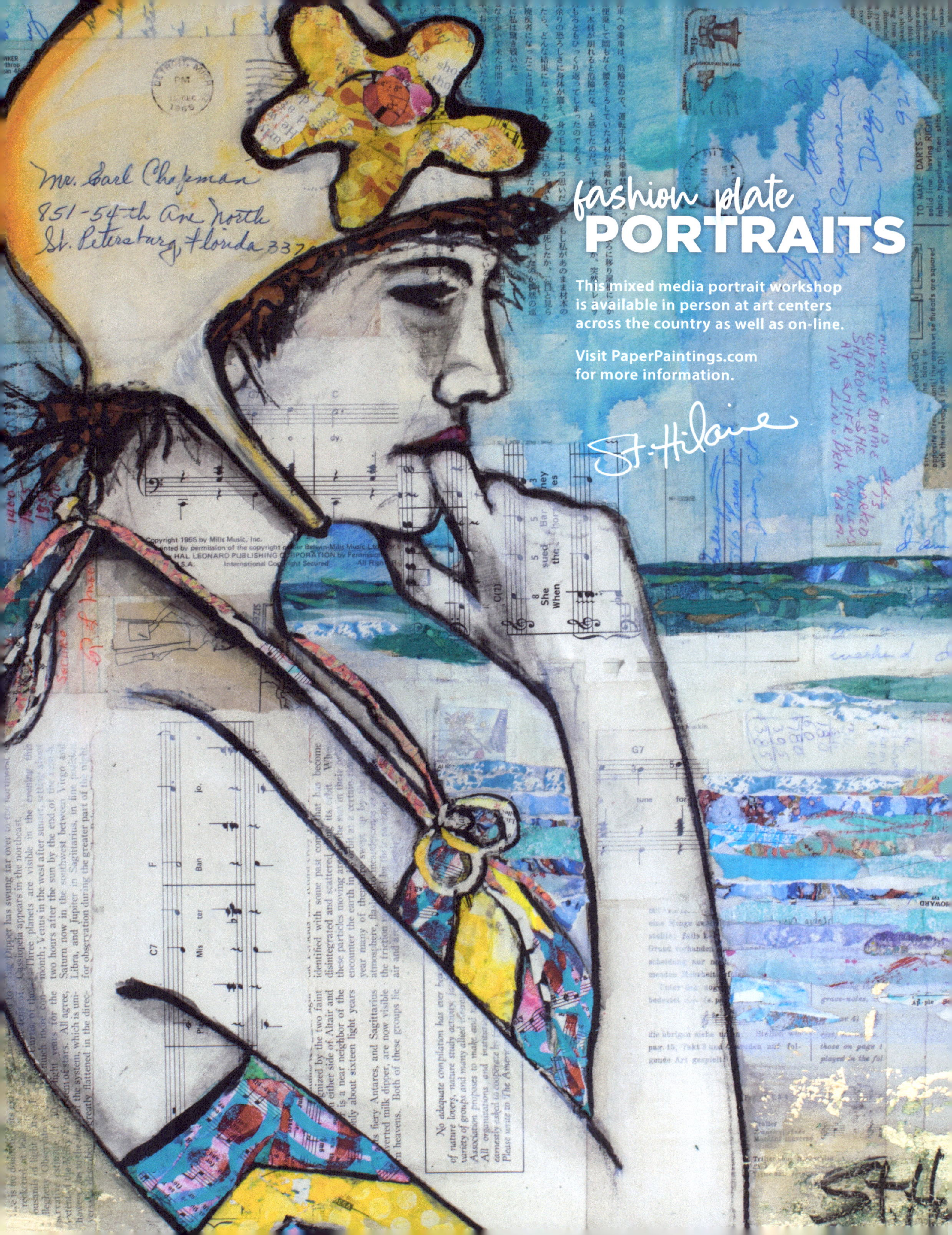

fashion plate
PORTRAITS
This mixed media portrait workshop
is available in person at art centers
across the country as well as on-line.

Visit PaperPaintings.com
for more information.

St. Hilaire